W9-CZB-234

THE AMERICAN
REVOLUTIONARY WAR
AND THE WAR OF 1812

PEOPLE, POLITICS, AND POWER

AMERICA AT WAR

THE AMERICAN REVOLUTIONARY WAR
AND THE WAR OF 1812

PEOPLE, POLITICS, AND POWER

EDITED BY JEFF WALLENFELDT, MANAGER, GEOGRAPHY AND HISTORY

Britannica®
Educational Publishing

IN ASSOCIATION WITH

ROSEN
EDUCATIONAL SERVICES

Published in 2010 by Britannica Educational Publishing
(a trademark of Encyclopædia Britannica, Inc.)
in association with Rosen Educational Services, LLC
29 East 21st Street, New York, NY 10010.

Distributed exclusively by Rosen Educational Services.
For a listing of additional Britannica Educational Publishing titles, call toll free (800) 237-9932.

First Edition

Britannica Educational Publishing
Michael I. Levy: Executive Editor
Marilyn L. Barton: Senior Coordinator, Production Control
Steven Bosco: Director, Editorial Technologies
Lisa S. Braucher: Senior Producer and Data Editor
Yvette Charboneau: Senior Copy Editor
Kathy Nakamura: Manager, Media Acquisition
Jeff Wallenfeldt: Manager, Geography and History

Rosen Educational Services
Hope Lourie Killcoyne: Senior Editor and Project Manager
Alexandra Hanson-Harding: Editor
Nelson Sá: Art Director
Matthew Cauli: Designer
Introduction by Alexandra Hanson-Harding

Library of Congress Cataloging-in-Publication Data

The American Revolutionary War and the War of 1812: people, politics, and power / edited by Jeff Wallenfeldt.—1st ed.
    p. cm.—(America at war)
"In association with Britannica Educational Publishing, Rosen Educational Services."
Includes index and bibliographical references.
ISBN 978-1-61530-022-8 (library binding)
1. United States—History—Revolution, 1775–1783. 2. United States—History—War of 1812.
3. United States—History—Revolution, 1775–1783—Campaigns. 4. United States—History—
War of 1812—Campaigns. 5. United States—Foreign relations—Great Britain. 6. Great
Britain—Foreign relations—United States. I. Wallenfeldt, Jeffrey H.
E208.A447 2010
973.3—dc22

                                                                    2009038296

Manufactured in the United States of America

On the cover: The Battle of Bunker Hill was the first major battle of the American Revolution. This illustration, after an oil painting by American painter John Trumbull, depicts the death of General Joseph Warren, June 17, 1775. *Hulton Archive/Getty Images*

CONTENTS

40

49

71

89

155

201

208

218

221

INTRODUCTION

When you think of the American Revolution, you may picture John Hancock signing the Declaration of Independence with a flourish. Perhaps you envision the fiery orations of Samuel Adams or imagine Minutemen firing muskets at Redcoats as they practice the form of guerrilla warfare they learned from their Indian neighbours. It can be hard to relate to these 18th-century people, with their powdered perukes, their lofty, ornate language, and what may seem to some as their willingness to fight to the death over the inconvenience of paying some small taxes imposed on them without consent. Indeed, it may seem puzzling that the colonists would choose to separate themselves from a powerful empire that not only came to their defense in the French and Indian War just two decades earlier but was also a ready trading partner for American goods. But the individuals who fought in the American Revolution were not merely quaint figures in a book. They were real people who risked death for a vision of what America could be and what kinds of rights free people deserved.

Today the United States and Great Britain are close allies who share a language, culture, and a similar outlook on the world. But in the early days of the United States they fought two fierce wars against each other. In this book, you will learn what factors led up to these wars, the American Revolution and the War of 1812. You will discover their major causes and get an overview of each war's actions. You will encounter the major battles and meet the extraordinary people—both military and civilian—who led the nation through each conflict. As you read, you will see how the business of separating from Britain was not truly settled until after the War of 1812, which some have called "The Second War of American Independence."

In this book, you will discover how belonging to the British Empire gave the American colonists a sense of identity, a reliable trading partner, and an army to protect them. You will also learn that, when the British required the American colonists to pay taxes, outraged Americans refused because they lacked representation in Britain's Parliament. At first it might seem strange that Americans would fight a war over something as modest as taxes. Certainly other peoples in the history of the world have suffered greater indignity and oppression but there were good reasons why "taxation without representation" became a rallying cry that led to the war.

When King George III of England was young, his mother told him, "George, be a King." He grew up determined to assert that royal power and

American seamstress Betsy Ross is said to have created the original 13-star flag used by the colonies. On June 14, 1777, the Continental Congress adopted the Stars and Stripes as the national flag of the United States. © www.istockphoto.com/Nic Taylor

became an old-fashioned, inflexible ruler. Unfortunately, he came of age in a time when change was in the air. The 18th century was the time of the Age of Enlightenment. During that era, philosophers questioned the traditional order of society. Instead of valuing blind obedience to a sovereign, they championed individual rights, what they termed "natural rights." Americans came to feel particularly strongly about their rights. Because they lived so far from their ruling home country—an ocean voyage could easily take two months—the colonists had a long history of governing themselves with little interference from the king or Parliament.

The colonists' road to independence started with a series of escalating boycotts and protests. When Britain tried to tax legal documents, colonists rioted. When the British taxed cloth, colonists made their own homespun fabric. When they taxed tea, colonists dumped a shipment of tea in Boston Harbor. Americans had rarely been taxed before and felt that paying a tax they hadn't agreed to was the first step in submitting to treatment other British subjects would not tolerate. Even worse, Parliament passed a law explicitly stating that it had the right to make laws for the colonies in all matters. Thomas Jefferson called acts like these nothing less than "a deliberate systematical plan of reducing us to slavery." Furious colonists wrote angry newspaper articles. Mobs rioted. In England, Parliamentary leaders were angry at the colonials' insubordination. To punish the defiant Boston residents, the British government enacted the Boston Port Bill, which closed the city's ocean-going trade pending payment for the dumped tea, and occupied the city. This harsh response made many Americans question the wisdom of their loyalty to Britain even more.

As these tensions grew, representatives from the 13 colonies met as the Second Continental Congress in Philadelphia. They decided to send the king the Olive Branch Petition, a last-ditch effort to explain the colonists' complaints and find common ground. But they were rebuffed, and finally, there was no turning back. Written primarily by Thomas Jefferson and signed by the delegates, the Declaration of Independence asserted that "all men are created equal" and established the colonists' claims to what they considered their God-given rights to "life liberty, and the pursuit of happiness." It laid out America's claim to be an independent country, as well as its grievances with Britain's monarch—though in fact, much of the colonists' anger was actually directed at its Parliament. The war had officially begun.

By the time the Declaration of Independence was signed, the war was already more than a year old. It had started on April 19, 1775, when colonial Minutemen fought fiercely against British soldiers dispatched to seize the Americans' stores of ammunition in Lexington, Mass. This first battle was a

View of The ATTACK on BUNKER'S HILL, with the Burning of CHARLES TOWN, June 17. 1775.

This engraving depicts the attack on Bunker Hill and the burning of Charlestown in Boston Harbor, 1775. The first major battle of the war, Bunker Hill was a Pyrrhic victory for the British. MPI/Hulton Archive/Getty Images

shock to the British, who believed that the ill-trained American farmers could not seriously challenge them. Realizing that the Americans meant business, the British called for reinforcements. Meanwhile, Americans also prepared for war by sending Gen. George Washington to Boston as the head of the newly formed Continental Army.

A few months later, the two sides clashed again at the Battle of Bunker Hill near Boston where the Americans were given the famous command, "Don't shoot until you see the whites of their eyes!" The British were led by Gen. William Howe, an experienced soldier who had opposed Parliament's coercive legislation toward the colonies and favoured reconciliation yet eventually took command of the British forces in North America. Though the colonists were forced to retreat, the British had more than 1,000 casualties. The loss of so many men deeply affected Howe, who wrote of the outcome, "The success is too dearly bought."

As you continue to read, you'll meet some of the other fighters who changed the course of the war. One of them was American Col. Henry Knox, a former bookseller who led an expedition to haul 60 tons of captured British artillery 300 miles (482 kilometres) through ice and snow from Fort Ticonderoga, in New York, to Boston. The cannons were placed on a hill overlooking the city, which the British were forced to abandon in March 1776.

Later that year, the British and Americans fought over control of New York City. In November 1776, the Americans were forced to flee south to Pennsylvania. Every day more demoralized soldiers deserted. Of that dark moment, the patriot propagandist Thomas Paine wrote, "These are the times that try men's souls." In a letter to his brother, Washington wrote, "I think the game is pretty near up." Desperate, he decided to attack Trenton, N.J. After crossing the ice-choked Delaware River at night, several thousand men under Washington's command captured more than 1,000 Hessian mercenaries the next day. In the succeeding days Washington's troops scored other stunning victories in New Jersey that reenergized the American cause.

But in late 1777 the outlook was grim for the Continental Army once again. The British had conquered Philadelphia and Washington's army spent a desperate winter at Valley Forge, Pa., where they nearly starved. Despite their well-trained army and mighty navy, the British faced some serious disadvantages. Transporting troops and orders across the Atlantic Ocean was difficult and time consuming. Moreover, the British had to battle America's rough, unfamiliar terrain. But the largest obstacle they encountered was the Revolutionary cause's popularity with the majority of Americans. As John Adams would later say, "The Revolution was effected before the war commenced. The Revolution was in the minds and hearts of the people."

The war reached a turning point in autumn 1777 when the Americans won the Battle of Saratoga. Impressed by this victory, France threw its support behind the Americans. With French help the Americans won a decisive battle at Yorktown, Va., in 1781, and the British surrendered. The Treaty of Paris, which officially ended the war, was signed in 1783.

In the following years, the United States underwent many changes. With the drafting and enactment of the Constitution and the Bill of Rights the nature of American citizenship and of the U.S. government were defined. The country's population boomed and more settlers

The original handwritten draft of "The Star Spangled Banner," by American poet and attorney Francis Scott Key. Getty Images

O say can you see ~~through the~~ by the dawn's early light
What so proudly we hail'd at the twilight's last gleaming,
Whose broad stripes & bright stars through the perilous fight
O'er the ramparts we watch'd, were so gallantly streaming?
And the rocket's red glare, the bombs bursting in air
Gave proof through the night that our flag was still there
O say does that star spangled banner yet wave
O'er the land of the free & the home of the brave?

On the shore dimly seen through the mists of the deep,
Where the foe's haughty host in dread silence reposes,
What is that which the breeze, o'er the towering steep,
As it fitfully blows half conceals half discloses?
Now it catches the gleam of the morning's first beam,
In full glory reflected now shines in the stream,
'Tis the star-spangled banner — O long may it wave
O'er the land of the free & the home of the brave!

And where is that band who so vauntingly swore,
That the havoc of war & the battle's confusion
A home & a Country should leave us no more?
~~Their~~ ~~blood~~
Their blood has wash'd out their foul footsteps pollution
No refuge could save the hireling & slave
From the terror of flight or the gloom of the grave,
And the star-spangled banner in triumph doth wave
O'er the land of the free & the home of the brave.

O thus be it ever when freemen shall stand
Between their lov'd home & the war's desolation!
Blest with vict'ry & peace may the heav'n rescued land
Praise the power that hath made & preserv'd us a nation!
Then conquer we must when our cause it is just,
And this be our motto — "In God is our trust"
And the star-spangled banner in triumph shall wave
O'er the land of the free & the home of the brave.

moved west. It became a competitive trading nation.

In spite of America's growing power, however, Britain repeatedly meddled in U.S. affairs in ways that deeply offended Americans. The British were again in a major struggle with France and its powerful ruler Napoleon, and they took actions to prevent the United States from trading with France. Moreover, to the great resentment of Americans, the British Navy was boarding American ships forcibly to seize alleged Royal Navy deserters and in the process impressing American citizens into service on British ships.

The United States and Great Britain also disagreed about the future of western North America. The Americans wanted to see that land settled; the British advocated creating a large neutral Indian state in the region that now includes the states of Illinois, Indiana, Michigan, Ohio, and Wisconsin. Americans believed that Britain was funneling arms to the Indians through Canada.

In this book, you will get an overview of the War of 1812, which was declared in June 1812. Despite the fact that the British were preoccupied with their struggle against Napoleon, the war did not start well for the Americans. The U.S. forces invaded Canada early in the conflict, but they had little success. One of the Americans' most resounding early failures came at the hands of Maj. Gen. Sir Isaac Brock, who commanded Britain's forces of Upper Canada. He tricked American Brig. Gen. William Hull into thinking that the British had more

soldiers there than they actually did. Frightened, Hull surrendered Michigan's Fort Detroit without firing a shot. Brock's clever trick caused the Americans to lose Michigan for much of the war. Another debacle followed when an American attack on Montreal was halted because of a lack of cooperation from troops from New England, many of whom opposed the war.

Not until Sept. 13, 1813, was there good news for the Americans, when Commodore Oliver Hazard Perry of the Great Lakes fleet wrote to Pres. James Madison, "We have met the enemy and he is ours." The Americans had defeated the British in the Battle of Lake Erie. After this battle, America controlled the lake for the rest of the war. In the summer, Americans also won the important Battle of Plattsburgh.

Nevertheless, the British captured Washington on Aug. 25, 1814, and burned the Capitol and the Executive Mansion (now called the White House). When she fled the onslaught First Lady Dolley Madison was carrying a rolled up portrait of George Washington for safekeeping.

A month later, the British attacked Baltimore. Francis Scott Key, an American lawyer who was on a British ship to negotiate an American prisoner's release, witnessed the battle. Trapped on the water during the doomed Battle of Baltimore, he watched helplessly as British ships bombarded Fort McHenry. Afterwards, he saw an American flag still waving and wrote "The Star-Spangled Banner," the poem that would eventually provide the lyrics for the U.S. national anthem.

Although the United States did not fight the War of 1812 brilliantly, the job was done well enough to eventually prompt the British—exhausted from their long struggle against Napoleon—to quit. Both parties signed the Treaty of Ghent in December 1814.

Some have questioned if the war was necessary. But when the War of 1812 was over, America's place in the world had changed. Unchecked by British interference, white Americans pushed west, first forcing Indians out of the Northwest Territories and eventually pushing on all the way to California. Tragically, in the process most of the United States' Native American population was killed by war or disease or else forced onto reservations. The Treaty of Ghent also clarified the relationship between Britain and the United States, beginning a long peace between the two countries. The war promoted a strong sense of nationalism leading to a period called "The Era of Good Feelings."

Founding father John Adams said, "I always consider the settlement of America with reverence and wonder, as the opening of a grand scene and design in providence, for the illumination of the ignorant and the emancipation of the slavish part of mankind all over the earth." As you read this book, you will understand how these two wars can be seen as part of that grand scheme. The Revolutionary War and the War of 1812 made it clear that America meant to become and remain independent and to police its own borders. In the wake of the Revolution the Founding Fathers laid out the philosophical framework for the U.S. government. After the War of 1812, free to expand across the continent, the United States became one of the richest and most powerful nations the world has ever known. These two wars and the living, breathing people who fought them helped to make America what it is today.

CHAPTER 1

PRELUDE TO THE AMERICAN REVOLUTION

Although the dates 1775 and 1783 are cemented into history as the beginning and end, respectively, of the American Revolution, the struggle for American democracy and independence began long before the "shot heard round the world" rang out in Concord, Mass., and in many ways continued well after the signing of the Peace of Paris. The founding of the United States of America came about not as the consequence of a single event but as the confluence of a variety of struggles and ideals. In some ways it was an accidental by-product of the great power conflict between France and Great Britain, but just as certainly it was a premeditated construct based on the ideals of the Enlightenment—particularly those of natural rights and the social contract. American independence was won in a bloody, grueling, and protracted contest with the world's preeminent military power, but the battle for international respect and for the survival of the United States continued for two decades and was not finally won until Britain was confronted again in the War of 1812, characterized by many historians, appropriately, as the second American Revolution. These two wars, fought 20 years apart, were finally part of the same struggle to create a lasting democratic American republic, and they set the United States down the path toward power and prosperity.

LEGACY OF THE GREAT WAR FOR THE EMPIRE

The Great War for the Empire—or the French and Indian War, as it is known to Americans—was but another round in a century of warfare between the major European powers. First in King William's War (1689-97), then in Queen Anne's War (1702-13), and later in King George's War (1744-48; the American phase of the War of the Austrian Succession), Englishmen and Frenchmen had vied for control over the Indians, for possession of the territory lying to the north of the North American colonies, for access to the trade in the Northwest, and for commercial superiority in the West Indies. In most of these encounters, France had been aided by Spain. Because of its own holdings immediately south and west of the British colonies and in the Caribbean, Spain realized that it was in its own interest to join with the French in limiting British expansion. The culmination of these struggles came in 1754 with the Great War for the Empire and in 1756 with the outbreak of the Seven Years' War, in which France and Britain's continuing conflict was part of a more complex European war. British Prime Minister William Pitt determined that the conflict should be in every sense a national war and a war at sea. He revived the militia, reequipped and reorganized the navy, and sought to unite all parties and public opinion behind a coherent and intelligible war policy. He seized upon America and

India as the main objects of British strategy. Whereas previous contests between Great Britain and France in North America had been mostly provincial affairs, with American colonists doing most of the fighting for the British, the Great War for the Empire saw sizable commitments of British troops to America. Pitt's strategy was to allow Britain's ally, Prussia, to carry the brunt of the fighting in Europe and thus free Britain to concentrate its troops in America.

Despite the fact that they were outnumbered 15 to 1 by the British colonial population in America, the French were nevertheless well equipped to hold their own. They had a larger military organization in America than did the English; their troops were better trained; and they were more successful than the British in forming military alliances with the Indians. The early engagements of the war went to the French and made it seem as if the war would be a short and unsuccessful one for the British. By 1758, however, with both men and material up to a satisfactory level, Britain began to implement the larger strategy that would lead to its ultimate victory: sending a combined land and sea force to gain control of the St. Lawrence River and a large land force aimed at Fort Ticonderoga to eliminate French control of Lake Champlain. The other major players in this struggle for control of North America were, of course, the American Indians. When the French and Indian War culminated in the expulsion of France from

Canada, the Indians no longer could play the diplomatic card of agreeing to support whichever king—the one in London or the one in Paris—would restrain westward settlement.

Britain's victory over France in the Great War for the Empire had been won at very great cost. British government expenditures, which had amounted to nearly £6.5 million (over $10.5 million) annually before the war, rose to about £14.5 million (over $23.5 million) annually during the war. As a result, the burden of taxation in England was probably the highest in the country's history, much of it borne by the politically influential landed classes. Furthermore, with the acquisition of the vast domain of Canada and the prospect of holding British territories both against the various nations of Indians and against the Spaniards to the south and west, the costs of colonial defense could be expected to continue indefinitely. Parliament, moreover, had voted to give Massachusetts a generous sum in compensation for its war expenses. It therefore seemed reasonable to British opinion that some of the future burden of payment should be shifted to the colonists themselves—who

until then had been lightly taxed and indeed lightly governed.

The prolonged wars had also revealed the need to tighten the administration of the loosely run and widely scattered elements of the British Empire. If the course of the war had confirmed the necessity, the end of the war presented the opportunity. The acquisition of Canada required officials in London to take responsibility for the unsettled western territories, now freed from the threat of French occupation. The British soon moved to take charge of the whole field of Indian relations. By the royal Proclamation of 1763, a line was drawn down the Appalachians marking the limit of

Benjamin Franklin encouraged the colonies to unite together for protection from the French in this 1754 political cartoon. Library of Congress Serial and Government Publications Division

settlement from the British colonies, beyond which Indian trade was to be conducted strictly through British-appointed commissioners. The proclamation sprang in part from a respect for Indian rights. After Indian grievances had resulted in the start of Pontiac's War (the rebellion led by the Ottawa chief Pontiac in 1763–64), British authorities were determined to subdue intercolonial rivalries and abuses. To this end, the proclamation organized new British territories in America—the provinces of Quebec, East and West Florida, and Grenada (in the Windward Islands)—and a vast British-administered Indian reservation west of the Appalachians, from south of Hudson Bay to north of the Floridas. It forbade settlement on Indian territory, ordered those settlers already there to withdraw, and strictly limited future settlement. For the first time in the history of European colonization in the New World, the proclamation formalized the concept of Indian land titles, prohibiting issuance of patents to any lands claimed by a tribe unless the Indian title had first been extinguished by purchase or treaty.

From London's viewpoint, leaving a lightly garrisoned West to the fur-gathering Indians also made economic and imperial sense. The proclamation, however, caused consternation among British colonists for two reasons. It meant that limits were being set to the prospects of settlement and speculation in western lands, and it took control of the west out of colonial hands. The most ambitious men in the colonies thus saw the proclamation as a loss of power to control their own fortunes. Indeed, the British government's huge underestimation of how deeply the halt in westward expansion would be resented by the colonists was one of the factors in sparking the 12-year crisis that led to the American Revolution. Indian efforts to preserve a terrain for themselves in the continental interior might still have had a chance with British policy makers, but they would be totally ineffective when the time came to deal with a triumphant United States of America.

THE TAX CONTROVERSY

George Grenville, who was named prime minister in 1763, was soon looking to meet the costs of defense by raising revenue in the colonies. The first measure was the Plantation Act of 1764, usually called the Revenue, or Sugar, Act, which reduced to a mere threepence the duty on molasses imported into the colonies from non-British Caribbean sources but linked with this a high duty on refined sugar and a prohibition on foreign rum. Actually a reinvigoration of the largely ineffective Molasses Act of 1733, the Sugar Act granted a virtual monopoly of the American market to British West Indies sugar planters. The 1733 act had not been firmly enforced, but this time the government set up a system of customhouses, staffed by British officers. The protected price of British sugar actually benefited New England distillers, though they did not appreciate it. More objectionable to the colonists were the stricter bonding regulations for shipmasters, whose cargoes were subject to seizure and confiscation by British customs commissioners and who were placed under the authority of the Vice Admiralty Court in distant Nova Scotia if they violated the trade rules or failed to pay duties. The court heard very few cases, but in principle it appeared to threaten the cherished British privilege of trials by local juries. Boston further objected to the tax's revenue-raising aspect on constitutional grounds, but, despite some expressions of anxiety, the colonies in general acquiesced. Owing to this act,

A satirical representation of an official stamp as required by the Stamp Act of 1765. Library of Congress Humanities and Social Sciences Division

the earlier clandestine trade in foreign sugar, and thus much colonial maritime commerce, was severely hampered.

Parliament next affected colonial economic prospects by passing a Currency Act (1764) to withdraw paper currencies, many of them surviving from the war period, from circulation. This was not done to restrict economic growth so much as to take out currency that was thought to be unsound, but it did severely reduce the circulating medium during the difficult postwar period and further indicated that such matters were subject to British control.

Grenville's next move was a stamp duty, to be raised on a wide variety of transactions, including legal writs, newspaper advertisements, and ships' bills of lading. The colonies were duly consulted and offered no alternative suggestions. The feeling in London, shared by Benjamin Franklin, was that, after making formal objections, the colonies would accept the new taxes as they had the earlier ones. But the Stamp Act (1765) hit harder and deeper than any previous parliamentary measure. As some agents had already pointed out, because of postwar economic difficulties the colonies were short of ready funds. (In Virginia this shortage was so serious that the province's treasurer, John Robinson, who was also speaker of the assembly, manipulated and redistributed paper money that had been officially withdrawn from circulation by the Currency Act; a large proportion of the landed gentry benefited from this largesse.) The Stamp Act struck at vital points of colonial economic operations, affecting transactions in trade. It also affected many of the most articulate and influential people in the colonies (lawyers, journalists, bankers). It was, moreover, the first "internal" tax levied directly on the colonies by Parliament. Previous colonial taxes had been levied by local authorities or had been "external" import duties whose primary aim could be viewed as regulating trade for the benefit of the empire as a whole rather than raising revenue. Yet no one, either in Britain or in the colonies, fully anticipated the uproar that followed the imposition of these duties. Mobs in Boston and other towns rioted and forced appointed stamp distributors to renounce their posts; legal business was largely halted. Several colonies sent delegations to a Congress in New York in the summer of 1765, where the Stamp Act was denounced as a violation of the Englishman's right to be taxed only through elected representatives, and plans were adopted to impose a nonimportation embargo on British goods.

A change of ministry facilitated a change of British policy on taxation. Parliamentary opinion was angered by what it perceived as colonial lawlessness, but British merchants were worried about the embargo on British imports. The marquis of Rockingham, succeeding Grenville, was persuaded to repeal the Stamp Act—for domestic reasons rather than out of any sympathy with colonial protests—and in 1766 the repeal was passed. On the same day, however, Parliament also passed the Declaratory Act, which declared that Parliament had the power to bind or legislate the colonies "in all cases whatsoever." Parliament would not have voted the repeal without this assertion of its authority.

This crisis focused attention on the unresolved question of Parliament's relationship to a growing empire. The act particularly illustrated British insensitivity to the political maturity that had developed in the American provinces during the 18th century. The colonists, jubilant at the repeal of the Stamp Act, drank innumerable toasts, sounded peals of cannon, and were prepared to ignore

IN FOCUS: THE SONS OF LIBERTY

Among those who opposed the Stamp Act were the Sons of Liberty. Formed in the summer of 1765, this organization took its name from a speech given in February 1765 in the British Parliament by Isaac Barré, in which he referred to the colonials who had opposed unjust British measures as the "sons of liberty." They rallied support for colonial resistance through the use of petitions, assemblies, and propaganda, and they sometimes resorted to violence against officials of the mother country. Instrumental in preventing the enforcement of the Stamp Act, they remained an active pre-Revolutionary force against the crown.

the Declaratory Act as face-saving window dressing. John Adams, however, warned in his *Dissertation on the Canon and Feudal Law* that Parliament, armed with this view of its powers, would try to tax the colonies again; and this happened in 1767 when Charles Townshend became chancellor of the Exchequer in a ministry formed by Pitt, now earl of Chatham. The problem was that Britain's financial burden had not been lifted. Townshend, claiming to take literally the colonial distinction between external and internal taxes, imposed external duties on a wide range of necessities, including lead, glass, paint, paper, and tea, the principal domestic beverage. One ominous result was that colonists now began to believe that the British were developing a long-term plan to reduce the colonies to a subservient position, which they were soon calling "slavery." This view was ill-informed, however. Grenville's measures had been designed as a carefully considered package; apart from some tidying-up legislation, Grenville had had no further plans for the colonies after the Stamp Act. His successors developed further measures, not as extensions of an original plan but because the Stamp Act had been repealed.

Nevertheless, the colonists were outraged. In Pennsylvania the lawyer and legislator John Dickinson wrote a series of essays that, appearing in 1767 and 1768 as *Letters from a Farmer in Pennsylvania*, were widely reprinted and exerted great influence in forming a united colonial opposition. Dickinson agreed that Parl-

iament had supreme power where the whole empire was concerned, but he denied that it had power over internal colonial affairs; he quietly implied that the basis of colonial loyalty lay in its utility among equals rather than in obedience owed to a superior.

It proved easier to unite on opinion than on action. Gradually, after much maneuvering and negotiation, a wide-ranging nonimportation policy against British goods was brought into operation. Agreement had not been easy to reach, and the tensions sometimes broke out in acrimonious charges of noncooperation. In addition, the policy had to be enforced by newly created local committees, a process that put a new disciplinary power in the hands of local men who had not had much previous experience in public affairs. There were, as a result, many signs of discontent with the ordering of domestic affairs in some of the colonies—a development that had obvious implications for the future of colonial politics if more action was needed later.

CONSTITUTIONAL DIFFERENCES WITH BRITAIN

Very few colonists wanted or even envisaged independence at this stage. (Dickinson had hinted at such a possibility with expressions of pain that were obviously sincere.) The colonial struggle for power, although charged with intense feeling, was not an attempt to change government structure but an argument over legal interpretation. The core of the colonial case was that, as British subjects, they were entitled to the same privileges as their fellow subjects in Britain. They could not constitutionally be taxed without their own consent; and, because they were unrepresented in the Parliament that voted the taxes, they had not given this consent. James Otis, in two long pamphlets, ceded all sovereign power to Parliament with this proviso. Others, however, began to question whether Parliament did have lawful power to legislate over the colonies. These doubts were expressed by the late 1760s, when James Wilson, a Scottish immigrant lawyer living in Philadelphia, wrote an essay on the subject. Because of the withdrawal of the Townshend round of duties in 1770, Wilson kept this essay private until new troubles arose in 1774, when he published it as Considerations on the Nature and Extent of the Legislative Authority of the British Parliament. In this he fully articulated a view that had been gathering force in the colonies (it was also the opinion of Franklin) that Parliament's lawful sovereignty stopped at the shores of Britain.

PRIMARY SOURCE: JOHN DICKINSON'S *LETTERS FROM A FARMER IN PENNSYLVANIA*

In 1765, Parliament passed a Quartering Act that required colonial legislatures to pay for specified articles used by British troops in the colonies. Among the legislatures refusing to obey the Quartering Act was that of New York. As New York was the headquarters of the British army, Parliament decided to make an example of the colony, and on July 2, 1767, suspended the Colonial Assembly until it complied with the Act.

Letters from a Farmer in Pennsylvania, written by John Dickinson, though conciliatory in tone, did much to formulate the sense of wrong in British policies that led the colonies at last to strike for independence. Published first in newspapers, the Letters were later brought out in a pamphlet that went rapidly through at least ten editions. In his letter of Nov. 5, 1767, Dickinson discussed Parliament's suspension of the New York Assembly. Source: Memoirs of the Historical Society of Pennsylvania, Vol. XIV, Philadelphia, 1895, pp. 307-312.

My Dear Countrymen,

I am a farmer, settled after a variety of fortunes near the banks of the River Delaware in the province of Pennsylvania. I received a liberal education and have been engaged in the busy scenes of life; but am now convinced that a man may be as happy without bustle as with it. My farm is small; my servants are few and good; I have a little money at interest; I wish for no more; my employment in my own affairs is easy; and with a contented, grateful mind . . . I am completing the number of days allotted to me by divine goodness.

Being generally master of my time, I spend a good deal of it in a library, which I think the most valuable part of my small estate; and being acquainted with two or three gentlemen of abilities and learning who honor me with their friendship, I have acquired, I believe, a greater share of knowledge in history and the laws and constitution of my country than is generally attained by men of my class, many of them not being so fortunate as I have been in the opportunities of getting information.

From infancy I was taught to love humanity and liberty. Inquiry and experience have since confirmed my reverence for the lessons then given me by convincing me more fully of their truth and excellence. Benevolence toward mankind excites wishes for their welfare, and such wishes endear the means of fulfilling them. These can be found in liberty only, and therefore her sacred cause ought to be espoused by every man, on every occasion, to the utmost of his power. As a charitable but poor person does not withhold his mite because he cannot relieve all the distresses of the miserable, so should not any honest man suppress his sentiments concerning freedom, however small their influence is likely to be. Perhaps he may "touch some wheel" that will have an effect greater than he could reasonably expect.

These being my sentiments, I am encouraged to offer to you, my countrymen, my thoughts on some late transactions that appear to me to be of the utmost importance to you. Conscious of my defects, I have waited some time in expectation of seeing the subject treated by persons much better qualified for the task; but being therein disappointed, and apprehensive that longer delays will be injurious, I venture at length to request the attention of the public, praying that these lines may be read with the same zeal for the happiness of British America with which they were written.

With a good deal of surprise I have observed that little notice has been taken of an act of Parliament, as injurious in its principle to the liberties of these colonies as the Stamp Act was: I mean the act for suspending the legislation of New York.

The assembly of that government complied with a former act of Parliament, requiring certain provisions to be made for the troops in America, in every particular, I think, except the articles of salt, pepper, and vinegar. In my opinion they acted imprudently, considering all circumstances, in not complying so far as would have given satisfaction as several colonies did. But my dislike of their conduct in that instance has not blinded me so much that I cannot plainly perceive that they have been punished in a manner pernicious to American freedom and justly alarming to all the colonies.

If the British Parliament has a legal authority to issue an order that we shall furnish a single article for the troops here and to compel obedience to that order, they have the same right to issue an order for us to supply those troops with arms, clothes, and every necessary, and to compel obedience to that order also; in short, to lay any burdens they please upon us. What is this but taxing us at a certain sum and leaving to us only the manner of raising it? How is this mode more tolerable than the Stamp Act? Would that act have appeared more pleasing to Americans if, being ordered thereby to raise the sum total of the taxes, the mighty privilege had been left to them of saying how much should be paid for an instrument of writing on paper, and how much for another on parchment?

An act of Parliament commanding us to do a certain thing, if it has any validity, is a tax upon us for the expense that accrues in complying with it, and for this reason, I believe, every colony on the continent that chose to give a mark of their respect for Great Britain, in complying with the act relating to the troops, cautiously avoided the mention of that act, lest their conduct should be attributed to its supposed obligation.

The matter being thus stated, the assembly of New York either had or had not a right to refuse submission to that act. If they had, and I imagine no American will say they had not, then the Parliament had no right to compel them to execute it. If they had not that right, they had no right to punish them for not executing it; and therefore had no right to suspend their legislation, which is a punishment. In fact, if the people of New York cannot be legally taxed but by their own representatives, they cannot be legally deprived of the privilege of legislation, only for insisting on that exclusive privilege of taxation. If they may be legally deprived in such a case of the privilege of legislation, why may they not, with equal reason, be deprived of every other privilege? Or why may not every colony be treated in the same manner, when any of them shall dare to deny their assent to any impositions that shall be directed? Or what signifies the repeal of the Stamp Act, if these colonies are to lose their other privileges by not tamely surrendering that of taxation?

There is one consideration arising from the suspension which is not generally attended to but shows its importance very clearly. It was not necessary that this suspension should be caused by an act of Parliament. The Crown might have restrained the governor of New York even from calling the assembly together, by its prerogative in the royal governments. This step, I suppose, would have been taken if the conduct of the assembly of New York had been regarded as an act of disobedience to the Crown alone. But it is regarded as an act of "disobedience to the authority of the British legislature." This gives the suspension a consequence vastly more affecting. It is a parliamentary assertion of the supreme authority of the British legislature over these colonies in the point of taxation; and it is intended to compel New York into a submission to that authority. It seems therefore to me as much a violation of the liberty of the people of that province, and consequently of all these colonies, as if the Parliament had sent a number of regiments to be quartered upon them, till they should comply.

For it is evident that the suspension is meant as a compulsion; and the method of compelling is totally indifferent. It is indeed probable that the sight of red coats and the hearing of drums would have been most alarming, because people are generally more influenced by their eyes and ears than by their reason. But whoever seriously considers the matter must perceive that a dreadful stroke is aimed at the liberty of these colonies. I say of these colonies; for the cause of one is the cause of all. If the Parliament may lawfully deprive New York of any of her rights, it may deprive any or all the other colonies of their rights; and nothing can possibly so much encourage such attempts as a mutual inattention to the interest of each other. To divide and thus to destroy is the first political maxim in attacking those who are powerful by their union. He certainly is not a wise man who folds his arms and reposes himself at home, seeing with unconcern the flames that have invaded his neighbor's house without using any endeavors to extinguish them. When Mr. Hampden's ship-money cause for 3s. 4d. was tried, all the people of England, with anxious expectations, interested themselves in the important decision; and when the slightest point touching the freedom of one colony is agitated, I earnestly wish that all the rest may with equal ardor support their sister. Very much may be said on this subject, but I hope more at present is unnecessary.

With concern I have observed that two assemblies of this province have sat and adjourned without taking any notice of this act. It may perhaps be asked: What would have been proper for them to do? I am by no means fond of inflammatory measures. I detest them. I should be sorry that anything should be done which might justly displease our sovereign or our mother country. But a firm, modest exertion of a free spirit should never be wanting on public occasions. It appears to me that it would have been sufficient for the assembly to have ordered our agents to represent to the Kings ministers their sense of the suspending act and to pray for its repeal. Thus we should have borne our testimony against it; and might therefore reasonably expect that on a like occasion we might receive the same assistance from the other colonies.

Small things grow great by concord.

A Farmer

The official British reply to the colonial case on representation was that the colonies were "virtually" represented in Parliament in the same sense that the large voteless majority of the British public was represented by those who did vote. To this Otis snorted that, if the majority of the British people did not have the vote, they ought to have it. The idea of colonial members of Parliament, several times suggested, was never a likely solution because of problems of time and distance and because, from the colonists' point of view, colonial members would not have adequate influence.

The standpoints of the two sides to the controversy could be traced in the language used. The principle of parliamentary sovereignty was expressed in the language of paternalistic authority; the British referred to themselves as parents and to the colonists as children. Colonial Tories, who accepted Parliament's case in the interests of social stability, also used this terminology. From this point of view, colonial insubordination was "unnatural," just as the revolt of children against parents was unnatural. The colonists replied to all this in the language of rights. They held that Parliament could do nothing in the colonies that it could not do in Britain because the Americans were protected by all the common-law rights of the British. (When the First Continental Congress met in September 1774, one of its first acts was to affirm that the colonies were entitled to the common law of England.)

Rights, as Richard Bland of Virginia insisted in *The Colonel Dismounted* (as early as 1764), implied equality. And here he touched on the underlying source of colonial grievance. Americans were being treated as unequals, which they not only resented but also feared would lead to a loss of control of their own affairs. Colonists perceived legal inequality when writs of assistance—essentially, general search warrants—were authorized in Boston in 1761 while closely related "general warrants" were outlawed in two celebrated cases in Britain. Townshend specifically legalized writs of assistance in the colonies in 1767. Dickinson devoted one of his *Letters from a Farmer* to this issue.

When Lord North became prime minister early in 1770, George III had at last found a minister who could work both with himself and with Parliament. British government began to acquire some stability. In 1770, in the face of the American policy of nonimportation, the Townshend tariffs were withdrawn—all except the tax on tea, which was kept for symbolic reasons. Relative calm returned, though it was ruffled on the New England coastline by frequent incidents of defiance of customs officers, who could get no support from local juries. These outbreaks did not win much sympathy from other colonies, but they were serious enough to call for an increase in the number of British regular forces stationed in Boston.

THE BOSTON MASSACRE

One of the most violent clashes occurred in Boston on March 5, 1770, just before the repeal of the Townshend duties. The incident, which became known as the Boston Massacre, was the climax of a series of brawls in which local workers and sailors clashed with British soldiers quartered in Boston. Harassed by a mob, the troops opened fire. Crispus Attucks, a black sailor and former slave, was shot first and died along with four others. Samuel Adams, a skillful propagandist of the day, shrewdly depicted the affair as a battle for American liberty. His cousin John Adams, however, successfully defended the British soldiers tried for murder in the affair.

The other serious quarrel with British authority occurred in New York, where the assembly refused to accept all the British demands for quartering troops. Before a compromise was reached, Parliament had threatened to suspend the assembly. The episode was ominous because it indicated that Parliament was taking the Declaratory Act at its word; on no previous occasion had the British legislature intervened in the operation of the constitution in an American colony. (Such interventions, which were rare, had come from the crown.)

THE INTOLERABLE ACTS

In retaliation to the Boston Massacre and other provocations, including the Boston Tea Party (see sidebar), in the spring of 1774, with hardly any opposition,

This depiction of the Boston Massacre was engraved by famous Revolutionary Paul Revere. Library of Congress Prints and Photographs Division

In Focus: The Boston Tea Party

The Townshend Acts passed by Parliament in 1767 imposed duties on various products imported into the British colonies and raised such a storm of colonial protest and noncompliance that they were repealed in 1770, saving the duty on tea, which was retained by Parliament to demonstrate its presumed right to raise such colonial revenue without colonial approval. The merchants of Boston circumvented the act by continuing to receive tea smuggled in by Dutch traders. In 1773 Parliament passed a Tea Act designed to aid the financially troubled East India Company by granting it (1) a monopoly on all tea exported to the colonies, (2) an exemption on the export tax, and (3) a "drawback" (refund) on duties owed on certain surplus quantities of tea in its possession. The tea sent to the colonies was to be carried only in East India Company ships and sold only through its own agents, bypassing the independent colonial shippers and merchants. The company thus could sell the tea at a less-than-usual price in either America or Britain; it could undersell anyone else. This plan naturally affected colonial merchants, and many colonists denounced the act as a plot to induce Americans to buy—and therefore pay the tax on—legally imported tea. The perception of monopoly drove the normally conservative colonial merchants into an alliance with radicals led by Samuel Adams and his Sons of Liberty. Boston was not the only port to threaten to reject the casks of taxed tea, but its reply was the most dramatic—and provocative.

In such cities as New York, Philadelphia, and Charleston, tea agents resigned or canceled orders, and merchants refused consignments. In Boston, however, the royal governor Thomas Hutchinson determined to uphold the law and maintained that three arriving ships, the Dartmouth, Eleanor, and Beaver, should be allowed to deposit their cargoes and that appropriate duties should be honoured. On the night of Dec. 16, 1773, a group of about 60 men, encouraged by a large crowd of Bostonians, donned blankets and Indian headdresses, marched to Griffin's wharf, boarded the ships, and dumped 342 tea chests, belonging to the East India Company and valued at £18,000 ($29,500), into the water. The British opinion was outraged, and America's friends in Parliament were immobolized. American merchants in other cities were also disturbed. Property was property.

On Dec. 16, 1773, Bostonians dressed in Native American clothing threw imported tea into Boston Harbor in protest against the Tea Act. MPI/Hulton Archive/Getty Images

Parliament passed the Coercive Acts, four punitive measures designed to reduce Massachusetts to order and imperial discipline. The first of these measures, which became known in the colonies as the Intolerable Acts, was the Boston Port Bill, closing that city's harbour until restitution was made for the destroyed tea. In the second, the Massachusetts Government Act, Parliament abrogated the colony's

PRIMARY SOURCE: THE QUARTERING ACT

One of the "Intolerable Acts" was the Quartering Act of June 2, 1774, which applied to all British America and gave colonial governors the right to requisition unoccupied buildings to house British troops. However, in Massachusetts the British troops were forced to remain camped on the Boston Common until the following November because the Boston patriots refused to allow workmen to repair the vacant buildings Gen. Thomas Gage had obtained for quarters. Source: The Statutes at Large [of Great Britain], Danby Pickering, ed., Cambridge (England), various dates, Vol. XXX.

Whereas doubts have been entertained whether troops can be quartered otherwise than in barracks, in case barracks have been provided sufficient for the quartering of all the officers and soldiers within any town, township, city, district, or place within His Majesty's dominions in North America; and whereas it may frequently happen from the situation of such barracks that, if troops should be quartered therein they would not be stationed where their presence may be necessary and required: be it therefore enacted by the King's Most Excellent Majesty, by and with the advice and consent of the Lords … and Commons, in this present Parliament assembled … that, in such cases, it shall and may be lawful for the persons who now are, or may be hereafter, authorized by law, in any of the provinces within His Majesty's dominions in North America, and they are hereby respectively authorized, empowered, and directed, on the requisition of the officer who, for the time being, has the command of His Majesty's forces in North America, to cause any officers or soldiers in His Majesty's service to be quartered and billeted in such manner as is now directed by law where no barracks are provided by the colonies.

2. And be it further enacted by the authority aforesaid that, if it shall happen at any time that any officers or soldiers in His Majesty's service shall remain within any of the said colonies without quarters for the space of twenty-four hours after such quarters shall have been demanded, it shall and may be lawful for the governor of the province to order and direct such and so many uninhabited houses, outhouses, barns, or other buildings as he shall think necessary to be taken (making a reasonable allowance for the same) and make fit for the reception of such officers and soldiers, and to put and quarter such officers and soldiers therein for such time as he shall think proper.

3. And be it further enacted by the authority aforesaid that this act, and everything herein contained, shall continue and be in force in all His Majesty's dominions in North America, until March 24, 1776.

charter of 1691, reducing it to the level of a crown colony, substituting a military government under Gen. Thomas Gage. It also outlawed town meetings—the famous gatherings that had been forums for radical thinkers—as political bodies.

The third act, the Administration of Justice Act, was aimed at protecting British officials charged with capital offenses during law enforcement by allowing them to go to England or another colony for trial. The fourth Coercive Act included new arrangements for housing British troops in occupied American dwellings, thus reviving the indignation that surrounded the earlier Quartering Act, which had been allowed to expire in 1770.

To make matters worse, Parliament also passed the Quebec Act. Under consideration since 1773, this act removed all the territory and fur trade between the Ohio and Mississippi rivers from possible colonial jurisdiction and awarded it to Upper Canada (the southern section that would eventually become the province of Quebec), permanently blocking the prospect of American control of western settlement. By establishing French civil law and the Roman Catholic religion in the coveted area, Britain acted liberally toward Quebec's settlers but raised the spectre of popery before the mainly Protestant colonies to Canada's south.

The Intolerable Acts represented an attempt to reimpose strict British control over the American colonies, but after 10 years of vacillation, the decision to be firm had come too late. Rather than cowing Massachusetts and separating it from the other colonies, the oppressive measures became the justification for convening the First Continental Congress later in 1774.

CHAPTER 2

INDEPENDENCE

THE FIRST CONTINENTAL CONGRESS

There was widespread agreement that the intervention in colonial government represented by the Intolerable Acts could threaten other provinces and could be countered only by collective action. After much intercolonial correspondence, a Continental Congress came into existence, meeting in Philadelphia in September 1774. Every colonial assembly except that of Georgia appointed and sent a delegation. The Virginia delegation's instructions were drafted by Thomas Jefferson and were later published as *A Summary View of the Rights of British America* (1774). Jefferson insisted on the autonomy of colonial legislative power and set forth a highly individualistic view of the basis of American rights. This belief that the American colonies and other members of the British Empire were distinct states united under the king and thus subject only to the king and not to Parliament was shared by several other delegates, notably James Wilson and John Adams, and strongly influenced the Congress.

The Congress, comprising 56 deputies, convened on Sept. 5, 1774. Peyton Randolph of Virginia was unanimously elected president, thus establishing usage of that term as well as "Congress." Charles Thomson of Pennsylvania was elected secretary and served in that office during the 15-year life of the Congress.

George Washington (standing) *surrounded by members of the Continental Congress, lithograph by Currier & Ives, c. 1876.* Currier & Ives Collection, Library of Congress, Neg. No. LC-USZC2-3154

The Congress's first important decision was one on procedure: whether to vote by colony, each having one vote, or by wealth calculated on a ratio with population. The decision to vote by colony was made on practical grounds—neither wealth nor population could be satisfactorily ascertained—but it had important consequences. Individual colonies, no matter what their size, retained a degree of autonomy that translated immediately into the language and prerogatives of sovereignty.

The First Continental Congress included Patrick Henry, George Washington, John and Samuel Adams, John Jay, and John Dickinson. Meeting in secret session, the body rejected a plan for reconciling British authority with colonial freedom. Under Massachusetts's influence, the Congress adopted the Suffolk Resolves, recently voted in Suffolk County, Mass., which for the first time put natural rights into the official colonial argument (hitherto all remonstrances had been based on common law and constitutional rights). Because representative provincial government had been dissolved in Massachusetts, delegates from Boston and neighbouring towns in Suffolk county met at Dedham and later at Milton to declare their refusal to obey either the acts or the officials responsible for them. They urged fellow citizens to cease paying taxes or trading with Britain and to undertake militia drill each week. Passed unanimously, the resolves were carried by Paul Revere to Philadelphia. The Congress adopted a declaration of personal rights, including life, liberty, property, assembly, and trial by jury. The declaration also denounced taxation without representation and the maintenance of

IN FOCUS: REGULATORS OF NORTH CAROLINA

The Regulators were a vigilance society dedicated to fighting exorbitant legal fees and the corruption of appointed officials in the frontier counties of North Carolina during the 1760s and '70s. Deep-seated economic and social differences had produced a distinct east-west sectionalism in North Carolina. The colonial government was dominated by the eastern areas, and even county governments were controlled by the royal governor through his power to appoint local officers. Backcountry (western) people who suffered from excessive taxes, dishonest officials, and exorbitant fees also became bitter about multiple office holdings. They formed an association called the Regulators, which sought vainly to obtain reforms. They then refused to pay taxes or fees, punished public officials, and interfered with the courts. Finally, the Regulator insurrection was crushed by Gov. William Tryon at the Battle of Alamance (May 16, 1771). Many frontiersmen fled to Tennessee, but the legacy of bitterness induced many Regulators to side with the loyalists during the American Revolution, in addition to continuing their own futile agitation for five more years.

the British army in the colonies without their consent. Parliamentary regulation of American commerce, however, was willingly accepted, and the prevailing mood was cautious.

The Congress's aim was to put such pressure on the British government that it would redress all colonial grievances and restore the harmony that had once prevailed. The Congress thus adopted an Association that committed the colonies to a carefully phased plan of economic pressure, beginning with nonimportation, moving to nonconsumption, and finishing the following September (after the rice harvest had been exported) with nonexportation. In October 1774 the Congress petitioned the crown for a redress of grievances accumulated since 1763. A few New England and Virginia delegates were looking toward independence, but the majority went home hoping that these steps, together with new appeals to the king and to the British people, would avert the need for any further such meetings. Its last act was to set a date for another Congress to meet on May 10, 1775, to consider further steps if these measures failed.

Behind the unity achieved by the Congress lay deep divisions in colonial society. In the mid-1760s upriver New York was disrupted by land riots, which also broke out in parts of New Jersey; much worse disorder ravaged the backcountry of both North and South Carolina, where frontier people were left unprotected by legislatures that taxed

them but in which they felt themselves unrepresented. A pitched battle at Alamance Creek in North Carolina in 1771 ended that rising, known as the Regulator Insurrection, and was followed by executions for treason.

Although without such serious disorder, the cities also revealed acute social tensions and resentments of inequalities of economic opportunity and visible status. New York provincial politics were riven by intense rivalry between two great family-based factions, the DeLanceys, who benefited from royal government connections, and their rivals, the Livingstons. (The politics of the quarrel with Britain affected the domestic standing of these groups and eventually eclipsed the DeLanceys.) Another phenomenon was the rapid rise of dissenting religious sects, notably the Baptists; although they carried no political program, their style of preaching suggested a strong undercurrent of social as well as religious dissent. There was no inherent unity to these disturbances, but many leaders of colonial society were reluctant to ally themselves with these disruptive elements even in protest against Britain. They were concerned about the domestic consequences of letting the protests take a revolutionary turn; power shared with these elements might never be recovered.

THE SECOND CONTINENTAL CONGRESS

Before the Second Continental Congress assembled in May 1775 at the Pennsylvania

Image of the Declaration of Independence (1776) taken from an engraving made by printer William J. Stone in 1823. National Archives, Washington, D.C.

State House (now Independence Hall), in Philadelphia, hostilities had already broken out between Americans and British troops at Lexington and Concord, Mass., on April 19. New members of the Second Congress included Benjamin Franklin and Thomas Jefferson. John Hancock and John Jay were among those who served as president. Although most colonial leaders still hoped for reconciliation with Britain, the news of fighting stirred the delegates to more radical action. Steps were taken to put the continent on a war footing. The Congress "adopted" the New England military forces that had converged upon Boston and appointed Gen. George Washington commander in chief of the Continental Army on June 15, 1775. While a further appeal was addressed to the British people (mainly at Dickinson's insistence), Congress adopted a *Declaration of the Causes and Necessity of Taking Up Arms*, and appointed committees to deal with domestic supply and foreign affairs. In August 1775 the king declared a state of rebellion; by the end of the year, all colonial trade had been banned. Even yet, Washington, still referred to the British troops as "ministerial" forces, indicating a civil war, not a war looking to separate national identity.

Then in January 1776 the publication of Thomas Paine's irreverent pamphlet *Common Sense* abruptly shattered this hopeful complacency and put independence on the agenda. Paine's eloquent, direct language spoke people's unspoken thoughts; no pamphlet had ever made such an impact on colonial opinion. While the Congress negotiated urgently, but secretly, for a French alliance, power struggles erupted in provinces where conservatives still hoped for relief. The only form relief could take, however, was British concessions; as public opinion hardened in Britain, where a general election in November 1774 had returned a strong majority for Lord North, the hope for reconciliation faded. In the face of British intransigence, men committed to their definition of colonial rights were left with no alternative, and the substantial portion of colonists—about one-third according to John Adams, although contemporary historians believe the number to have been much smaller—who preferred loyalty to the crown, with all its disadvantages, were localized and outflanked. Where the British armies massed, they found plenty of loyalist support, but, when they moved on, they left the loyalists feeble and exposed.

The most dramatic internal revolution occurred in Pennsylvania, where a strong radical party, based mainly in Philadelphia but with allies in the country, seized power in the course of the controversy over independence itself. Opinion for independence swept the colonies in the spring of 1776.

On April 12, 1776, the Revolutionary convention of North Carolina specifically authorized its delegates in Congress to vote for independence. On May 15 the Virginia convention instructed its deputies to offer the motion, which was brought forward in the Congress by Richard Henry Lee on June 7. By that time the Congress had already taken long steps toward severing ties with Britain. It had denied Parliamentary sovereignty over the colonies as early as Dec. 6, 1775, and it had declared on May 10, 1776, that the authority of the king ought to be "totally suppressed," advising all the several colonies to establish governments of their own choice.

The passage of Lee's resolution was delayed for several reasons. Some of the delegates had not yet received authorization to vote for separation; a few were opposed to taking the final step; and several men, among them John Dickinson, believed that the formation of a central government, together with attempts to secure foreign aid, should precede it. However, a committee consisting of Thomas Jefferson, John Adams, Benjamin Franklin, Roger Sherman, and Robert R. Livingston was promptly chosen on June 11 to prepare a statement justifying the decision to assert independence, should it be taken.

THE DECLARATION OF INDEPENDENCE

This document was written largely by Jefferson, who had displayed talent as a political philosopher and polemicist in his *A Summary View of the Rights of British America* (1774). At the request of his fellow committee members he wrote the first draft. The members of the committee made a number of merely semantic changes and also expanded somewhat the list of charges against the king.

The Congress also made substantial changes (notably removing a denunciation of the slave trade). The resulting Declaration of Independence consisted of two parts. The preamble set the claims of the United States on a basis of natural rights, with a dedication to the principle of equality (famously proclaiming: "We hold these truths to be self-evident, that all men are created equal, that they are endowed by their Creator with certain unalienable Rights, that among these are Life, Liberty and the pursuit of Happiness."). The second part of the document was a long list of grievances against the crown—not Parliament now, since the argument was that Parliament had no lawful power in the colonies.

It can be said, as John Adams did, that the declaration contained nothing really novel in its political philosophy, which was derived from John Locke, Algernon Sidney, and other English theorists. It may also be asserted that the argument offered was not without flaws in history and logic. But even with its defects, the Declaration of Independence was in essence morally just and politically valid. If its invocation of the right and duty of revolution cannot be established on historical grounds, it nevertheless rests solidly upon ethical ones.

On July 1 nine delegations voted for separation, despite warm opposition on

IN FOCUS: LIBERTY BELL

Legend has it that the Liberty Bell, one of the most recognizable traditional symbols of American freedom, was rung on July 4, 1776, to signal the Continental Congress's adoption of the Declaration of Independence. In fact it was not rung until four days later, on July 8, to celebrate the first public reading of the document.

Commissioned in 1751 by the Pennsylvania Provincial Assembly to hang in the new State House (renamed Independence Hall) in Philadelphia, the now famous bell was cast in London by the Whitechapel Bell Foundry, purchased for about £100 ($164), and delivered in August 1752. It was

cracked by a stroke of the clapper while being tested and was twice recast in Philadelphia before being hung in the State House steeple in June 1753. It weighs about 2,080 pounds (943 kg), is 12 feet (3.7 metres) in circumference around the lip, and measures 3 feet (1 metre) from lip to crown. It bears the motto, "Proclaim liberty throughout all the land unto all the inhabitants thereof" (Leviticus 25:10).

In 1777, when British forces entered Philadelphia, the bell was hidden in an Allentown, Pa., church. Restored to Independence Hall, it cracked, according to tradition, while tolling for the funeral of Chief Justice John Marshall in 1835. The name "Liberty Bell" was first applied in 1839 in an abolitionist pamphlet. It was rung for the last time for George Washington's birthday in 1846, during which it cracked irreparably. On Jan. 1, 1976, the bell was moved to a pavilion about 100 yards (91 metres) from Independence Hall. In 2003 it was relocated to the newly built Liberty Bell Center, which is part of Independence National Historic Park. Some two million people visit the bell each year.

The cracked Liberty Bell on display in Philadelphia, Pa. Shutterstock.com

the part of Dickinson. On the following day, with the New York delegation abstaining only because it lacked permission to act, the Lee resolution calling for final separation was voted on and endorsed. On July 4 the Congress adopted the Declaration of Independence. (The convention of New York gave its consent on July 9, and the New York delegates voted affirmatively on July 15.) On July 19 the Congress ordered the document to be engrossed as "The Unanimous Declaration of the Thirteen United States of America." It was accordingly put on parchment, probably by Timothy Matlack of Philadelphia. Members of the Congress present on August 2 affixed their signatures to this parchment copy on that day, and others later. The last signer was Thomas McKean of Delaware, whose name was not placed on the document before 1777.

CHAPTER 3

THE AMERICAN REVOLUTION: AN OVERVIEW

LAND CAMPAIGNS TO 1778

Americans fought the war on land essentially with two types of organization, the Continental (national) Army and the state militias. The total number of the former provided by quotas from the states throughout the conflict was 231,771 men; the militias totaled 164,087. At any given time, however, the American forces seldom numbered over 20,000; in 1781 there were only about 29,000 insurgents under arms throughout the country. The war was therefore one fought by small field armies. Militias, poorly disciplined and with elected officers, were summoned for periods usually not exceeding three months. The terms of Continental Army service were only gradually increased from one to three years, and not even bounties and the offer of land kept the army up to strength. Reasons for the difficulty in maintaining an adequate Continental force included the colonists' traditional antipathy to regular armies, the objections of farmers to being away from their fields, the competition of the states with the Continental Congress to keep men in the militia, and the wretched and uncertain pay in a period of inflation.

By contrast, the British army was a reliable, steady force of professionals. Since it numbered only about 42,000, heavy recruiting programs were introduced. Many of the enlisted men were farm boys, as were most of the Americans. Others were

George Washington, commander in chief of the Continental Army, on horseback in Trenton, N.J. Library of Congress Prints and Photographs Division

IN FOCUS: MINUTEMEN

The first minutemen (ready to fight "at a minute's warning") were organized in Worcester County, Mass., in September 1774, when Revolutionary leaders sought to eliminate Tories from the old militia by requiring the resignation of all officers and reconstituting the men into seven regiments with new officers. One-third of the members of each regiment were to be ready to assemble under arms at instant call and were specifically designated "Minutemen." Other counties began adopting the same system, and, when Massachusetts' Provincial Congress met in Salem in October, it directed that the reorganization be completed. The first great test of the Minutemen was at the Battles of Lexington and Concord on April 19, 1775. On July 18, 1775, the Continental Congress recommended that other colonies organize units of Minutemen; Maryland, New Hampshire, and Connecticut are known to have complied.

unemployed persons from the urban slums. Still others joined the army to escape fines or imprisonment. The great majority became efficient soldiers owing to sound training and ferocious discipline. The officers were drawn largely from the gentry and the aristocracy and obtained their commissions and promotions by purchase. Though they received no formal training, they were not so dependent on a book knowledge of military tactics as were many of the Americans. British generals, however, tended toward a lack of imagination and initiative, while those who demonstrated such qualities often were rash.

Because troops were few and conscription unknown, the British government, following a traditional policy, purchased about 30,000 troops from various German princes. The Landgrave of Hesse furnished approximately three-fifths of this total. Few acts by the crown roused so much antagonism in America as this use of these foreign "Hessian" mercenaries.

The role of black soldiers on both sides of the conflict has received increasing attention from historians. For slaves the issue was their personal freedom from bondage rather than notions of political sovereignty, and they were willing to take up arms for whomever promised them emancipation. It has been estimated that some 5,000 blacks fought for the side of the Revolution, while about twice as many fought for the British, who seem to have more actively recruited slaves to arms.

The war began in Massachusetts when Gen. Thomas Gage sent a force from Boston to destroy rebel military stores at Concord. Fighting occurred at Lexington and Concord on April 19, 1775, and only the arrival of reinforcements saved the British original column. Rebel militia then converged on Boston from all over New England. Their entrenching on Breed's Hill led to a British frontal assault on June 17 under Gen. William Howe, who won the hill but at the cost of more than 40 percent of the assault force.

Gen. George Washington, the commander in chief of the American forces, not only had to contain the British in Boston, but he had also to recruit a Continental army. During the winter of 1775–76 recruitment lagged so badly that fresh drafts of militia were called up to help maintain the siege. The balance shifted in late winter, when Gen. Henry Knox arrived with artillery from Fort Ticonderoga in New York, which had been captured from the British in May 1775. Mounted on Dorchester Heights, above Boston, the guns forced Howe, who had replaced Gage in command, to evacuate the city on March 17, 1776. Howe then repaired to Halifax to prepare for an invasion of New York, and Washington moved units southward for its defense.

Meanwhile, action flared in the north. In the fall of 1775 the Americans invaded Canada. One force under Gen. Richard Montgomery captured Montreal on November 13. Another under Benedict Arnold made a remarkable march through the Maine wilderness to Quebec. Unable to take the city, Arnold was presently joined by Montgomery, many of whose troops had gone home because their enlistments had expired. An attack on the city on the last day of the year failed, Montgomery was killed, and many troops were captured. The Americans maintained a siege of the city but withdrew with the arrival of British reinforcements in the spring. Pursued by

the British and decimated by smallpox, the Americans fell back to Ticonderoga. Gen. Guy Carleton's hopes of moving quickly down Lake Champlain, however, were frustrated by Arnold's construction of a fighting fleet. Forced to build one of his own, Carleton destroyed most of the American fleet in October 1776 but considered the season too advanced to bring Ticonderoga under siege.

As the Americans suffered defeat in Canada, so did the British in the South. North Carolina patriots trounced a body of loyalists at Moore's Creek Bridge on Feb. 27, 1776. Charleston, S.C., was successfully defended against a British assault by sea in June.

Having made up its mind to crush the rebellion, the British government sent General Howe and his brother, Richard, Admiral Lord Howe, with a large fleet and 34,000 British and German troops to New York. It also gave the Howes a commission to treat with the Americans. The Continental Congress, which had proclaimed the independence of the colonies, at first thought the Howes were empowered to negotiate peace terms but discovered that they were authorized only to accept submission and assure pardons.

Their peace efforts getting nowhere, the Howes turned to force. Under his brother's guns, General Howe landed troops on Long Island and on August 27 scored a smashing victory. Washington evacuated his army from Brooklyn to Manhattan that night under cover of a

PRIMARY SOURCE: HORATIO GATES'S INSTRUCTIONS FOR RECRUITING TROOPS

As the theatre of war expanded in America, the need became evident for an intercolonial military establishment. Established by the Second Continental Congress in 1775 and led by Gen. George Washington, the Continental Army initially comprised the scattered colonial forces outside Boston. As military organization was developed and funds were raised, fresh units were authorized to supplement the forces already in the field. Horatio Gates, adjutant general of the army, issued instructions to the recruiters on July 10, 1775. Source: Principles and Acts of the Revolution in America, *Hezekiah Niles, ed., New York, 1876 (first published Baltimore, 1822), "Instruction of Adjutant General Horatio Gates for Recruiting Troops, Massachusetts Bay, July 10, 1775."*

You are not to enlist any deserter from the ministerial army, nor any stroller, Negro, or vagabond, or person suspected of being an enemy to the liberty of America, nor any under eighteen years of age.

As the cause is the best that can engage men of courage and principle to take up arms, so it is expected that none but such will be accepted by the recruiting officer; the pay, provision, etc., being so ample, it is not doubted but the officers set upon this service will without delay complete their respective corps, and march the men forthwith to the camp.

You are not to enlist any person who is not an American born, unless such person has a wife and family, and is a settled resident in this country.

The person you enlist must be provided with good and complete arms.

Given at the headquarters at Cambridge, this 10th day of July, 1775.

fog. On September 15 Howe followed up his victory by invading Manhattan. Though checked at Harlem Heights the next day, he drew Washington off the island in October by a move to Throg's Neck and then to New Rochelle, northeast of the city. Leaving garrisons at Fort Washington on Manhattan and at Fort Lee on the opposite shore of the Hudson River, Washington hastened to block Howe. The latter, however, defeated him on October 28 at Chatterton Hill near White Plains. Howe slipped between the American army and Fort Washington and stormed the fort on November 16, seizing nearly 3,000 prisoners, guns, and supplies. British forces under Lord Cornwallis then took Fort Lee and on November 24 started to drive the American army across New Jersey. Though Washington escaped to the west bank of the Delaware River, his army nearly disappeared. Howe then put his army into winter quarters, with outposts at towns such as Bordentown and Trenton.

On Christmas night Washington struck back with a brilliant riposte. Crossing the ice-strewn Delaware with

4,000 men, he fell upon the Hessian garrison at Trenton at dawn and took nearly 1,000 prisoners. Though almost trapped by Cornwallis, who recovered Trenton on Jan. 2, 1777, Washington made a skillful escape during the night, won a battle against British reinforcements at Princeton the next day, and went into winter quarters in the defensible area around Morristown. The Trenton-Princeton campaign roused the country and saved the struggle for independence from collapse.

Britain's strategy in 1777 aimed at driving a wedge between New England and the other colonies. An army under Gen. John Burgoyne was to march south from Canada and join forces with Howe on the Hudson. But Howe seems to have concluded that Burgoyne was strong enough to operate on his own and left New York in the summer, taking his army by sea to the head of Chesapeake Bay. Once ashore, he defeated Washington badly but not decisively at Brandywine Creek on September 11. Then, feinting westward, he entered Philadelphia, the American capital, on September 25. The Continental Congress fled to York. Washington struck back at Germantown on October 4 but, compelled to withdraw, went into winter quarters at Valley Forge.

In the north the story was different. Burgoyne was to move south to Albany with a force of about 9,000 British, Germans, Indians, and American loyalists; a smaller force under Lieut. Col. Barry St. Leger was to converge on Albany through the Mohawk valley. Burgoyne

took Ticonderoga handily on July 5 and then, instead of using Lake George, chose a southward route by land. Slowed by the rugged terrain, strewn with trees cut down by American axmen under Gen. Philip Schuyler, and needing horses, Burgoyne sent a force of Germans to collect them at Bennington, Vt. The Germans were nearly wiped out on August 16 by New Englanders under Gen. John Stark and Col. Seth Warner. Meanwhile, St. Leger besieged Fort Schuyler (present-day Rome, N.Y.), ambushed a relief column of American militia at Oriskany on August 6, but retreated as his Indians gave up the siege and an American force under Arnold approached. Burgoyne himself reached the Hudson, but the Americans, now under Gen. Horatio Gates, checked him at Freeman's Farm on September 19 and, thanks to Arnold's battlefield leadership, decisively defeated him at Bemis Heights on October 7. Ten days later, unable to get help from New York, Burgoyne surrendered at Saratoga.

The most significant result of Burgoyne's capitulation was the entrance of France into the war. The French had secretly furnished financial and material aid since 1776. Now they prepared fleets and armies, although they did not formally declare war until June 1778.

LAND CAMPAIGNS FROM 1778

Meanwhile, the Americans at Valley Forge survived a hungry winter, which was made worse by quartermaster and

Primary Source: "Yankee Doodle"

France, Spain, the Netherlands, Germany, and Hungary have all claimed "Yankee Doodle," but the melody seems to have come first from England, where it was a children's game song called "Lucy Locket." Brought to America by the English soldiers who fought in the French and Indian War, the song became popular among the colonists, each settlement having its own set of lyrics. During the Revolutionary War, the British soldiers used a derisive set of lyrics to mock the shabby colonial soldiers, and the colonists in turn had another set of words that eventually became their battle cry. "Yankee" was a contemptuous nickname the British used for the New Englanders, and "doodle" meant "dope, half-wit, fool."

Father and I went down to camp
Along with Captain Gooding,
And there we saw the men and boys
As thick as hasty pudding.
Yankee Doodle keep it up,
Yankee Doodle Dandy,
Mind the music and the step,
And with the girls be handy.
There was Captain Washington
Upon a slapping stallion
A-giving orders to his men —
There must have been a million.
Then I saw a swamping gun
As large as logs of maple
Upon a very little cart,
A load for Father's cattle.
Every time they shot it off
It took a horn of powder
And made a noise like father's gun
Only a nation louder.
There I saw a wooden keg
With heads made out of leather;
They knocked upon it with some sticks
To call the folks together.
Then they'd fife away like fun
And play on cornstalk fiddles,
And some had ribbons red as blood
All bound around their middles.

I can't tell you all I saw —
They kept up such a smother.
I took my hat off, made a bow,
And scampered home to mother.

The Spirit of '76 *or* Yankee Doodle, *as it is sometimes called, was painted by Archibald Willard on the occasion of the nation's centennial.* Library of Congress Prints and Photographs Division

PRIMARY SOURCE: BENJAMIN RUSH ON THE PROGRESS OF THE WAR

Dr. Benjamin Rush was a member of the Second Continental Congress and a signer of the Declaration of Independence. He made the following cautious appraisal of the war's progress in a letter to Richard Henry Lee, who was serving in Congress at the time. The letter was written on Dec. 30, 1776, while Rush was stationed with the American army in New Jersey. Source: Richard H. Lee, Memoir of the Life of Richard Henry Lee, etc., etc., *Philadelphia, 1825, Vol. II, pp. 161–163.*

There is no soil so dear to a soldier as that which is marked with the footsteps of a flying enemy—everything looks well. Our army increases daily, and our troops are impatient to avenge the injuries done to the state of New Jersey; the Tories fly with the precipitation of guilty fear to General Howe. A detachment from our body yesterday took four of them, and killed one; two of the former were officers of Howe's new militia establishment.

We suffer much for the want of intelligence, which can only be procured by money that will pass in both camps. Howe owes the superiority and regularity of his intelligence above ours, not so much to the voluntary information of the Tories as to the influence of his gold. Pray send £ 2,000 or £ 3,000 in hard money immediately to General Washington; it will do you more service than twenty new regiments. Let not this matter be debated and postponed in the usual way for two or three weeks; the salvation of America, under God, depends upon its being done in an instant.

I beg leave for a moment to call off your attention from the affairs of the public to inform you that I have heard from good authority that my much honored father-in-law, who is now a prisoner with General Howe, suffers many indignities and hardships from the enemy, from which not only his rank but his being a man ought to exempt him. I wish you would propose to Congress to pass a resolution in his favor similar to that they have passed in favor of General Lee; they owe it to their own honor as well as to a member of their body. I did not want this intelligence to rouse my resentment against the enemy, but it has increased it. Every particle of my blood is electrified with revenge, and if justice cannot be done to him in any other way, I declare I will, in defiance of the authority of the Congress and the power of the army, drive the first rascally Tory I meet with a hundred miles barefooted through the first deep snow that falls in our country.

Two small brigades of New England troops have consented to serve a month after the time of their enlistments expire. There is reason to believe all the New England troops in their predicament will follow their example. We have just learned that the enemy are preparing to retreat from Princeton. Adieu. General Washington must be invested with dictatorial power for a few months, or we are undone. The vis inertiae of the Congress has almost ruined this country.

commissary mismanagement, graft of contractors, and unwillingness of farmers to sell produce for paper money. Order and discipline among the troops were improved by the arrival of Baron von Steuben, a Prussian officer in the service of France. Steuben instituted a training program in which he emphasized drilling by officers, marching in column, and using firearms more effectively.

The program paid off at Monmouth Courthouse, N.J., on June 28, 1778, when Washington attacked the British, who were withdrawing from Philadelphia to New York. Although Sir Henry Clinton, who had replaced Howe, struck back hard, the Americans stood their ground.

French aid now materialized with the appearance of a strong fleet under the comte d'Estaing. Unable to enter New York harbour, d'Estaing tried to assist Maj. Gen. John Sullivan in dislodging the British from Newport, R.I. Storms and British reinforcements thwarted the joint effort.

Action in the North was largely a stalemate for the rest of the war. The British raided New Bedford, Mass., and New Haven and New London, Conn., while loyalists and Indians attacked settlements in New York and Pennsylvania. On the other hand, the Americans under Anthony Wayne stormed Stony Point, N.Y., on July 16, 1779, and "Light-Horse Harry" Lee took Paulus Hook, N.J., on August 19. More lasting in effect was Sullivan's

expedition of August 1779 against Britain's Indian allies in New York, particularly the destruction of their villages and fields of corn. Farther west, Col. George Rogers Clark seized Vincennes and other posts north of the Ohio River in 1778.

Potentially serious blows to the American cause were Arnold's defection in 1780 and the army mutinies of 1780 and 1781. Arnold's attempt to betray West Point to the British miscarried. Mutinies were sparked by misunderstandings over terms of enlistment, poor food and clothing, gross arrears of pay, and the decline in the purchasing power of the dollar. Suppressed by force or negotiation, the mutinies shook the morale of the army.

The Americans also suffered setbacks in the South. British strategy from 1778 called for offensives that were designed to take advantage of the flexibility of sea power and the loyalist sentiment of many of the people. British forces from New York and St. Augustine, Fla., occupied Georgia by the end of January 1779 and successfully defended Savannah in the fall against d'Estaing and a Franco-American army. Clinton, having withdrawn his Newport garrison, captured Charleston—and an American army of 5,000 under Gen. Benjamin Lincoln—in May 1780. Learning that Newport was threatened by a French expeditionary force under the comte de Rochambeau, Clinton returned to New York, leaving Cornwallis at Charleston.

Cornwallis, however, took the offensive. On August 16 he shattered General

Primary source: Henry Wadsworth Longfellow's "Paul Revere's Ride"

In 1863, at a point in the Civil War when it seemed that the Confederacy might triumph, Henry Wadsworth Longfellow published a collection of story-poems, Tales of a Wayside Inn, *modeled after Chaucer's* Canterbury Tales. *The first poem in the collection, "Paul Revere's Ride," became a national favorite. Although Paul Revere's ride—warning of the advance of British troops on the military stores of American colonists at Concord, Mass., in April 1775—was, of course, almost ancient history by this time, the last stanza of the poem sounded the same alarm in the Union's present hour of darkness. The crisis that Revere had faced was now faced, in Longfellow's opinion, by everyone in the country. Source:* Complete Poetical Works, Cambridge Edition, *Boston, 1893.*

On April 18, 1775, Paul Revere warned American militia in Lexington that British troops were coming.
MPI/Hulton Archive/Getty Images

Listen, my children, and you shall hear
Of the midnight ride of Paul Revere,
On the eighteenth of April, in seventy-five;
Hardly a man is now alive
Who remembers that famous day and year.
He said to his friend, "If the British march
By land or sea from the town tonight,
Hang a lantern aloft in the belfry arch
Of the North Church tower as a signal light—

One, if by land, and two, if by sea;
And I on the opposite shore will be,
Ready to ride and spread the alarm
Through every Middlesex village and farm,
For the country folk to be up and to arm."
Then he said, "Good-night!" and with muffled oar
Silently rowed to the Charlestown shore,
Just as the moon rose over the bay,
Where swinging wide at her moorings lay

The Somerset, British man-of-war;
A phantom ship, with each mast
and spar
Across the moon like a prison bar,
And a huge black hulk, that was
magnified
By its own reflection in the tide.
Meanwhile, his friend, through alley
and street,
Wanders and watches with eager ears,
Till in the silence around him
he hears
The muster of men at the barrack door,
The sound of arms, and the tramp
of feet,
And the measured tread of the
grenadiers,
Marching down to their boats on
the shore.
Then he climbed the tower of the Old
North Church,
By the wooden stairs, with
stealthy tread,
To the belfry chamber overhead,
And startled the pigeons from
their perch
On the somber rafters, that round
him made
Masses and moving shapes of shade —
By the trembling ladder, steep and tall,
To the highest window in the wall,
Where he paused to listen and
look down
A moment on the roofs of the town,
And the moonlight flowing over all.
Beneath, in the churchyard, lay
the dead,
In their night encampment on
the hill,
Wrapped in silence so deep and still

That he could hear, like a
sentinel's tread,
The watchful night wind, as it went
Creeping along from tent to tent,
And seeming to whisper, "All is well!"
A moment only he feels the spell
Of the place and the hour, and the
secret dread
Of the lonely belfry and the dead;
For suddenly all his thoughts are bent
On a shadowy something far away,
Where the river widens to meet the bay —
A line of black that bends and floats
On the rising tide, like a bridge
of boats.
Meanwhile, impatient to mount
and ride,
Booted and spurred, with a heavy stride
On the opposite shore walked
Paul Revere.
Now he patted his horse's side,
Now gazed at the landscape far
and near,
Then, impetuous, stamped the earth,
And turned and tightened his
saddle-girth;
But mostly he watched with
eager search
The belfry tower of the Old
North Church,
As it rose above the graves on the hill,
Lonely and spectral and somber
and still.
And lo! as he looks, on the
belfry's height
A glimmer, and then a gleam of light!
He springs to the saddle, the bridle
he turns,
But lingers and gazes, till full on
his sight

A second lamp in the belfry burns!
A hurry of hoofs in a village street,
A shape in the moonlight, a bulk in
the dark,
And beneath, from the pebbles, in
passing, a spark
Struck out by a steed flying fearless
and fleet:
That was all! And yet, through the
gloom and the light,
The fate of a nation was riding
that night;
And the spark struck out by that steed,
in his flight,
Kindled the land into flame with
its heat.
He has left the village and mounted
the steep,
And beneath him, tranquil and broad
and deep,
Is the Mystic, meeting the ocean tides;
And under the alders that skirt
its edge,
Now soft on the sand, now loud on
the ledge,
Is heard the tramp of his steed as
he rides.
It was twelve by the village clock
When he crossed the bridge into
Medford town.
He heard the crowing of the cock,
And the barking of the farmer's dog,
And felt the damp of the river fog
That rises after the sun goes down.
It was one by the village clock
When he galloped into Lexington.
He saw the gilded weathercock
Swim in the moonlight as he passed,
And the meetinghouse windows, blank
and bare,

A depiction of a British Grenadier of the 57th Regiment. MPI/Hulton Archive/ Getty Images

Gaze at him with a spectral glare,
As if they already stood aghast
At the bloody work they would
look upon.
It was two by the village clock
When he came to the bridge in
Concord town.
He heard the bleating of the flock,
And the twitter of birds among
the trees,
And felt the breath of the
morning breeze
Blowing over the meadows brown.
And one was safe and asleep in his bed
Who at the bridge would be first to fall,
Who that day would be lying dead,
Pierced by a British musket ball.
You know the rest. In the books you
have read
How the British regulars fired and fled—
How the farmers gave them ball
for ball,

From behind each fence and
farmyard wall,
Chasing the redcoats down the lane,
Then crossing the fields to emerge again
Under the trees at the turn of the road,
And only pausing to fire and load.
So through the night rode Paul Revere;
And so through the night went his cry
of alarm
To every Middlesex village and farm—
A cry of defiance and not of fear,
A voice in the darkness, a knock at
the door,
And a word that shall echo
forevermore!
For, borne on the night wind of the past,
Through all our history, to the last,
In the hour of darkness and peril and need,
The people will waken and listen to hear
The hurrying hoofbeats of that steed,
And the midnight message of
Paul Revere.

Gates's army at Camden, S.C. The destruction of a force of loyalists at Kings Mountain on October 7 led him to move against the new American commander, Gen. Nathanael Greene. When Greene put part of his force under Gen. Daniel Morgan, Cornwallis ordered pursuit of Morgan by his cavalry leader, Col. Banastre Tarleton, whose ruthlessness and ferocity on the battlefield earned him (perhaps somewhat undeservedly, some have argued) the nickname "the Butcher of the Carolinas." At Cowpens on Jan. 17, 1781, Morgan destroyed practically all of Tarleton's column. Subsequently, on March 15, Greene and Cornwallis fought at Guilford Courthouse, N.C. Cornwallis won but suffered heavy casualties. After withdrawing to Wilmington, he marched into Virginia to join British forces sent there by Clinton.

Greene then moved back to South Carolina, where he was defeated by Lord Rawdon at Hobkirk's Hill on April 25 and at Ninety Six in June and by Lieut. Col. Alexander Stewart at Eutaw Springs on September 8. In spite of this, the British, harassed by partisan leaders such as Francis Marion, Thomas Sumter, and Andrew Pickens, soon retired to the coast and remained locked up in Charleston and Savannah.

PRIMARY SOURCE: GEORGE WASHINGTON ON THE APPOINTMENT OF FOREIGN OFFICERS

Unemployed professional soldiers were plentiful in Europe, and when war broke out in America they were eager to serve in the Continental Army. Securing passage money and letters of recommendation from Benjamin Franklin, the American representative in France, they came to America and offered their services to the army. Congress appointed these mercenaries to ranks as high as major general, leaving it to Gen. George Washington, as commander of the Continental Army, to find something for them to do. Most of them were given positions on Washington's staff because some Americans disliked serving under foreigners. With this situation in view, Washington addressed a letter to Gouverneur Morris, from White Plains, N.Y., on July 24, 1778. Source: John P. Sanderson, The Views and Opinions of American Statesmen on Foreign Immigration, *Philadelphia, 1856, pp. 108–109.*

The design of this is to touch cursorily upon a subject of very great importance to the being of these states; much more so than will appear at first view, I mean the appointment of so many foreigners to offices of high rank and trust in our service.

The lavish manner in which rank has hitherto been bestowed on these gentlemen will certainly be productive of one or the other of these two evils, either to make us despicable in the eyes of Europe, or become a means of pouring them in upon us like a torrent, and adding to our present burden.

But it is neither the expense nor the trouble of them I most dread; there is an evil more extensive in its nature and fatal in its consequence to be apprehended, and that is the driving of all our officers out of the service, and throwing not only our own Army, but our military councils entirely into the hands of foreigners.

The officers, my dear sir, on whom you must depend for the defense of the cause, distinguished by length of service and military merit, will not submit much, if any, longer to the unnatural promotion of men over them who have nothing more than a little plausibility, unbounded pride and ambition, and a perseverance in the application to support their pretensions, not to be resisted but by uncommon firmness; men who, in the first instance, say they wish for nothing more than the honor of serving so glorious a cause as volunteers, the next day solicit rank without pay; the day following want money advanced to them; and in the course of a week, want further promotion. The expediency and policy of the measure remain to be considered, and whether it is consistent with justice or prudence to promote these military fortune hunters at the hazard of our Army.

Baron Steuben, I now find, is also wanting to quit his inspectorship for a command in the line. This will be productive of much discontent. In a word, although I think the Baron an excellent officer, I do most devoutly wish that we had not a single foreigner among us except the Marquis de Lafayette, who acts upon very different principles from those which govern the rest. Adieu.

Meanwhile, Cornwallis entered Virginia. Sending Tarleton on raids across the state, he started to build a base at Yorktown, at the same time fending off American forces under Wayne, Steuben, and the marquis de Lafayette.

Learning that the comte de Grasse had arrived in the Chesapeake with a large fleet and 3,000 French troops, Washington and Rochambeau moved south to Virginia. By mid-September the Franco-American forces had placed Yorktown under siege, and British rescue efforts proved fruitless. Cornwallis surrendered his army of more than 7,000 men on October 19. Thus, for the second time during the war the British had lost an entire army.

Thereafter, land action in America died out, though the war persisted in other theatres and on the high seas. Eventually Clinton was replaced by Sir Guy Carleton. While the peace treaties were under consideration and afterward, Carleton evacuated thousands of loyalists from America, including many from Savannah on July 11, 1782, and others from Charleston on December 14. The last British forces finally left New York on Nov. 25, 1783. Washington then reentered the city in triumph.

THE WAR AT SEA

Although the colonists ventured to challenge Britain's naval power from the outbreak of the conflict, the war at sea in its later stages was fought mainly between Britain and America's European allies, the American effort being reduced to privateering.

The importance of sea power was recognized early. In October 1775 the Continental Congress authorized the creation of the Continental Navy and established the Marine Corps in November. The navy, taking its direction from the naval and marine committees of the Congress, was only occasionally effective. In 1776 it had 27 ships against Britain's 270; by the end of the war, the British total had risen close to 500, and the American had dwindled to 20. Many of the best seamen available went off privateering, and both Continental Navy commanders and crews suffered from a lack of training and discipline.

The first significant blow by the navy was struck by Cdre. Esek Hopkins, who captured New Providence (Nassau) in the Bahamas in 1776.

Other captains, such as Lambert Wickes, Gustavus Conyngham, and John Barry, also enjoyed successes, but the Scottish-born John Paul Jones was especially notable. As captain of the *Ranger*, Jones scourged the British coasts in 1778, capturing the man-of-war *Drake*. As captain of the *Bonhomme Richard* in 1779, he intercepted a timber convoy and captured the British frigate *Serapis*.

More injurious to the British were the raids by American privateers on their shipping. American ships, furnished with letters of marque by the Congress or the states, swarmed about the British Isles. By the end of 1777 they had taken 560 British vessels, and by the end of the

PRIMARY SOURCE: JOHN ADAMS ON AN ALLIANCE WITH FRANCE

France had been giving aid secretly to the American cause for at least two years. However, the French were unwilling to enter into an open alliance until it became certain that there would be no reconciliation between America and Britain. George Washington's conduct of the war in the winter of 1777-78 convinced France of the practicability of a treaty. On Feb. 6, 1778, two agreements were signed with France: a treaty of alliance and a treaty of amity and commerce. On July 28, John Adams, then commissioner to France, discussed the merits of the alliance in a letter to Samuel Adams. Source; The Revolutionary Diplomatic Correspondence of the United States, Francis Wharton, ed., Washington, 1889, Vol. II, pp. 667-668.

The sovereign of Britain and his Council have determined to instruct their commissioners to offer you independence, provided you will disconnect yourselves from France. The question arises, how came the King and Council by authority to offer this? It is certain that they have it not.

In the next place, is the treaty of alliance between us and France now binding upon us? I think there is not room to doubt it; for declarations and manifestos do not make the state of war — they are only publications of the reasons of war. Yet the message of the King of Great Britain to both houses of Parliament, and their answers to that message, were as full a declaration of war as ever was made, and, accordingly, hostilities have been frequent ever since. This proposal, then, is a modest invitation to a gross act of infidelity and breach of faith. It is an observation that I have often heard you make that "France is the natural ally of the United States." This observation is, in my opinion, both just and important. The reasons are plain. As long as Great Britain shall have Canada, Nova Scotia, and the Floridas, or any of them, so long will Great Britain be the enemy of the United States, let her disguise it as much as she will.

It is not much to the honor of human nature, but the fact is certain that neighboring nations are never friends in reality. In the times of the most perfect peace between them their hearts and their passions are hostile, and this will certainly be the case forever between the thirteen United States and the English colonies. France and England, as neighbors and rivals, never have been and never will be friends. The hatred and jealousy between the nations are eternal and irradicable. As we, therefore, on the one hand, have the surest ground to expect the jealousy and hatred of Great Britain, so on the other we have the strongest reasons to depend upon the friendship and alliance of France, and no one reason in the world to expect her enmity or her jealousy, as she has given up every pretension to any spot of ground on the continent.

The United States, therefore, will be for ages the natural bulwark of France against the hostile designs of England against her, and France is the natural defense of the United States against the rapacious spirit of Great Britain against them. France is a nation so vastly eminent, having been for so many centuries what they call the dominant power of

Europe, being incomparably the most powerful at land, that united in a close alliance with our states, and enjoying the benefit of our trade, there is not the smallest reason to doubt but both will be a sufficient curb upon the naval power of Great Britain.

This connection, therefore, will forever secure a respect for our states in Spain, Portugal, and Holland too, who will always choose to be upon friendly terms with powers who have numerous cruisers at sea, and indeed, in all the rest of Europe. I presume, therefore, that sound policy as well as good faith will induce us never to renounce our alliance with France, even although it should continue us for some time in war. The French are as sensible of the benefits of this alliance to them as we are, and they are determined as much as we to cultivate it.

In order to continue the war, or at least that we may do any good in the common cause, the credit of our currency must be supported. But how? Taxes, my dear sir, taxes! Pray let our countrymen consider and be wise; every farthing they pay in taxes is a farthing's worth of wealth and good policy. If it were possible to hire money in Europe to discharge the bills, it would be a dreadful drain to the country to pay the interest of it. But I fear it will not be. The house of Austria has sent orders to Amsterdam to hire a very great sum, England is borrowing great sums, and France is borrowing largely. Amidst such demands for money, and by powers who offer better terms, I fear we shall not be able to succeed.

war they had probably seized 1,500. More than 12,000 British sailors also were captured. One result was that, by 1781, British merchants were clamouring for an end to hostilities.

Most of the naval action occurred at sea. The significant exceptions were Arnold's battles against General Carleton's fleet on Lake Champlain at Valcour Island on October 11 and off Split Rock on Oct. 13, 1776. Arnold lost both battles, but his construction of a fleet of tiny vessels, mostly gondolas (gundalows) and galleys, had forced the British to build a larger fleet and hence delayed their attack on Fort Ticonderoga until the following spring. This delay contributed significantly to Burgoyne's capitulation in October 1777.

The entrance of France into the war, followed by that of Spain in 1779 and the Netherlands in 1780, effected important changes in the naval aspect of the war. The Spanish and Dutch were not particularly active, but their role in keeping British naval forces tied down in Europe was significant. The British navy could not maintain an effective blockade of both the American coast and the enemies' ports. Owing to years of economy and neglect, Britain's ships of the line were neither modern nor sufficiently numerous. An immediate result was that France's Toulon fleet under d'Estaing got safely away to America, where it appeared off New York and later assisted General Sullivan in the unsuccessful siege of Newport. A fierce battle off Ushant, Fr., in July 1778 between the Channel fleet under Adm. Augustus Keppel and the Brest fleet under the comte d'Orvilliers proved inconclusive. Had Keppel won decisively, French aid to the Americans would have diminished and Rochambeau might never have been able to lead his expedition to America.

In the following year England was in real danger. Not only did it have to face the privateers of the United States, France, and Spain off its coasts, as well as the raids of John Paul Jones, but it also lived in fear of invasion. The combined fleets of France and Spain had acquired command of the Channel, and a French army of 50,000 waited for the propitious moment to board their transports. Luckily for the British, storms, sickness among the allied crews, and changes of plans terminated the threat.

Despite allied supremacy in the Channel in 1779, the threat of invasion, and the loss of islands in the West Indies, the British maintained control of the North American seaboard for most of 1779 and 1780, which made possible their southern land campaigns. They also reinforced Gibraltar, which the Spaniards had brought under siege in the fall of 1779, and sent a fleet under Admiral Sir George Rodney to the West Indies in early 1780. After fruitless maneuvering against the comte de Guichen, who had replaced d'Estaing, Rodney sailed for New York.

While Rodney had been in the West Indies, a French squadron slipped out of Brest and sailed to Newport with Rochambeau's army. Rodney, instead of trying to block the approach to Newport, returned to the West Indies, where, upon receiving instructions to attack Dutch possessions, he seized Sint Eustatius, the Dutch island that served as the principal depot for war materials shipped from Europe and transshipped into American vessels. He became so involved in the disposal of the enormous booty that he dallied at the island for six months.

In the meantime, a powerful British fleet relieved Gibraltar in 1781, but the price was the departure of the French fleet at Brest, part of it to India, the larger part under Admiral de Grasse to the West Indies. After maneuvering indecisively against Rodney, de Grasse received a request from Washington and Rochambeau to come to New York or the Chesapeake.

Earlier, in March, a French squadron had tried to bring troops from Newport to the Chesapeake but was forced to return by Adm. Marriot Arbuthnot, who had succeeded Lord Howe. Soon afterward Arbuthnot was replaced by Thomas Graves, a conventional-minded admiral.

Informed that a French squadron would shortly leave the West Indies, Rodney sent Samuel Hood north with a powerful force while he sailed for England, taking with him several formidable ships that might better have been left with Hood.

Soon after Hood dropped anchor in New York, de Grasse appeared in the Chesapeake, where he landed troops to help Lafayette contain Cornwallis until Washington and Rochambeau could arrive. Fearful that the comte de Barras, who was carrying Rochambeau's artillery train from Newport, might join de Grasse, and hoping to intercept him, Graves sailed with Hood to the Chesapeake. Graves had 19 ships of the line against de Grasse's 24. Though the battle that began on September 5 off the Virginia capes was not a skillfully managed affair, Graves had the worst of it and retired to New York. He ventured out again on October 17 with a strong contingent of troops and 25 ships of the line, while de Grasse, reinforced by Barras, now had 36 ships of the line. No battle occurred, however, when Graves learned that Cornwallis had surrendered.

Although Britain subsequently recouped some of its fortunes, by Rodney defeating and capturing de Grasse in the Battle of the Saintes off Dominica in 1782 and British land and sea forces inflicting defeats in India, the turn of events did not significantly alter the situation in America as it existed after Yorktown. A new government under Lord Shelburne tried to get the American commissioners to agree to a separate peace, but, ultimately, the treaty negotiated with the Americans was not to go into effect until the formal conclusion of a peace with their European allies.

CHAPTER 4

THE BATTLES OF THE AMERICAN REVOLUTION

At first, it seemed inevitable that the British would put a quick end to the colonists' rebellion that had begun in Lexington and Concord on April 19, 1775. After all, the British Empire had arguably the best-trained army and mightiest navy in the world, while the American troops were poorly paid, undisciplined, and led by inexperienced generals. Indeed, Gen. George Washington made a number of serious strategic blunders in the early days of the war.

Yet, the Americans had their own advantages. They knew their vast, complex terrain and capitalized on that familiarity by using guerrilla tactics. Unlike the British, the Americans were not dependent on the transatlantic shipment of men and materiel, and could fight a defensive war. Even if the British won battles and had Loyalist support, they could not win over the great majority of the people. As war destroyed lives and property in the colonies, opinion hardened against the British. Furthermore, as the fighting dragged on, opinion against the war hardened in Britain as well. Although Britain triumphed in many individual battles, this mighty, war-tested country ultimately lost the war.

BATTLES OF LEXINGTON AND CONCORD

Acting on orders from London to suppress the rebellious colonists, Gen. Thomas Gage, recently appointed royal governor

A print by engraver Cornelius Tiebout depicting Minutemen firing on the British at the Battle of Lexington. Library of Congress Prints and Photographs Division

of Massachusetts, ordered his troops to seize the colonists' military stores at Concord. En route from Boston, on April 19, 1775, the British force of 700 men was met on Lexington Green by 77 local Minutemen and others who had been forewarned of the raid by the colonists' efficient lines of communication, including the ride of Paul Revere. It is unclear who fired the first shot. Resistance melted away at Lexington, and the British moved on to Concord. Most of the American military supplies had been hidden or destroyed before the British troops arrived. A British covering party at Concord's North Bridge was finally confronted by 320 to 400 American patriots and forced to withdraw. The march back to Boston was a genuine ordeal for the British, with Americans continually firing on

them from behind roadside houses, barns, trees, and stone walls. This experience established guerrilla warfare as the colonists' best defense strategy against the British. Total losses were British 273, American 95. The Battles of Lexington and Concord confirmed the alienation between the majority of colonists and the mother country, and it roused some 15,000 New Englanders to join forces and begin the Siege of Boston, resulting in its evacuation by the British the following March.

BATTLE OF BUNKER HILL

The first major battle of the American Revolution, the Battle of Bunker Hill, occurred on June 17, 1775, in Charlestown (now part of Boston) during the Siege of Boston. Although the British eventually

The British Army storming Bunker Hill in Charlestown, Mass., June 17, 1775. Library of Congress Prints and Photographs Division

won the battle, it was a Pyrrhic victory that lent considerable encouragement to the Revolutionary cause.

Within two months after the Battles of Lexington and Concord (April 19, 1775), more than 15,000 troops from Massachusetts, Connecticut, New Hampshire, and Rhode Island had assembled in the vicinity of Boston to confront the British army of 5,000 or more stationed there. Gen. Artemas Ward, commander in chief of the Massachusetts troops, served as the senior New England officer. There were two obvious points from which Boston was vulnerable to artillery fire: Dorchester Heights, and two high hills, Bunker's and Breed's, in Charlestown, about a quarter of a mile across the Charles River from the north shore of Boston. By the middle of June, hearing that British Gen. Thomas Gage was about to occupy Dorchester Heights, the colonists decided to fortify the hills. By the time they were discovered, Col. William Prescott and his men had completed a redoubt atop Breed's Hill (which was an indefensible decision in the eyes of many historians, since Breed's Hill was lower and less impregnable than Bunker Hill). Despite a cannonade from British men-of-war in the harbour and from a battery across the river in north Boston, the colonists continued to strengthen their position.

Gage then dispatched about 2,300 troops under Maj. Gen. William Howe against Prescott. Landing without opposition under artillery protection, the British were stopped by heavy fire from the colonial troops barricaded behind rail fences that had been stuffed with grass, hay, and brush. On the second or third advance, however, the attackers carried the redoubt and forced the surviving defenders, mostly exhausted and weaponless, to flee. Casualties numbered more than 1,000 British and about 450 American soldiers.

If the British had followed this victory with an attack on Dorchester Heights to the south of Boston, it might have been worth the heavy cost. But, presumably because of their severe losses and the fighting spirit displayed by the rebels, the British commanders abandoned or indefinitely postponed such a plan. Consequently, after Gen. George Washington took colonial command two weeks later, enough heavy guns and ammunition had been collected that he was able in March 1776 to seize and fortify Dorchester Heights and compel the British to evacuate Boston and the harbour. Also, the heavy losses inflicted on the British in

the Battle of Bunker Hill bolstered the Americans' confidence and showed that the relatively inexperienced colonists could indeed fight on par with the mighty redcoats of the British army. The encounter is primarily remembered as the Battle of Bunker Hill, but because most of the fighting took place on Breed's Hill, it is also known as the Battle of Breed's Hill, and it is Breed's Hill that is the site of the Bunker Hill Monument, a 221-foot (67-metre) granite obelisk that commemorates the conflict.

BATTLE OF TICONDEROGA

Held by the British since 1759, Fort Ticonderoga (in New York) was overrun on the morning of May 10, 1775, in a surprise attack by the Green Mountain Boys under Ethan Allen, assisted by Benedict Arnold. The artillery seized in the Battle of Ticonderoga was moved to Boston by Henry Knox for use against the British.

SIEGE OF BOSTON

After the Battles of Lexington and Concord (April 19, 1775), American militiamen besieged the British-held city of Boston from April 1775 to March 1776. By June 1775, 15,000 raw, undisciplined, ill-equipped colonials—by then called the Continental Army—surrounded a force of 6,500 British regulars commanded by Gen. Thomas Gage.

After the Battle of Bunker Hill (June 17, 1775), Gen. George Washington assumed command of American forces, while, in

October of that year, Gen.William Howe succeeded Gage as British commander. Fighting remained stalemated for months, with both sides hesitant to attack. Finally, on March 4, 1776, Washington seized Dorchester Heights and trained his cannon—newly arrived from Fort Ticonderoga—on the city and harbour. Howe was forced to evacuate Boston by ship (March 17), and the siege ended.

BATTLE OF QUEBEC

In the winter of 1775–76, American Revolutionary leaders detached some of their forces from the Siege of Boston to mount an expedition through Maine with the aim of capturing the British stronghold of Quebec. On Dec. 31, 1775, under Gen. Richard Montgomery and Col. Benedict Arnold, an inadequate force of roughly 1,675 Americans assaulted the fortified city, only to meet with complete defeat in the Battle of Quebec. Montgomery was killed, and large numbers of colonials were captured. Demonstrations against Canada were soon discontinued, and Arnold withdrew the remnant of his army in May 1776.

BATTLE OF MOORE'S CREEK BRIDGE

In defeating a force of North Carolina loyalists on Feb. 27, 1776, in the Battle of Moore's Creek, North Carolina Revolutionaries helped thwart a British invasion of the southern colonies. Gen. Donald McDonald, who had amassed some 1,600 Scottish Highlanders and North Carolina Regulators, marched toward Wilmington, N.C., to join British troops coming by sea from Boston and England. A rebel militia, about 1,000 strong, under Colonels Alexander Lillington and Richard Caswell, was assembled and positioned at Moore's Creek Bridge, 18 miles (29 km) northwest of Wilmington. The loyalists attacked the rebel force at the bridge but were quickly defeated. The rebels, of whom only one was killed and one wounded, captured or killed more than half of the loyalist forces and seized arms, supplies, and £15,000 ($24,673) sterling.

BATTLE OF LONG ISLAND

The Battle of Long Island, fought on August 27, initiated the British campaign of 1776 to seize control of New York and thereby isolate New England from the rest of the colonies. After the British evacuation from Boston in March, the British Gen. Lord Howe moved to occupy New York City under the protection of a British fleet that commanded the surrounding waters. To protect his left flank, the defending American general, George Washington, stationed one-third of his troops (numbering no more than 20,000 trained soldiers) on the Long Island side of the East River, where they erected fortifications.

From his encampment on Staten Island, Howe attacked Washington's isolated wing by landing 20,000 men at

Gravesend Bay, Long Island, on August 22. After four days' reconnaissance, Howe drove the Americans back and inflicted heavy losses (1,200 American prisoners were taken, and about 400 men on each side were killed or wounded). Howe might have captured Washington's entire force on Long Island at this point, but instead he elected to lay siege. The following week Washington took advantage of this delay to retreat across the river to Manhattan, a successful move that helped repair low American morale.

BATTLE OF WHITE PLAINS

In late 1776 the British were engaged in a campaign to defeat Gen. George Washington's main American army or isolate the New England colonies by gaining military control of New York. From his strengthened position facing the American lines on Harlem Heights, at the northern tip of Manhattan Island, British Gen. Sir William Howe moved most of his army into Westchester county via amphibious landings at Throg's Neck (October 12) and then Pell's Point (October 18). To prevent his army's being surrounded, Washington left a garrison at Fort Washington, his main redoubt on Harlem Heights, and marched most of his force north into Westchester, finally setting up fortified lines near White Plains. Following some small actions, Howe advanced his force of 10,000– 15,000 in two columns toward Washington's positions. On October 28,

in a brief, sharp action that became known as the Battle of White Plains, a Continental brigade was defeated at Chatterton Hill. Howe's plan for further action over the next few days was delayed by a heavy rain, and Washington was able to withdraw his 14,000 men farther north to more secure ground. Howe then withdrew most of his men to Manhattan and prepared to attack Fort Washington.

BATTLES OF TRENTON AND PRINCETON

After the capture of Fort Washington on Manhattan Island in November 1776, the British Gen. Sir William Howe forced the Americans to retreat through New Jersey and across the Delaware River into Pennsylvania. Howe then went into winter quarters, leaving the Hessian colonel Johann Rall at Trenton with about 1,400 men.

Although Gen. George Washington's Continental Army was discouraged by the year's disasters, its morale was not crushed, and it now numbered 6,000 effectives. Ascertaining that the Hessians were virtually unsupported, Washington determined to attempt their capture. Despite the ice floes in the Delaware, Washington crossed the river on December 25 and surprised the enemy, the next day capturing more than 900 men. Four days later he occupied Trenton. Hearing of Washington's move, Lord Cornwallis confronted the Continentals east of the city with about 7,000 troops

George Washington standing with the flags captured from the British in the Battle of Trenton. Library of Congress Prints and Photographs Division

on Jan. 2, 1777, driving them back. Unable to find boats for an escape, Washington called a council of war that confirmed his bold plan to break camp quietly that night and take a byroad to Princeton. The maneuver succeeded, and three British regiments that met him there on January 3 were all driven back or retreated. As a result, Washington continued his march to Morristown, N.J., where he flanked British communications with New York. Cornwallis retired to New Brunswick.

Besides succeeding in breaking through Howe's lines, Washington had placed himself in an advantageous position for recruiting his army and maintaining a strong defensive in the next campaign.

The effect of these early American victories in the battles of Trenton and Princeton, the first successes won by Washington in the open field, was marked. Following close upon a series of defeats, they put new life into the

American cause and renewed confidence in Washington as commander of the Revolutionary Army.

BATTLES OF SARATOGA

The closely related engagements in the fall of 1777 known as the Battles of Saratoga are often characterized as the turning point of the war in favour of the Americans. The failure of the American invasion of Canada in 1775–76 had left a large surplus of British troops along the St. Lawrence River. In 1777 these troops were to move south and join forces with Gen. Sir William Howe's troops along the Hudson River.

Leading a force of about 8,000 British troops southward, Gen. John Burgoyne forced the surrender of Fort Ticonderoga (July 6) and Fort Edward on the upper Hudson (July 31). He left nearly 1,000 men behind to garrison Fort Ticonderoga. Having collected 30 days' rations, Burgoyne crossed the Hudson and encamped near Saratoga, N.Y. Gen. Horatio Gates, the American commander, was camped four miles away with 12,000 men and was receiving daily reinforcements.

On September 19 Burgoyne's army moved south and engaged the Continental forces at the Battle of Freeman's Farm, or the First Battle of Saratoga. Burgoyne failed to pierce Gates's lines, however, and thus open a way to Albany. On October 7 he led 1,500 of his men out on reconnaissance but met with a fierce American counterattack under Gen.

Benedict Arnold. This engagement was called the Battle of Bemis Heights, also known as the Second Battle of Freeman's Farm or the Second Battle of Saratoga. By now Burgoyne's army had been reduced to about 5,000 effective troops, and his supplies were running low. On October 8 Burgoyne began his retreat, but Gates, who had 20,000 men by now, surrounded him at Saratoga. On October 17 Burgoyne surrendered his troops under the Convention of Saratoga, which provided for the return of his men to Great Britain on condition that they would not serve again in North America during the war.

The American victory in the Battles of Saratoga helped to induce the French to recognize American independence and to give open military assistance, thus marking a turning point in the uprising and making possible its ultimate success.

BATTLE OF ORISKANY

The Battle of Oriskany, between British troops and American defenders of the Mohawk Valley, on Aug. 6, 1777, contributed to the failure of the British campaign in the North. British troops under Lieut. Col. Barry St. Leger were marching eastward across central New York to join with British forces at Albany. En route, they arrived at Fort Stanwix (also called Fort Schuyler; now Rome, N.Y.) and demanded its surrender. Attempting to come to the fort's rescue, 800 colonial militiamen under Gen. Nicholas Herkimer were ambushed two miles west of Oriskany Creek by a force of about 1,200 British and their Iroquois allies. The battle that followed resulted in heavy casualties for both sides. St. Leger was unable to capture the fort and retreated to Oswego on August 22.

BATTLE OF BENNINGTON

Fought on Aug.16, 1777, the Battle of Bennington was an important victory for American militiamen defending colonial military stores in Bennington, Vt., against a British raiding party.

In early August the British commander, Gen. John Burgoyne, hoped to capture needed supplies and overawe New Englanders by dispatching a well-equipped regiment to Bennington under the German colonel Friedrich Baum. On the 16th, Baum's force of 800 British, Germans, loyalists, and Indians was decisively defeated by about 1,600 colonial troops gathered from neighbouring militia by Ethan Allen and Seth Warner and led by Gen. John Stark. Reinforcements on both sides arrived too late to influence the outcome, and about 700 of the British forces were taken prisoner. The outcome of this engagement went far in enhancing American morale.

The battle, which took place at the site of the present village of Walloomsac, N.Y. (several miles west of Bennington), contributed to the eventual defeat of Burgoyne. It is commemorated by a historical park near Walloomsac and by a 306-foot (93-metre) obelisk at the village of Old Bennington.

BATTLE OF THE BRANDYWINE

On Sept. 11, 1777, near Philadelphia, the British army defeated the American forces in the Battle of the Brandywine but failed to destroy the Revolutionary army. The British Gen. Sir William Howe had been lured to Philadelphia in the belief that its large Tory element would rise up when joined by a British army and thus virtually remove Pennsylvania from the war. That move left the forces of Gen.John Burgoyne in northern New York to fend for themselves, directly resulting in the British disaster at the Battle of Saratoga.

Embarking from New York City in July 1777, Howe's army of about 15,000 troops met Gen. George Washington's Continental Army of about 11,000 in the vicinity of Chadds Ford, on Brandywine Creek in southeastern Pennsylvania, about 25 miles (40 km) southwest of Philadelphia. In the end, the British troops occupied the battlefield, but they neither destroyed Washington's army nor cut it off from the capital at Philadelphia. Thus the American army was kept intact and the Revolution remained alive.

BATTLE OF GERMANTOWN

Not discouraged by his recent defeat at the Battle of the Brandywine, Gen. George Washington conceived a daring and imaginative plan to attack the 9,000 British regulars stationed at Germantown (now part of Philadelphia) under Gen. Sir William Howe. The plan called for Washington's force of 11,000 troops to attack simultaneously from four different directions. The surprise raid at dawn on Oct. 4, 1777, failed partly because it was too complicated and partly because of a dense fog that confused the Americans into firing on one of their own columns. British losses in the Battle of Germantown were set at 535, American at about twice that number. Combined with the American victory at Saratoga (September–October 1777), the Germantown engagement, by impressing the French with Washington's strategic ability, was credited with influencing the French to come to America's aid in the war.

VALLEY FORGE

Following the American failures at the nearby battles of Brandywine and Germantown, Washington led 11,000

George Washington and the Marquis de Lafayette surveying the troops in Valley Forge, Pa., during the particularly harsh winter of 1777–78. Library of Congress Prints and Photographs Division

regulars to take up winter quarters from Dec. 19, 1777, to June 19, 1778, at Valley Forge on the west bank of the Schuylkill River, 22 miles (35 km) northwest of Philadelphia (which at the time was occupied by the British). The site was considered a defensible one, strategically located on leading trade routes and near farm supplies.

During that unusually harsh winter, the force of Washington's leadership held together the dwindling American army, which was suffering from the bitter cold, lack of clothes, semistarvation, gross mismanagement in the commissary and transport departments, Congressional neglect, and public criticism. More adequate money and supplies were forthcoming after the Franco-American Alliance became known in late spring 1778. Although its ranks were decimated by rampant disease, the Continental Army was reorganized, and it emerged the following June as a well-disciplined and efficient fighting force, largely because of the efficient drilling methods introduced by Frederick William, Baron von Steuben.

BATTLE OF MONMOUTH

Having evacuated Philadelphia, the British under Sir Henry Clinton were marching through New Jersey to Sandy Hook. After a 40-hour halt at Monmouth Court House, the army moved out, leaving a small covering force. In order to strike a vigorous blow at the retreating enemy, Gen. George Washington ordered Charles Lee, commanding the advance guard, to attack the British rear on June 28, 1778. When Lee attempted to surround the small force at the courthouse, he was surprised by the arrival of Lord Cornwallis's rear guard, which Clinton had ordered back to resist the attackers. Rather than risk fighting a delaying action on difficult terrain, Lee ordered a retreat but was tardy giving Washington notice. When Washington arrived, he was therefore surprised and indignant to find his Continental forces retreating in much disorder. He immediately rallied the troops and checked the British advances. Cornwallis fell back and withdrew undetected at night, joining the main British army on safe ground. Washington did not follow.

Having about equal forces, both sides claimed to have won victory at the Battle of Monmouth, but the British claim seems more valid since Clinton was able to complete his march without molestation. Washington presently marched to the Hudson River to join the Continental Army there, while Clinton's forces returned to New York. The combatants thus resumed the positions held two years before.

ENGAGEMENT BETWEEN *BONHOMME RICHARD* AND *SERAPIS*

Challenged by a large combined French and Spanish fleet, the British navy was too preoccupied to prevent American interference with its merchant marine in the Atlantic. Operating from French bases, Capt. John Paul Jones led a small fleet around the British Isles from August to October 1779. On September 23, Jones's *Bonhomme Richard* sighted two enemy ships of war conveying merchantmen loaded with naval stores and

engaged the British frigate *Serapis*, commanded by Capt. Richard Pearson, in a memorable three and a half hour duel that proved to be an important naval victory for the Americans.

The American commander answered a challenge to surrender early in the battle with the famous quotation, "I have not yet begun to fight!" The slaughter on

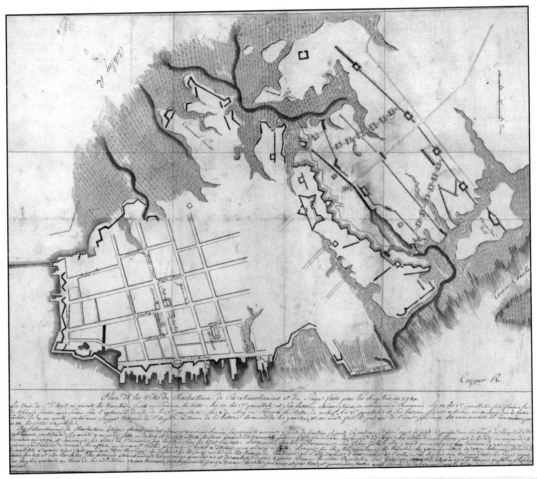

Early map of the city of Charleston, S.C., at the time of the siege by the British in 1780. Library of Congress Geography and Map Division

both sides was great; an estimated 150 Americans and nearly as many British were killed or wounded. Despite the fact that his ship was sinking (later Jones moved his command to the *Serapis*), Jones outlasted his adversary and forced a surrender.

SIEGE OF CHARLESTON

In 1776 Charleston, S.C., the principal port city of the southern American colonies, had withstood attack on Fort Sullivan (renamed Fort Moultrie because its defense had been overseen by Gen. William Moultrie) by British naval and army forces commanded by Adm. Peter Parker and Gen. Henry Clinton. In 1779 it had repulsed another, led by Gen. Augustus Prevost. But in the spring of 1780 a British land and sea campaign directed by Clinton cut off and forced the surrender of Charleston.

At this stage of the Revolution, the British war effort was refocused from New York and New Jersey to the south, where it was believed the large number of loyalists could be roused to take action against the rebellion. By 1778 an expedition to Savannah, Ga., had resulted in British control of most of Georgia. In December 1779 a British fleet bearing a large force led by Clinton embarked from New York. After encountering stormy weather, the fleet was forced to regroup in Savannah. In February 1780 Clinton's reconstituted army landed about 30 miles (50 km) south of Charleston and began its assault on the city, whose defense was commanded by Gen. Benjamin Lincoln.

In the coming weeks the British army advanced on and isolated Charleston. In the meantime the British fleet entered Charleston Harbor, where the small American naval flotilla had scuttled its ships and removed their cannon. The British land forces began constructing siege battlements in early April, and by April 14 the victory of a British force led by Lieut. Col. Banastre Tarleton at Moncks Corner cut off Charleston from potential colonial reinforcement. On May 12 Lincoln was forced to surrender. The British paroled the militiamen under Lincoln's command but made prisoners of the large contingent of the Continental Army that had defended the city.

BATTLE OF CAMDEN

The British victory in the Battle of Camden, fought in South Carolina on Aug. 16, 1780, was one of the most crushing defeats ever inflicted upon an American army.

After the fall of Charleston, S.C., to the British in May 1780, Gen. Horatio Gates marched upon the British stronghold at the town of Camden with a force of 1,400 regulars and more than 2,000 militia. With his army weakened by hunger and dysentery, Gates was surprised north of Camden by a British force of 2,200 troops under Lord Cornwallis. At the first attack, the untried colonial militia fled, and the regulars were soon surrounded and almost wiped out.

Though only 324 British were killed, the Americans suffered more than 2,000 casualties and lost large amounts of military supplies. While enhancing the reputation of Cornwallis, the battle ruined the career of Gates, who was replaced. The victory opened the way to a subsequent British invasion of North Carolina. The British stopped a second American attack on Camden under Gen. Nathanael Greene on April 25, 1781, at Hobkirk's Hill, but, worn down by colonial guerrilla harassment, they burned and evacuated the town the following month.

BATTLE OF KINGS MOUNTAIN

To stem the British advance into North Carolina, a force of about 2,000 colonial frontiersmen had been gathered from neighbouring states to replace the Continental forces that had been lost in South Carolina at the battles of Charleston (May 1780) and Camden (August 1780). The frontiersmen felt particularly bitter against the 1,100 soldiers, under Maj. Patrick Ferguson, who were mostly New Yorkers and South Carolinians loyal to the British. On Oct. 7, 1780, about a mile and a half south of the North Carolina–South Carolina boundary, the frontiersmen surrounded the loyalists on Kings Mountain and killed or captured almost the entire force. The Battle of Kings Mountain was noted as the first of a series of setbacks that ended in the eventual collapse of the British effort to hold North America.

BATTLE OF COWPENS

Fought on the northern border of South Carolina on Jan. 17, 1781, the Battle of Cowpens was a brilliant American victory that slowed Lord Cornwallis's campaign to invade North Carolina. From his headquarters at Charlotte, N.C., the new American commander in the South, Gen. Nathanael Greene, had divided his army and sent a force of 1,000 men under Gen. Daniel Morgan to the southwest to intercept Cornwallis's advance. At Cowpens, Morgan confronted about 1,150 troops under Col. Banastre Tarleton and inflicted a surprise defeat upon them. British casualties were set at about 600, while the Americans lost only 72. Not discouraged by what he described as a "very unexpected and severe blow," Cornwallis pushed on into North Carolina.

BATTLE OF GUILFORD COURTHOUSE

The strategic victory for the Americans at the Battle of Guilford Courthouse in North Carolina on March 15, 1781, played a crucial role in obliging the British to abandon control of the Carolinas.

After the Battle of Cowpens (Jan. 17, 1781), the American commander Nathanael Greene united both wings of his 4,400-man southern army at Guilford Courthouse. There Lord Cornwallis, with a force of 1,900 British veterans, caught up with the Americans, and a battle ensued. American casualties were light; British casualties were heavy. Wishing to avoid another defeat such as the one suffered by Gen. Horatio Gates at Camden, S.C., the previous August, Greene withdrew his forces intact.

Declining to pursue the Americans into the backcountry, Cornwallis temporarily retired to Hillsboro, N.C.. Acknowledging his failure to destroy patriot resistance in the South, Cornwallis abandoned the heart of the state a few weeks later and marched to the coast at Wilmington to recruit and refit his command.

BATTLE OF VIRGINIA CAPES

In late summer 1781 Lord Cornwallis led the main British army of the South onto the Yorktown Peninsula, Va., where he confidently awaited rescue by reinforcements from the British fleet. In the meantime the French admiral comte de Grasse proceeded with his entire fleet of 24 ships from the West Indies to Chesapeake Bay.

Sailing from New York, a British fleet of 19 ships under the command of Adm. Thomas Graves confronted the French at Virginia Capes on September 5. Only the leading squadrons of the two fleets engaged in moderate fighting in the late afternoon. Although British losses were heavier, the Battle of Virginia Capes was by and large undecided, and the two partly becalmed fleets drifted along parallel courses for the next three days without incident. Then, reinforced by

additional vessels and siege guns from Newport, R.I., the French sailed back into Chesapeake Bay to take final control of the harbour, while the British fleet returned to New York. The outcome of the battle was indispensable to the successful Franco-American Siege of Yorktown from August to October. Indeed, British naval historian Sir William M. James labeled this the "decisive battle of the war," one that sealed the fate of Cornwallis and of the British cause in America.

BATTLE OF EUTAW SPRINGS

On Sept. 8, 1781, British troops under Lieut. Col. Alexander Stewart clashed with American forces commanded by Gen. Nathanael Greene near Charleston, S.C., in the Battle of Eutaw Springs. Greene wished to prevent Stewart from joining Gen. Lord Cornwallis in the event of that leader's retreat south from Yorktown. About 2,000 American troops, many ill-clad and barefoot, were slightly outnumbered. In the early fighting the British were more successful; on September 9, however, Stewart withdrew his forces to Charleston, where they remained until the end of the war.

SIEGE OF YORKTOWN

After a series of reverses and the depletion of his forces' strength, the British commander in the southern colonies, Lord Cornwallis, moved his army from

Wilmington, N.C., eastward to Petersburg, Va., on the Atlantic coast, in May 1781. Cornwallis had about 7,500 men and was confronted in the region by only about 4,500 American troops under the marquis de Lafayette, Gen. Anthony Wayne, and Baron von Steuben. In order to maintain his seaborne lines of communication with the main British army of Gen. Henry Clinton in New York City, Cornwallis then retreated through Virginia, first to Richmond, next to Williamsburg, and finally, near the end of July, to

Yorktown and the adjacent promontory of Gloucester, both of which he proceeded to fortify.

Gen. George Washington ordered Lafayette to block Cornwallis's possible escape from Yorktown by land. In the meantime Washington's 2,500 Continental troops in New York were joined by 4,000 French troops under the comte de Rochambeau. This combined allied force left a screen of troops facing Clinton's forces in New York while the main Franco-American force, beginning on

This Currier and Ives lithograph of the John Trumbull painting, The Surrender of Lord Cornwallis at Yorktown, Virginia, October 19th, 1781 *(1820), shows British General Lincoln and his officers flanked by French and American troops.* Library of Congress Prints and Photographs Division

August 21, undertook a rapid march southward to the head of Chesapeake Bay, where it linked up with a French fleet of 24 ships under the comte de Grasse. This fleet had arrived from the West Indies and was maintaining a sea blockade of Cornwallis's army. Cornwallis's army waited in vain for rescue or reinforcements from the British navy while de Grasse's fleet transported Washington's troops southward to Williamsburg, Va., whence they joined Lafayette's forces in the siege of Yorktown. Washington was thus vindicated in his hopes of entrapping Cornwallis on the Yorktown Peninsula.

Meanwhile, a smaller British fleet under Adm. Thomas Graves was unable to counter French naval superiority at the Battle of Virginia Capes and felt forced to return to New York. A British rescue fleet, two-thirds the size of the French, set out for Virginia on October 17 with some 7,000 British troops, but it was too late. Throughout early October Washington's 14,000 Franco-American troops steadily overcame the British army's fortified positions at Yorktown. Surrounded, outgunned, and running low on food, Cornwallis surrendered his entire army on October 19. (The Siege of Yorktown is usually dated from September 28 to October 19.) The total

number of British prisoners taken was about 8,000, along with about 240 guns. Casualties on both sides were relatively light. The victory at Yorktown ended fighting in the Revolution and virtually assured success to the American cause.

BATTLE OF THE SAINTES

A major British naval victory, the Battle of the Saintes, fought on April 12, 1782, ended the French threat to British possessions in the West Indies. Setting out from Martinique on April 8, a French fleet of 35 warships and 150 merchantmen under the comte de Grasse intended to descend upon Jamaica with Spanish help. They were intercepted at the Saintes Passage, between the islands of Dominica and Guadeloupe, by a British fleet of 36 ships commanded by Adm. Sir George Rodney. After preliminary skirmishing, the main action took place on April 12, when a shift in the wind altered the course of two French ships, causing gaps in their line of battle that were quickly entered by the British. The French fleet was thus scattered and the ensuing British victory at the Saintes helped restore Britain's naval prestige. As a result, in the Treaty of Paris (Sept. 3, 1783) Britain regained most of its islands in the West Indies.

CHAPTER 5

MILITARY FIGURES OF THE AMERICAN REVOLUTION

At the beginning of the American Revolution, the Continental Army had few career soldiers. The American military had to invent itself step by step. It took time for this coalition—a collection of landowners, millworkers, farmers, foreign aristocrats, southerners, and Yankees—to learn to work together. But when they did, they became a formidable fighting force.

THE AMERICAN SIDE

ETHAN ALLEN
(b. Jan. 21, 1738, Litchfield, Conn.—d. Feb. 12, 1789, Burlington, Vt.)

Soldier and frontiersman Ethan Allen was the leader of the patriot militia known as the Green Mountain Boys.

After fighting in the French and Indian War (1754–63), Allen settled in what is now Vermont. At the outbreak of the Revolution, he raised his force of Green Mountain Boys (organized in 1770) and Connecticut troops and helped capture the British fort at Ticonderoga, New York (May 10, 1775). Later, as a volunteer in Gen. Philip Schuyler's forces, he conducted a foolhardy attempt to take Montreal (September 1775), in the course of which he was captured by the British and held prisoner until May 6, 1778. Congress gave Allen the brevet rank of colonel with back pay, but he did not serve in the war after his release. Instead, he devoted his time to local affairs in Vermont, especially working for separate statehood from New York. Failing to achieve this, he attempted to negotiate the annexation of Vermont to Canada.

BENEDICT ARNOLD
(b. Jan. 14, 1741, Norwich, Conn.— d. June 14, 1801, London, Eng.)

Patriot officer Benedict Arnold served the cause of the Revolution until 1779, when he shifted his allegiance to the British; thereafter his name became an epithet for traitor in the United States.

Upon the outbreak of hostilities at Lexington, Mass., Arnold volunteered for service and participated with Ethan Allen in the successful colonial attack on British-held Fort Ticonderoga, N.Y., the following month. That autumn he was appointed by Gen. George Washington to command an expedition to capture Quebec. He marched with 700 men by way of the Maine wilderness, a remarkable feat of woodsmanship and endurance, and, reinforced by Gen. Richard Montgomery, attacked the well-fortified city. The combined assault (Dec. 31, 1775) failed, Montgomery was killed, and Arnold was severely wounded.

Promoted to the rank of brigadier general, Arnold constructed a flotilla on Lake Champlain and inflicted severe losses on a greatly superior enemy fleet near Valcour Island, N.Y. (Oct. 11, 1776). He returned a hero, but his rash courage

and impatient energy had aroused the enmity of several officers. When in February 1777 Congress created five new major generalships, Arnold was passed over in favour of his juniors. Arnold resented this affront, and only Washington's personal persuasion kept him from resigning.

Two months later he repelled a British attack on Danbury, Conn., and was made a major general, but his seniority was not restored and Arnold felt his honour

Benedict Arnold was an officer in the Continental Army as well as a traitor to the Revolution. MPI/Hulton Archive/ Getty Images

impugned. Again he tried to resign, but in July he accepted a government order to help stem the British advance into upper New York. He won a victory at Fort Stanwix (now Rome) in August 1777 and commanded advance battalions at the Battle of Saratoga that autumn, fighting brilliantly until seriously wounded. For his services he was restored to his proper relative rank.

Crippled from his wounds, Arnold was placed in command of Philadelphia (June 1778), where he socialized with families of loyalist sympathies and lived extravagantly. To raise money, he violated several state and military regulations, arousing the suspicions and, finally, the denunciations of Pennsylvania's supreme executive council. These charges were then referred to Congress, and Arnold asked for an immediate court-martial to clear himself.

Meanwhile, in April 1779, Arnold married Margaret (Peggy) Shippen, a young woman of loyalist sympathies. Early in May he made secret overtures to British headquarters, and a year later he informed the British of a proposed American invasion of Canada. He later revealed that he expected to obtain the command of West Point, N.Y., and asked the British for £20,000 for betraying this post. When his British contact, Maj. John André, was captured by the Americans, Arnold escaped on a British ship, leaving André to be hanged as a spy. The sacrifice of André made Arnold odious to loyalists, and his reputation was further tarnished among his former neighbours when he led a raid on New London, Conn, in September 1781.

At the end of 1781 Arnold went to England, where he remained, inactive, ostracized, and ailing, for the rest of his life.

JOHN BARRY
(b. 1745, County Wexford, Ire.— d. Sept. 13, 1803, Philadelphia, Pa.)

American naval officer John Barry won significant maritime victories during the Revolution and trained so many young officers who later became celebrated in the country's history that he was often called the "Father of the Navy."

A merchant shipmaster out of Philadelphia at the age of 21, Barry outfitted the first Continental fleet at the outbreak of the Revolution. Commissioned captain of the brig *Lexington* in 1776, he early distinguished himself by capturing the British tender *Edward* after a short engagement. He fought with distinction in the campaign around Trenton, N.J. (1776), and was then commissioned captain of the frigate *Effingham*, which he was forced to scuttle to avoid capture by the British.

In the winter of 1777–78 Barry commanded a spectacular boat foray that ran the British batteries at Philadelphia and raided enemy shipping in the Delaware River and Bay. Next commanding the frigate *Raleigh* out of Boston, he fought a vigorous but futile battle against superior enemy forces but managed to save most of his crew from capture.

Commanding the frigate *Alliance* in 1780, he was assigned to convey Col. John Laurens on a diplomatic mission to France. En route he took several prizes and in returning engaged in a notable battle with two British sloops of war, eventually subduing them.

On the final cruise of the *Alliance* (beginning in 1782), Barry ranged the shipping lanes from Bermuda to Cape Sable and captured four British ships. He fought the last battle of the war (March 1783) in the Straits of Florida, where he beat off three British frigates seeking to intercept him.

After the war Barry was recalled to active service as senior captain of the new U.S. Navy. In the quasi-war with France (1798–1800), he was twice in command of all U.S. ships in the West Indies. By the end of his career he was senior officer of the navy.

GEORGE ROGERS CLARK
(b. Nov. 19, 1752, Albemarle County, Va.—d. Feb. 13, 1818, near Louisville, Ky.)

The battlefield successes of frontier military leader George Rogers Clark during the Revolution were crucial to the awarding of the Old Northwest to the United States in the Treaty of Paris, concluding the war.

Trained by his grandfather, Clark engaged in surveying along the Ohio River in the mid-1770s. He became interested in the Kentucky country around Harrodsburg and opposed those who sought to establish an independent colony of Transylvania there. At the outbreak of the Revolution, Clark persuaded the Virginia government to make Kentucky a separate county and to authorize him to enlist troops for its defense against the British and Indians along the frontier.

In May 1778 Clark, with an expedition of about 175 men, took two Mississippi River settlements—Kaskaskia and Cahokia, both in present-day Illinois. At Kaskaskia, Clark gained the friendship of Pierre Gibault, who induced the French at Vincennes on the Wabash River to change their allegiance. When reinforcements promised from Virginia failed to arrive, Clark withdrew to Fort Nelson (now Louisville) on the Ohio River and made that his base for the rest of the war. In 1780 he helped defeat a British expedition sent against the Spanish settlement at St. Louis. That same year, in what is now Ohio, he destroyed the Shawnee Indian towns of Chillicothe and Piqua; in 1782 he razed Shawnee villages and destroyed crops in the Miami River valley.

Throughout the war Clark and his men received no pay for their services. Furthermore, Clark was held responsible for debts incurred for supplies, since Virginia, despite its promises, never reimbursed him.

Clark was appointed an Indian commissioner after the war, and in 1786 he helped negotiate a treaty with the Shawnees. The same year, he led an expedition against the Wabash tribes and seized goods taken to Vincennes by Spanish traders.

James Wilkinson, a double agent in the pay of Spain, coveted Clark's command and his post of Indian commissioner. After a deliberate campaign to discredit Clark, Wilkinson was appointed Indian commissioner and Clark was relieved of his military command. Thereafter Clark became involved in a scheme to found a Spanish colony west of the Mississippi River. In 1793 he accepted a French major general's commission in connection with French emissary Edmond-Charles Genet's mission to involve the United States in hostilities between France and England. Clark returned to Louisville in 1799 and resided there until his death.

THOMAS CONWAY
(b. Feb. 27, 1735, Ireland—d. c. 1800)

Thomas Conway served as a general during the Revolution and is remembered for advocating that George Washington be replaced by Gen. Horatio Gates as the Continental Army's commander in chief.

Conway moved from Ireland to France at age six. In 1749 he joined the French army, and by 1772 he held the rank of colonel. In 1776 Conway was recommended for service in the American army, and he arrived in the United States the following year. Appointed a brigadier general, he saw action at Brandywine and Germantown. Although regarded as a skillful disciplinarian of infantry, Conway was refused promotion to major general—largely due to the opposition of Washington, who believed that there were older officers more deserving of the rank.

Conway then offered his resignation to Congress. Congress not only refused to accept it but commissioned him major general and—on the same day (Dec. 14, 1777)—inspector general. Believing Congress lacked confidence in Washington, Conway launched a secret correspondence with Gates, bolstering Gates's ambitions and criticizing Washington. The correspondence came to Washington's attention and the American commander wrote to both Conway and Gates (sending the Gates letter through Congress). With the "plot" exposed, congressional support for replacing Washington immediately evaporated. Although Conway himself played a minor role in the conspiracy, the entire event has been called the Conway Cabal.

In 1778 Conway intrigued to be named second in command to the marquis de Lafayette during an expedition to Canada, but Lafayette refused to go along with the plan. Conway did accompany the expedition—but as third in command. On April 22, 1778, Conway again offered his resignation to Congress. This time, to his surprise, Congress accepted it.

On July 4, 1778, in a duel brought on by his criticism of Washington, Conway was wounded. Believing himself about to die, he wrote a long letter of apology to Washington. But Conway recovered, returned to France, and rejoined the French army. He served in Flanders and India before returning to France after the start of the French Revolution. In 1793 he was forced to flee France because of support for the royalist cause. He died in exile.

GUSTAVUS CONYNGHAM
(b. c. 1747, County Donegal, Ire.— d. Nov. 27, 1819, Philadelphia, Pa.)

American naval officer Gustavus Conyngham fought the British in their own waters during the Revolution.

Conyngham was taken to America in his youth and apprenticed to a captain in the West Indian trade. Advancing to shipmaster, he was stranded in the Netherlands at the outbreak of the Revolution. The American commissioners in France supplied him with a commission and sent him forth from Dunkirk, Fr., in May in an armed lugger. He captured two ships, but Britain protested the flagrant violation of French neutrality. Conyngham and his crew were imprisoned; his captain's commission was confiscated. The commissioners, with French contrivance, secured his release and supplied him with a new commission and the cutter *Revenge*. Operating around the British Isles, off Spain, and in the West Indies, he took 27 prizes and sank another 30 ships in the next 18 months.

Despite this achievement, when Conyngham landed in Philadelphia in 1779, he was accused of corruption arising from his relationship with the American commissioners in France. The *Revenge* was confiscated, sold, and repurchased—still under Conyngham's command but now as a privateer. It was promptly taken by the British, and Conyngham, never especially concerned with either paperwork or neutral rights,

was threatened with death as a pirate for being unable to produce his original commission. Imprisoned in England, Conyngham escaped to the Netherlands, where in 1780 he joined John Paul Jones in a cruise in the frigate *Alliance*. Acquiring his own ship, Conyngham was once again captured (May 17, 1780). Released nine months later, he spent the rest of the war on the beach.

From the end of the war in 1783 until his death in Philadelphia in 1819, Conyngham waged a futile fight to gain compensation from Congress. Almost a century after his death, the commission that could have substantiated his claim was found in the collection of a Parisian autograph dealer.

RICHARD DALE
(b. Nov. 6, 1756, Norfolk County, Va.—d. Feb. 26, 1826, Philadelphia, Pa.)

Naval officer Richard Dale served on ships of both sides in the Revolution but ultimately distinguished himself as an American patriot.

Dale went to sea at age 12 and thereafter had a checkered career as a lieutenant in the Virginia provincial navy, a prisoner of war with the British fleet in Chesapeake Bay, and a mate on a loyalist brigantine. When the brigantine was taken by the U.S. captain John Barry (July 1776), Dale signed on Barry's Continental brigantine *Lexington* as a master's mate. He went to prison in England along with the rest of the crew when the *Lexington* was taken by the British in 1777.

Escaping to France more than a year later, Dale went on board the *Bonhomme Richard* under Capt. John Paul Jones. As first lieutenant, Dale distinguished himself at the taking of the *Serapis* near Flamborough Head, Yorkshire (September 1779). He followed Jones's fortunes on the *Alliance* and the *Ariel* and in August 1781 was on board the *Trumbull* when that frigate was captured by the British.

After the war Dale served in the new U.S. Navy and later in the merchant marine. In May 1801 he was recalled to duty and with a small force maintained a successful blockade off Tripoli, holding the Barbary pirates in check for six months. He resigned in 1802.

CHARLES-HECTOR, COMTE D'ESTAING
(b. Nov. 24, 1729, Ruvel, Auvergne, Fr.—d. April 28, 1794, Paris)

The comte d'Estaing was the commander of the first French fleet sent in support of the American colonists during the Revolution.

D'Estaing served in India during the Seven Years' War and was governor of the Antilles (1763–66). He was appointed vice admiral in 1767 and in 1778 attempted to surprise the English squadrons in North America and enable the colonists to resume the offensive. His blockade of Adm. Richard Howe in New York Bay proved unsuccessful (July 1778), and in

August storms prevented him from engaging the British fleet near Newport, R.I. In November he sailed for the Antilles, where, despite several opportunities, he failed to eliminate a much smaller British squadron. He was seriously wounded in an unsuccessful attack on Savannah, Ga. (September–October 1779), and returned to France with his squadron. D'Estaing was an energetic commander, but his lack of naval experience caused him to be diffident before smaller British forces. His caution and hesitancy greatly disappointed the colonists during a crucial phase of the war.

In France, d'Estaing was an enlightened reformer; he was elected to the Assembly of Notables in 1787. He was commander of the National Guard at Versailles at the outbreak of the French Revolution (1789) and was guillotined in Paris during the Reign of Terror.

HORATIO GATES
(b. *c.* 1728, Maldon, Essex, Eng.— d. April 10, 1806, New York, N.Y.)

English-born American general Horatio Gates played a pivotal role in turning the tide of victory in the Revolution on behalf of the Americans with his triumph over the British at the Battle of Saratoga (1777).

Gates first served in North America in the French and Indian War, emerged as a major, and returned to England. In 1772 he immigrated to the region that is now West Virginia. Sympathizing with colonial complaints against the crown, in

1775 he was made adjutant general of the Continental Army, and in 1777 he superseded Gen.Philip Schuyler in northern New York. In the two battles of Saratoga his army forced Gen. John Burgoyne to surrender, partly, however, because of the previous maneuvers of Schuyler and the initiative of Gen. Benedict Arnold. Congress next elected Gates president of the Board of War. At the same time a group of army officers, among them Gen.Thomas Conway, became involved in a plan to replace Gen. George Washington with Gates. The "Conway Cabal" soon collapsed, and in the spring of 1778 Gates returned to his command in New York. Transferred to the south (June 1780), Gates was disastrously defeated by Lord Cornwallis at the Battle of Camden, S.C., on August 16. An official inquiry into his conduct was ordered but charges were never pressed. After the war Gates freed his slaves, moved to New York, and served one term in the state legislature.

FRANÇOIS-JOSEPH-PAUL, COMTE DE GRASSE
(b. Sept. 13, 1722, Le Bar, Fr.— d. Jan. 11, 1788, Paris)

French naval commander the comte de Grasse played a major role during the Revolution by commanding the fleet whose actions at sea made possible the successful Siege of Yorktown.

De Grasse took service in 1734 on the galleys of the Knights of Malta, and in 1740 he entered the French service. Shortly after France and America joined forces in the Revolutionary War, he was dispatched to America as commander of a squadron. In 1779–80 he fought the English off the West Indies. In 1781 he was promoted to the rank of admiral and was successful in defeating Adm. Samuel Hood and in taking Tobago. When Gen. George Washington and the French general the comte de Rochambeau determined to march to Virginia to join forces with the marquis de Lafayette's army against the British commander Lord Cornwallis, Washington requested the cooperation of de Grasse's fleet. De Grasse therefore sailed from the West Indies to the Chesapeake River, where he was joined by a fleet under the comte de Barras. A British force under Adm. Thomas Graves attempted to prevent this juncture by engaging de Grasse's fleet when it arrived at the Chesapeake Bay but was unsuccessful. French naval supremacy in the waters off Yorktown was instrumental in the success of the siege of that city.

After Cornwallis's surrender, de Grasse returned to the West Indies, where he captured the island of St. Kitts in January 1782. In April, however, he was defeated by Adm. George Rodney and taken prisoner. On his return to France, de Grasse published *Mémoire du comte de Grasse* (1782; "Memoir of the Count of Grasse") and was acquitted by a court-martial in 1784.

NATHANAEL GREENE
(b. Aug. 7, 1742, Potowomut, R.I.—d. June 19, 1786, Mulberry Grove, Ga.)

A skilled strategist and tactician, Nathanael Greene was among the most important American generals during the Revolution.

After managing a branch of his father's iron foundry, Greene served several terms in the colonial legislature and was elected commander of the Rhode Island army, organized in 1775; he was made a major general in 1776. Greene served with George Washington in the Siege of Boston, in the fighting in and around New York City (1776), and in the retreat across New Jersey after the British capture of Fort Washington (November 1776). He also led troops at Trenton (December 1776) and, the following year, at Brandywine and Germantown.

After briefly serving as quartermaster general, Greene succeeded Gen. Horatio Gates as commander in chief of the southern army in October 1778. Opposed by a superior force under Lord Cornwallis, Greene developed a strategy that relied on mobility and maneuver. Irregular forces kept the British extended, while Greene preserved his small main army as a "force in being" to lure Cornwallis further away from his coastal bases. Greene ultimately risked dividing his own force, encouraging the British to divide theirs as well. His strategy led to Gen. Daniel Morgan's victory at Cowpens, S.C. (Jan. 17, 1781). Although Greene was defeated at the Battle of Guilford Courthouse, N.C. (March 15, 1781), the British were so weakened by their victory that Cornwallis abandoned his plan

General Nathanael Greene of the Continental Army. This portrait, c. 1780, shows Greene around the time he was given command of American forces in the south. MPI/Hulton Archive/Getty Images

to conquer North Carolina and instead marched north into Virginia.

Taking the offensive, by the end of June Greene had forced the British back to the South Carolina coast. On September 8 Greene engaged the British under Lieut. Col. Alexander Stewart at Eutaw Springs, where the British were so weakened that they withdrew to Charleston. He held them there during the remainder of the war.

Greene contributed significantly to restoring civil government and public order to a South wracked by years of guerrilla war. Committed to the rights of property, he opposed the dispossession and persecution of loyalists. South Carolina and Georgia recognized Greene's achievements by liberal grants of land and money. He settled in 1785 on an estate near Savannah—ironically the former property of a loyalist official.

As quartermaster general, Greene was accused of profiteering when inflation required paying more than authorized for goods. He supplied the southern army in part by cosigning notes with a contractor whose bankruptcy and death left Greene responsible. Greene denied charges of impropriety, which remain unproven in an 18th-century context of boundaries between public and private affairs that were at best hazy. He did his unsuccessful best to liquidate the debts until his early death in 1786 from what might well have been a stress-induced heart attack. Greene, however, is not remembered for his bookkeeping, but as Washington's designated successor and a strategist without peer on the American side of the Revolution.

GREEN MOUNTAIN BOYS

The Green Mountain Boys came into being in 1770 at present-day Bennington, Vermont, as an unauthorized militia organized to defend the property rights of local residents who had received land grants from New Hampshire. New York, which then claimed present-day Vermont, disputed New Hampshire's right to grant land west of the Green Mountains. The Green Mountain Boys stopped sheriffs from enforcing New York laws and terrorized settlers who had New York grants, burning buildings, stealing cattle, and administering occasional floggings with birch rods.

The Green Mountain Boys immediately joined the Revolution, and on May 10, 1775, fewer than 100 of them, under the joint command of Ethan Allen and Benedict Arnold, captured Fort Ticonderoga. Eventually they became part of the Continental Army and served in the abortive offensive against Canada. Reorganized despite an ongoing conflict with New York over jurisdiction, the Green Mountain Boys took the field against Gen. John Burgoyne in 1777, playing central roles at the battles of Hubbardton and Bennington. The latter action, which destroyed a detachment of Burgoyne's army as it sought to forage for supplies, was crucial to Burgoyne's eventual defeat.

Other Green Mountain Boys, under Allen's mercurial leadership, continued an internal war against "Yorkers," a campaign Allen is said by some accounts to have pursued to the point of negotiating for Vermont's return to British allegiance. His resignation from the Vermont militia in 1781 rendered the subject moot, and Vermont in 1791 joined the Union as its 14th state.

NATHAN HALE
(b. June 6, 1755, Coventry, Conn.—
d. Sept. 22, 1776, New York, N.Y.)

One of America's most legendary patriots, army officer Nathan Hale was hanged as a result of his attempt to spy on the British during the Revolution.

A graduate of Yale University (1773) and a schoolteacher, Hale joined a Con-

Nathan Hale, American patriot and spy, about to be hanged by British soldiers on Sept. 22, 1776. Before being executed, Hale uttered the famous line "I only regret that I have but one life to lose for my country". MPI/Hulton Archive/Getty Images

necticut regiment in 1775, served in the Siege of Boston, and was commissioned a captain (1776). He went to New York with William Heath's brigade and is said to have participated in the capture of a provision sloop from under the guns of a British man-of-war. Hale was captured by the British while attempting to return to his regiment, having penetrated the British lines on Long Island to obtain information. He was hanged without trial the next day.

Hale is regarded by American Revolutionary tradition as a hero and a martyr. He is supposed to have said before his death that his only regret was that he had but one life to lose for his country, a remark similar to one in Joseph Addison's play *Cato.*

EDWARD HAND
(b. Dec. 31, 1744, King's County, Ire.—
d. Sept. 3, 1802, Lancaster, Pa.)

Remembered for his skillful negotiations with and actions against Native Americans, army officer Edward Hand faced a variety of challenging tasks during his military service and is regarded as among the most accomplished of the Revolution's citizen-soldiers.

Trained as a doctor in Ireland, Hand served with the British army on the Pennsylvania frontier from 1767 to 1774, before resigning his commission to practice medicine in Lancaster. An early supporter of the American cause, Hand was commissioned a lieutenant colonel in the rifle battalion that Pennsylvania raised in 1775. He served at the Siege of Boston, the Battle of Long Island, and the battles of Trenton and Princeton, N.J., demonstrating tactical and administrative abilities that earned him promotion to brigadier general on April 1, 1777.

Assigned to Fort Pitt, in western Pennsylvania, Hand improved the effectiveness of the local militia and secured the neutrality of the Delaware Indians and some Shawnee clans. His proposals for active defense against hostile tribes foundered for lack of resources, and rising public criticism led him to request relief. In October 1777, he was reassigned to the northern frontier, where the next year he played a major role in the campaign against Britain's Iroquois Confederacy allies.

Returning to George Washington's main army, Hand in 1781 was appointed its adjutant general. He overhauled administrative and training procedures, but frustration with the indifference of the Continental Congress led him to threaten resignation. At Washington's urging, however, he continued in the post until the end of the war. A committed Federalist, Hand subsequently served in the Continental Congress and the Pennsylvania Assembly, helped suppress the Whiskey Rebellion of 1794, and was a customs inspector from 1791 to 1801. His success in a variety of challenging tasks places him among the best of the Revolution's citizen-soldiers.

NICHOLAS HERKIMER
(b. 1728, near Herkimer, N.Y.— d. Aug. 16, 1777, Little Falls, N.Y.)

Gen. Nicholas Herkimer distinguished himself during the Revolution as the calm, courageous commander of American militiamen in the Battle of Oriskany (Aug. 6, 1777).

Herkimer grew up in New York's Mohawk Valley, which during the Revolution was sharply divided between patriots and loyalists and was subject to ferocious Indian attacks. He became a lieutenant in the militia during the French and Indian War and rose to brigadier general at the outbreak of the Revolution.

In 1777 Herkimer commanded a force of about 800 militiamen in an effort to relieve Fort Stanwix, threatened by a combined force of loyalists and Indians. On August 6, near the present site of Oriskany, New York, Herkimer's force was ambushed, and the ensuing battle proved to be one of the bloodiest of the entire war. During the fight, Herkimer sustained a severe leg wound. He is said to have then directed his troops while sitting under a tree and smoking his pipe. The American militia retreated and carried Herkimer back to his home. There he died 10 days after the battle, following an ineptly performed amputation.

ESEK HOPKINS
(b. April 26, 1718, Providence, R.I.— d. Feb. 26, 1802, Providence)

Esek Hopkins's short tenure during the Revolution as the first commodore of the United States Navy might charitably be described as undistinguished.

Hopkins, who went to sea at the age of 20, proving his ability as a seaman and trader, and a marriage into wealth put him at the head of a large merchant fleet prior to the French and Indian War. By privateering during that war, he added to his fortune and won a considerable naval reputation. Rhode Island named him a brigadier general of its land forces at the outbreak of the Revolution, but a call from the Continental Congress, where his brother was chairman of the naval committee, induced him to forsake the army and accept the command (Dec. 22, 1775) of the first Continental fleet then outfitting at Philadelphia. Instructed to attack the British fleet under John Murray, 4th earl of Dunmore, in Chesapeake Bay, Hopkins considered his orders discretionary and the enemy too strong. He therefore sailed his fleet of eight armed vessels to the Bahamas, captured considerable war matériel at New Providence Island, and upon his return fought an inconclusive action with the British ship *Glasgow* (April 1776).

Dissatisfaction with the achievements of the fleet and its subsequent inactivity in Rhode Island led to an investigation by Congress. Censured for disobedience of orders, Hopkins returned to the fleet, but his continued inactivity and quarrels with his officers induced Congress to suspend him from his command in March

1777. He was dismissed from the navy in 1778 and thereafter played a prominent part in Rhode Island politics.

JOHN PAUL JONES
(b. July 6, 1747, Kirkbean, Kirkcudbright, Scot.—d. July 18, 1792, Paris, Fr.)

Renowned for the victory of the ship he commanded, *Bonhomme Richard*, over British ships, including the frigate *Serapis*, off the east coast of England on Sept. 23, 1779, Scottish-born John Paul Jones was the greatest American naval hero of the Revolution.

Apprenticed at age 12 to John Younger, a Scottish merchant shipper, John Paul sailed as a cabin boy on a ship to Virginia, where he visited his older brother William at Fredericksburg. When Younger's business failed in 1766, Paul found work as chief mate of a Jamaica-owned slaver brigantine. After two years he quit the slave trade and shipped passage for Scotland. When both master and chief mate died of fever en route, he brought the ship safely home and was appointed a master. In 1772 he purchased a vessel in the West Indies but the following year, after killing the ringleader of a mutinous crew, he fled the islands to escape trial and changed his name to John Paul Jones. Two years later he returned to Fredericksburg and when the Revolution broke out, he went to Philadelphia and was commissioned a senior lieutenant in the new Continental Navy.

American Naval Commander John Paul Jones, who commanded the flagship Bonhomme Richard *during the American Revolution.* Hulton Archive/ Getty Images

Assigned to the *Alfred*, flagship of the little fleet commanded by Commodore Esek Hopkins, Jones distinguished himself in action in the Bahamas and against the British ship *Glasgow* on the return trip. In 1776 he was in command of the *Providence*, and between August and October he ranged over the Atlantic from Bermuda to Nova Scotia, twice outwitting British frigates, manning and

sending in eight prizes, and sinking and burning eight more. Again in charge of the *Alfred*, later in the same year, he reached port unmolested with several prizes in tow.

Appointed by Congress to the newly built *Ranger* (June 1777), Jones made a spectacular cruise through St. George's Channel and the Irish Sea, where he took a number of prizes. Arriving at Brest, Fr., on May 8, 1778, he was hailed as a hero by the French.

In August 1779 Jones took command of the *Bonhomme Richard* and, accompanied by four small ships, sailed around the British Isles. In September the little squadron intercepted the Baltic merchant fleet under convoy of the British ships *Serapis* and *Countess of Scarborough*. What followed was one of the most famous naval engagements in American history. During the early stages of a gruelling gun battle, Jones answered an enemy challenge to surrender with the memorable words, "I have not yet begun to fight!" He won a stunning victory, though with a heavy loss of life, when the *Serapis* surrendered and was boarded by Jones and his crew. The *Bonhomme Richard* sank soon afterward from damage received in the engagement, and Jones sailed both the *Serapis* and the captured *Countess of Scarborough* to the Netherlands. In France Louis XVI rewarded him with a gold-hilted sword and made him a chevalier of France.

After receiving a Congressional gold medal in 1787, Jones was dispatched on official business to Denmark; while abroad he accepted an appointment to the Russian Navy as rear admiral. This period in his life was uniformly disappointing, and he was plagued with lack of recognition and false accusation. In 1790 he returned to Paris embittered and physically broken. He died soon after and was buried in an unmarked grave. More than a century later, however, U.S. warships escorted his remains back to his adopted country, and his grave at Annapolis, Md., was made a national shrine.

JOHANN KALB
(b. June 29, 1721, Hüttendorf, near Erlangen [Ger.]—d. Aug. 19, 1780, Camden, S.C.)

One of a number of prominent foreign officers who played crucial roles in the American military effort during the Revolution, Johann Kalb, a German national, weathered the difficult winter at Valley Forge, Pa., with the Continental Army but later died of wounds sustained in battle.

Of peasant antecedents, Kalb was schooled at Kriegenbronn and left home at age 16. He received his first military training in 1743 as a lieutenant in a German regiment of the French infantry, calling himself Jean de Kalb. After a number of years of outstanding service (notably in the War of the Austrian Succession and the Seven Years' War), he was asked, in 1768, by the duke de Choiseul, head of the French Foreign Ministry, to undertake a secret visit to the

13 British colonies in North America to ascertain their attitude toward Great Britain. His four-month investigation resulted in a number of detailed and astute reports. Eager to return to the New World after going back to Europe, Kalb in 1776 secured a promise of a commission in the Continental Army from Silas Deane, American commissioner to France. He reached Philadelphia in July 1777 and was eventually appointed a major general by the Continental Congress. He became a strong admirer of Gen. George Washington and served with him through the trying winter at Valley Forge. As second in command to the marquis de Lafayette, he participated in an abortive expedition against Canada (1778).

In April 1780 Kalb was ordered from Morristown, N.J., to the relief of Charleston, S.C., but the city fell to the British while he was marching south. At Deep River, N.C., he was joined in July by Gen. Horatio Gates, commander of the southern department. Kalb urged an immediate attack, but Gates waited until the British forces knew of his presence and then on August 14 marched against them at Camden. The British drove Gates from the field, but Kalb remained in the battle and died five days later from wounds received there.

HENRY KNOX
(b. July 25, 1750, Boston, Mass.— d. Oct. 25, 1806, Thomaston, Maine)

Gen. Henry Knox made important contributions to the American war effort throughout the Revolution, beginning with his heroics during the Siege of Boston and culminating in his role in the Siege of Yorktown.

Forced by family circumstances to leave school at age nine, Knox worked in a Boston bookstore and by age 21 had acquired his own store. He became active in the colonial militia and in 1775 joined the Continental Army at Cambridge, Mass. He was commissioned a colonel and placed in charge of the artillery. During the winter of 1775–76 Gen. George Washington sent him to Fort Ticonderoga, in New York, to bring back captured British artillery there. In a remarkable feat, Knox brought back artillery totaling 120,000 pounds (55,000 kg), using oxen, horses, and men to transport the guns over snow and ice 300 miles (480 km) to Boston. The weapons were used to drive the British from that besieged city and formed the basis for the Revolutionary artillery.

In the Philadelphia campaign (1778), Knox, then a brigadier general, distinguished himself in commanding the artillery at Monmouth, N.J. (June), and later at the decisive Siege of Yorktown (1781). He was made a major general and at the end of the war succeeded Washington as commander of the army (December 1783). Knox resigned his command early in 1784 and returned to Boston. He became secretary of war (1785) in the government under the Articles of Confederation and was carried over into President Washington's first cabinet (1789). He retired to a large estate at Thomaston, Maine, in 1795.

TADEUSZ KOŚCIUSZKO
(b. Feb. 4, 1746, Mereczowszczyzna, Pol.—d. Oct. 15, 1817, Solothurn, Switz.)

Polish patriot Tadeusz Kościuszko was yet another foreign national who fought on the American side during the Revolution. He studied military engineering in Paris and went to America in 1776, where he joined the colonial army. He helped build fortifications in Philadelphia, Pa., and at West Point, N.Y. As chief of engineers, he twice rescued the army of Gen. Nathanael Greene by directing river crossings. He also directed the blockade of Charleston, S.C. At the war's end he was awarded U.S. citizenship and made a brigadier general. He returned to Poland in 1784 and became a major general in the Polish army. In 1794 he led a rebellion against occupying Russian and Prussian forces, during which he defended Warsaw for two months, directing residents to build earthworks. He was jailed in Russia from 1794 to 1796, returned to the U.S. in 1797, and then left for France, where he continued efforts to secure Polish independence.

MARIE-JOSEPH-PAUL-YVES-ROCH-GILBERT DU MOTIER, MARQUIS DE LAFAYETTE
(b. Sept. 6, 1757, Chavaniac, Fr.— d. May 20, 1834, Paris)

French aristocrat and military leader the marquis de Lafayette served with great distinction during the American Revolution even before France entered the conflict with the British.

French aristocrat and officer in the Continental Army the Marquis de Lafayette served as a member of General George Washington's staff. MPI/Hulton Archive/Getty Images

major general by the colonists, he quickly struck up a lasting friendship with George Washington. Lafayette fought with distinction at the Battle of Brandywine, Pa., on Sept. 11, 1777, and, as a division commander, he conducted a masterly retreat from Barren Hill on May 28, 1778. Returning to France early in 1779, he helped persuade the government of Louis XVI to send a 6,000-man expeditionary army to aid the colonists. Lafayette arrived back in America in April 1780 and was immediately given command of an army in Virginia. After forcing the British commander Lord Cornwallis to retreat across Virginia, Lafayette entrapped him at Yorktown in late July. A French fleet and several additional American armies joined the siege, and on October 19 Cornwallis surrendered. The British cause was lost. Lafayette was hailed as "the Hero of Two Worlds," and on returning to France in 1782 he was promoted maréchal de camp (brigadier general). He became a citizen of several states on a visit to the United States in 1784.

Born into an ancient noble family, Lafayette had already inherited an immense fortune by the time he married the daughter of the influential duc d'Ayen in 1774. He joined the circle of young courtiers at the court of King Louis XVI but soon aspired to win glory as a soldier. Hence, in July 1777, 27 months after the outbreak of the American Revolution, he arrived in Philadelphia. Appointed a

HENRY LEE
(b. Jan. 29, 1756, Prince William county, Va.—d. March 25, 1818, Cumberland Island, Ga.)

Nicknamed "Light-horse Harry," Virginian Henry Lee was among the most dashing heroes of the American Revolution. He was also the father of Robert E. Lee, the Confederacy's leading general during the American Civil War.

A graduate of the College of New Jersey (now Princeton University), Lee joined Washington's army immediately upon the outbreak of the American Revolution (1775–83). In 1778 he advanced to the rank of major and commanded three troops of cavalry and three companies of infantry with which he won notable engagements and gained his nickname. His storming of Paulus Hook, N.J. (Aug. 19, 1779), won praise from Washington, and as a lieutenant colonel of dragoons in the Southern theatre (1780–81) he added further lustre to his name.

After the war Lee served in the Virginia legislature (1785–88; 1789–91), in the Congress under the Articles of Confederation (1785–88), in the Virginia Convention of 1788 that ratified the federal Constitution, and as governor of the state (1791–94). In 1794 his political career was interrupted while he commanded the army assembled to put down the Whiskey Rebellion, an uprising of farmers resisting the federal whiskey tax, in western Pennsylvania. From 1799 to 1801 he served in the U.S. House of Representatives.

After 1800 he became involved in unfortunate land speculation and was twice imprisoned for debt. In 1812 he was badly crippled in a Baltimore riot while defending the editor of an antiwar newspaper. The next year he went to the West Indies for his health, although some said he had gone to escape his creditors. He died while returning home.

Lee was the author of *Memoirs of the War in the Southern Department of the United States*, published in 1812 and reprinted in 1869 with a biographical sketch by Robert E. Lee. He was also the author of the resolution passed by Congress upon the death of George Washington containing the celebrated apothegm "first in war, first in peace, and first in the hearts of his countrymen."

BENJAMIN LINCOLN
(b. Jan. 24, 1733, Hingham, Mass.—d. May 9, 1810, Boston, Mass.)

Continental Army officer Benjamin Lincoln rendered distinguished service in the northern campaigns early in the war, but was forced to surrender with about 7,000 troops at Charleston, S.C., May 12, 1780.

A small-town farmer, Lincoln held local offices and was a member of the Massachusetts militia (1755–76). In May 1776 he was appointed major general in the Continental Army and in 1778 was placed in command of Continental forces in the South. He was widely criticized for the Charleston defeat, although no formal action was taken against him. Released in a prisoner exchange, he participated in the Yorktown campaign in 1781, then served the Continental Congress as secretary of war (1781–83). Shays's Rebellion (brought on in Massachusetts in 1786 by business depression and heavy taxes) was quelled by militiamen led by Lincoln. He was elected lieutenant governor of Massachusetts (1788) and was collector for the port of Boston (1789–1809).

FRANCIS MARION
(b. c. 1732, Winyah, S.C.—d. Feb. 26, 1795, Berkeley county, S.C.)

American military leader Francis Marion, nicknamed the "Swamp Fox" for his elusive tactics, menaced the British with guerrilla warfare during the Revolution.

Marion gained his first military experience fighting against the Cherokee Indians in 1759. Then, serving as a member of the South Carolina Provincial Congress (1775), he was commissioned a captain. It was after the surrender of Gen. Benjamin Lincoln to the British at Charleston, S.C. (1780), that he slipped away to the swamps, gathered together his band of guerrillas, and began leading his bold raids. Marion and his irregulars often defeated larger bodies of British troops by the surprise and rapidity of their movement over swampy terrain. For a daring rescue of Americans surrounded by the British at Parkers Ferry, S.C. (August 1781), Marion received the thanks of Congress. He was then appointed a brigadier general, and after the war he served in the senate of South Carolina (1782–90).

JAMES MONROE
(b. April 28, 1758, Westmoreland county, Va.—d. July 4, 1831, New York, N.Y.)

James Monroe, the fifth president of the United States (1817–25), left his studies at the College of William and Mary in 1776 to fight in the Revolution.

As a lieutenant he crossed the Delaware with Gen. George Washington for what became the Battle of Trenton. Suffering a near fatal wound in the shoulder, Monroe was carried from the field. Upon recovering, he was promoted to captain for heroism, and he took part in the Battles of the Brandywine and Germantown. Advanced to major, he became aide-de-camp to Gen. William Alexander and with him shared the suffering of the troops at Valley Forge in the cruel winter of 1777-78. Monroe was a scout for Washington at the Battle of

James Monroe, who would go on to be the fifth president of the United States, served with distinction at the Battle of Trenton in December 1776. MPI/Hulton Archive/Getty Images

Monmouth and served as Alexander's adjutant general.

In 1780, having resigned his commission in the army, he began the study of law under Thomas Jefferson, then governor of Virginia, and between the two men there developed an intimacy and a sympathy that had a powerful influence upon Monroe's later career. Jefferson also fostered a friendship between Monroe and James Madison. From 1783 to 1786 Monroe served in the Congress under the Articles of Confederation. In 1790 he was elected to the U.S. Senate, where he opposed the administration of George Washington. He nevertheless became Washington's minister to France in 1794, though he was recalled two years later for misleading the French about U.S. politics.

From 1799 to 1802 he served as governor of Virginia. In 1803 President Jefferson sent him to France to help negotiate the Louisiana Purchase; he was then appointed minister to Britain (1803–07). He returned to Virginia and was again elected governor in 1810, though he resigned the office after 11 months to serve as U.S. secretary of state (1811–17) and secretary of war (1814–15). On Aug. 24, 1814, while serving as secretary of state during the War of 1812, Monroe appeared at Bladensburg, Md., which was about to become a battlefield, and without authorization redeployed troops, an action some believe contributed to the American defeat that day and allowed the British to advance on and capture Washington, D.C.

Monroe served two terms as president, presiding in a period that became known as the Era of Good Feelings. He oversaw the Seminole War of 1817–18 and the acquisition of the Floridas (1819–21), and he signed the Missouri Compromise (1820). With Secretary of State John Quincy Adams, he developed the principles of U.S. foreign policy later called the Monroe Doctrine.

Daniel Morgan
(b. 1736, Hunterdon County, N.J.— d. July 6, 1802, Winchester, Va.)

American Gen. Daniel Morgan won an important victory against the British in one of the Revolution's pivotal clashes, the Battle of Cowpens (Jan. 17, 1781).

After moving to Virginia in 1753, Morgan was commissioned a captain of Virginia riflemen at the outbreak of the Revolution. During the following winter, he accompanied Gen. Benedict Arnold to Canada, and in the assault on Quebec (December 31) he and his riflemen penetrated well into the city, where he was hemmed in and forced to surrender. Late in 1776 he was released, and in September 1777 he joined Gen. Horatio Gates and took part in both Battles of Saratoga (New York) that fall.

Partly because of ill health, Morgan resigned from the army in 1779, but after the disastrous American defeat at the Battle of Camden, S.C. (1780), he agreed to join Gates at Hillsborough, N.C., where he took command of a corps and was made brigadier general. Aiming at slowing Lord Cornwallis's advance in the South, Morgan gradually retired northward and then turned suddenly to confront the British troops at Cowpens, where he won a brilliant and unexpected victory over a larger force under Colonel Banastre Tarleton.

In 1794 Morgan led Virginia militiamen into western Pennsylvania to help suppress the Whiskey Rebellion. He was a Federalist representative in Congress from 1797 to 1799.

WILLIAM MOULTRIE
(b. Dec. 4, 1730, Charleston, S. C.—
d. Sept. 27, 1805, Charleston)

American Gen. William Moultrie was celebrated for his skillful resistance to British incursions into the South during the Revolution.

Elected to the provincial assembly of South Carolina (1752–62), Moultrie gained early military experience fighting against the Cherokee Indians. A member of the provincial congress (1775–76) at the outbreak of the Revolution, he sided with the patriot cause and took command (March 1776) of a fort he had built of sand and palmetto logs on Sullivan's Island off Charleston. He held the fort against heavy British attack on June 28, and it was named Fort Moultrie in his honour. He received the thanks of the federal Congress and was made a brigadier general in the Continental Army that September.

Moultrie went on to campaign in Georgia and dislodged the British from Beaufort, S.C. (February 1779), but surrendered with the fall of Charleston (May 1780). He was a prisoner on parole until February 1782, when he was exchanged, and he then served until the end of hostilities. After the war he served two terms as governor of his state (1785–87, 1792–94) and in the state senate between terms. He was also a member of the state convention that ratified the federal Constitution.

TIMOTHY PICKERING
(b. July 17, 1745, Salem, Mass.—
d. Jan. 29, 1829, Salem)

Before serving with distinction (1795–1800) as a Federalist politician in the first two U.S. cabinets, Timothy Pickering was an officer in the Continental Army.

During the American Revolution, Pickering served in several capacities under Gen. George Washington, among them quartermaster general (1780–85). In 1786, after taking up residence in Philadelphia, he helped resolve the dispute with Connecticut settlers over claims to Pennsylvania's Wyoming Valley and helped develop the town of Wilkes-Barre. Pickering served as Indian commissioner (1790–95), postmaster general (1791–95), secretary of war (1795), and secretary of state (1795–1800). He was dismissed from office by Pres. John Adams after a policy dispute.

During the administrations of Jefferson and Madison, Pickering led the Federalist opposition in Congress, serving as senator from Massachusetts

(1803–11) and as a member of the House of Representatives (1813–17). Remaining friendly to England and fearing the power of Napoleon, he bitterly opposed the War of 1812. After his retirement from Congress, he devoted himself to agricultural experimentation and education.

CHARLES COTESWORTH PINCKNEY
(b. Feb. 25, 1746, Charleston, S.C.— d. Aug. 16, 1825, Charleston)

American soldier, statesman, and diplomat Charles Cotesworth Pinckney is remembered largely for his participation in the XYZ Affair, an unsavory diplomatic incident with France in 1798.

Pinckney entered public service in 1769 as a member of the South Carolina Assembly. He served in the first South Carolina Provincial Congress (1775) and later in both houses of the South Carolina legislature. During the Revolution he was an aide to George Washington at Brandywine and Germantown, Pa. (both 1777), and later commanded a regiment at Savannah, Ga.; he was promoted to brigadier general in 1783. He took part in the Constitutional Convention of 1787, along with his cousin Charles Pinckney.

Pinckney was appointed minister to France (1796) but was refused recognition by the French Directory and left Paris for Amsterdam. He returned to Paris the following year as a member of a commission that included John Marshall and Elbridge Gerry. When one of the group of French negotiators (later referred to in the correspondence as "X,Y, and Z") suggested that the U.S. representatives offer a gift, Pinckney is said to have replied, "No! No! Not a sixpence!" No treaty was negotiated, and an undeclared war with France ensued. Upon his return home Pinckney was made a major general. An unsuccessful Federalist candidate for vice president in 1800 and for president in 1804 and 1808, Pinckney spent his later years in law practice.

MOLLY PITCHER
(b. 1754, near Trenton, N.J.— d. Jan. 22, 1832, Carlisle, Pa.)

According to legend, at the Battle of Monmouth (June 28, 1778), Mary Hays, wife of artilleryman William Hays, carried water to cool both the cannon and the soldiers in her husband's battery, earning the nickname "Molly Pitcher." Legend also asserts that when William Hays collapsed or was wounded, she took her husband's place in the gun crew for the rest of the battle.

Patriotic prints and literature depicting the alleged event initially referred to "Captain Molly." The less martial and more nurturing "Molly Pitcher" did not appear as a cognomen until the mid-19th century. Neither image was identified with a specific person until 1876, when the citizens of Carlisle claimed a woman buried there was the literal heroine of Monmouth. Military records indicate that a William Hays did enlist in the artillery in 1776 and died about 1789. His wife

This engraving by J.C. Armytage (c. 1859) shows "Molly Pitcher"—who may have been Mary Hays McCauley (1754–1832)—taking over her wounded husband's role at his cannon at the Battle of Monmouth in June 1778. Rischgitz/ Hulton Archive/Getty Images

Mary remarried and eventually applied for a pension as a soldier's widow. Instead, on Feb. 21, 1822, Pennsylvania awarded her an annual grant of $40 "for services she rendered." The services were unspecified, though the wording of the pension bill suggests that she may have played some kind of direct role in the Revolution. Whether she was this particular woman

or not, monuments near the Monmouth battle site and at Mary Hays's grave recognize Molly Pitcher's contribution to American independence.

KAZIMIERZ PUŁASKI
(b. March 4, 1747, Winiary, Pol.—
d. Oct. 11?, 1779, at sea, between
Savannah, Ga., and Charleston, S.C.)

Polish patriot and American colonial army officer Kazimierz Pułaski (Casimir Pulaski) was a hero of both the Polish anti-Russian insurrection of 1768 (the Confederation of Bar) and of the American Revolution.

The son of Józef Pułaski (1704–69), one of the originators of the Confederation of Bar, the young Pułaski distinguished himself in the defense of Berdichev (1768) and Częstochowa (1770–71) against the Russians. He also unsuccessfully attempted to kidnap King Stanisław II to the Confederates' camp (October 1771) and was falsely accused of trying to murder the king. After the Prussian and Austrian invasion of Poland in the spring of 1772, Pułaski left Częstochowa for Saxony; he later moved to France and lived in financial straits.

In December 1776, in Paris, Pułaski met the American statesman Benjamin Franklin, who recommended him to Gen. George Washington. Pułaski landed in America in June 1777. In Washington's army he served at Brandywine, was made general and chief of cavalry by Congress, and fought at Germantown and in the winter campaign of 1777–78. The Pułaski

Legion, a mixed corps he formed in 1778, exploited his experience in guerrilla warfare. In May 1779 he defended Charleston. Wounded at Savannah on Oct. 9, 1779, he died aboard the *Wasp* en route to Charleston.

ISRAEL PUTNAM
(b. Jan. 7, 1718, Salem Village [now Danvers], Mass.—d. May 29, 1790, Pomfret, Conn.)

Israel Putnam was a general in the American army during the Revolution.

After moving to Pomfret, Conn., about 1740, Putnam became a prosperous farmer. He saw service throughout the French and Indian War, being captured by Indians and rising to the rank of lieutenant colonel in 1759. By this time his numerous adventures on the frontier had given him a formidable reputation for strength and bravery. At the outbreak of the American Revolution in 1775, he was appointed a major general in the Continental Army. He distinguished himself at the Battle of Bunker Hill in June 1775, but at the Battle of Long Island he commanded the divisions in Brooklyn that were defeated. In May 1777 he was put in charge of American defenses in the Hudson highlands, including Forts Montgomery and Clinton. When he abandoned these forts to the British soon afterward, he was faced with a court of inquiry, which nevertheless exonerated him. A paralytic stroke ended his active service in December 1779.

George Washington and others had originally placed high hopes in Putnam as a Continental commander, given his near-legendary feats as an Indian fighter. But Putnam proved disappointing as a tactician, being unable to plan and coordinate operations involving large numbers of troops. His dilatory execution of orders from Washington further diminished his effectiveness on the battlefield. Although brave, self-confident, and energetic, Putnam was not competent to fill the generalship that his popularity had brought him, and after 1777 Washington was forced to withhold important commands from him.

RUFUS PUTNAM
(b. April 9, 1738, Sutton, Mass.—d. May 4, 1824, Marietta, Ohio, U.S.)

Before playing a major role in the settlement of Ohio, Rufus Putnam made his mark as a soldier in the service of the Revolution.

Putnam fought in the French and Indian War from 1757 to 1760, worked as a millwright in 1761–68, and from then on until the outbreak of the American Revolution was a farmer and surveyor. In 1775 he entered the Continental Army as a lieutenant colonel. He organized the batteries and fortifications in Boston and New York City in 1776–77 and then successfully commanded a regiment under Gen. Horatio Gates at the Battle of Saratoga. In 1778 he built new fortifications at West Point, and in 1779 he served under Gen. Anthony Wayne. He was promoted to brigadier general in 1783.

After the war Putnam became interested in the settlement of the Western lands, and in 1786 he helped found the Ohio Company of Associates with the purpose of obtaining a land grant in the Ohio country for settlement by veterans of the American Revolution. The company obtained a grant from Congress of 1,500,000 acres (606,000 hectares) there, and Putnam was appointed the company superintendent of the colonizing activities. In 1788 he led a small party that founded Marietta, Ohio; this was the first white settlement in the Northwest Territory.

Putnam afterward served as a territorial judge in Ohio and as a brigadier general before being appointed surveyor general of the United States in 1796; his service in this post was less than satisfactory, however, owing to his deficiency in mathematics, and in 1803 he was dismissed by Pres. Thomas Jefferson. In 1802 he served as a member of the Ohio state constitutional convention.

Jean-Baptiste-Donatien de Vimeur, comte de Rochambeau
(b. July 1, 1725, Vendôme, Fr.—d. May 10, 1807, Thoré)

The comte de Rochambeau commanded French forces that helped defeat the British in the Siege of Yorktown, Va., in 1781.

Rochambeau was originally trained for the church but then entered a cavalry regiment. He fought in the War of the Austrian Succession, attaining the rank of colonel. He became a brigadier general and inspector of cavalry in 1761 and in 1776 was appointed governor of Villefranche-en-Roussillon. Four years later he was put in command of a French army of about 6,000 troops destined for North America to join the Continentals in their struggle for independence from the British.

Rochambeau and his troops arrived in Newport, R.I., July 1780 and waited nearly a year for the arrival of French naval support (which never came). Finally, in June 1781 he joined forces with Gen. George Washington in White Plains, N.Y., and together they made a swift descent to Yorktown, where Franco-American forces under the marquis de Lafayette were harassing the British. With the aid of French naval forces under Admiral de Grasse, the allies laid siege to Lord Cornwallis's forces, bottled them up on the peninsula, and forced Cornwallis to surrender on October 19, thus virtually ending the war.

Rochambeau remained in Virginia for another year and then embarked for Europe in January 1783. Acknowledging his distinctive contribution to the peace, King Louis XVI appointed him commander of Calais and later of the Alsace district. During the French Revolution he commanded the Army of the North (1790–91) and was created a marshal of

France (1791). Arrested during the Reign of Terror, he narrowly escaped the guillotine; but Napoleon then pensioned him.

PHILIP JOHN SCHUYLER
(b. Nov. 11, 1733, Albany, N.Y.—d. Nov. 18, 1804, Albany)

A soldier, political leader, and member of the Continental Congress, Philip John Schuyler was born into a prominent New York family. He served in the provincial army during the last French and Indian War (1755–60), rising to the rank of major. After the war he went to England (1761–63) to help negotiate the settlement of colonial war claims. He served in the New York Assembly (1768–75) and was a delegate to the Second Continental Congress in Philadelphia (1775–77). When the Revolutionary War broke out in 1775 he was commissioned one of the four major generals in the Continental Army.

Placed in command of the northern department, he made preparations for an invasion of Canada, but shortly after the expedition started, he fell ill, and the actual command devolved upon Gen. Richard Montgomery. Nonetheless, when the invasion proved a failure Schuyler's reputation suffered, and two years later, with the fall of Ft. Ticonderoga, N.Y., he was accused of incompetence and neglect of duty and was replaced by Gen. Horatio Gates. Court-martialled at his own insistence in 1778, Schuyler was acquitted of all charges, and resigned from the army the following year.

Schuyler was again a member of the Continental Congress (1778–80), and then served in the New York State Senate (1780–84, 1786–90). He campaigned actively in New York for ratification of the new U.S. Constitution, and was one of his state's first two U.S. senators (1789–91). In 1791 he was defeated for reelection by Aaron Burr, and returned to the state senate (1792–97). He recaptured his seat from Burr in 1797, but was forced by ill health to retire less than a year later.

JOHN SEVIER
(b. Sept. 23, 1745, New Market, Va.— d. Sept. 24, 1815, Fort Decatur, Mississippi Territory [now in Alabama])

Frontiersman John Sevier, who served as the first governor of the state of Tennessee, is also remembered for his heroism as a soldier during the Revolution.

In 1773 Sevier moved his family westward across the Allegheny Mountains to what is now eastern Tennessee. The next year he fought the Indians in Lord Dunmore's War (1773–74), and during the Revolution he became a hero for his part in the victory over loyalist forces in the Battle of Kings Mountain (1780).

In 1784 Sevier took part in the settlers' revolt against North Carolina that led to the formation of the separate state of Franklin. He was elected its first governor, but many of the settlers were hostile to him, and by 1790 the state of Franklin had collapsed. Denounced as a disturber of the peace, he fled to the mountains. The next year he regained favour and was elected to the North Carolina Senate and later served in the U.S. House of Representatives (1789–91).

After North Carolina ceded its western territory to the new federal government (1790), Sevier was a leader among the settlers of the region, and when it was admitted to the Union (1796) as the state of Tennessee, he served as governor from 1796 to 1801 and from 1803 to 1809. He was then elected to the state senate and finally to the U.S. House of Representatives (1811), where he served until his death.

DANIEL SHAYS

(b. c. 1747, Hopkinton, Mass.?—d. Sept. 29, 1825, Sparta, N.Y.)

Although he is best remembered as a leader of Shays's Rebellion (1786–87), Daniel Shays also served as an American officer during the Revolution.

Born to parents of Irish descent, Shays grew up in humble circumstances. At the outbreak of the Revolution he responded to the call to arms at Lexington and served 11 days (April 1775). He served as second lieutenant in a Massachusetts regiment from May to December 1775 and became captain in the 5th Massachusetts Regiment in January 1777. He took part in the Battle of Bunker Hill and in the expedition against Ticonderoga, and he participated in the storming of Stony Point and fought at Saratoga. In 1780 he resigned from the army, settling in Pelham, Mass., where he held several town offices.

Daniel Shays, a poor farmer from Massachusetts, served with distinction during the American Revolution. After the war, he led other poor farmers in an uprising in western Massachusetts in opposition to high taxes and stringent economic conditions that would come to be called Shays's Rebellion. Hulton Archive/ Getty Images

Prosperity reigned in America at the signing of the peace (1783) but was soon transformed into an acute economic depression. Property holders—apparently including Shays—began losing their possessions through seizures for overdue debts and delinquent taxes and became subject to debtor's imprisonment. Demonstrations ensued, with threats of violence against the courts handling the enforcements and indictments. Shays emerged as one of several leaders of what by chance came to be called Shays's Rebellion (1786–87), and after it was over he and about a dozen others were condemned to death by the Supreme Court of Massachusetts. In 1788 he petitioned for a pardon, which was soon granted.

At the end of the rebellion Shays had escaped to Vermont. Afterward he moved to Schoharie County, N.Y., and then, several years later, farther westward to Sparta, N.Y. In his old age, he received a federal pension for his services in the Revolution.

JOHN STARK
(b. Aug. 28, 1728, Londonderry, N.H.—d. May 8, 1822, Manchester, N.H.)

A prominent American general, John Stark led attacks that cost the British nearly 1,000 men and contributed to the surrender of British Gen. John Burgoyne at Saratoga by blocking his retreat line across the Hudson River (1777).

From 1754 to 1759, Stark served in the French and Indian War with Rogers' Rangers, first as a lieutenant and later as a captain. Made a colonel at the outbreak of the American Revolution, he fought at Bunker Hill (June 17, 1775), in the invasion of Canada, and in New Jersey.

In March 1777 Stark resigned his commission, but when Burgoyne invaded New York he was made brigadier general of militia. On August 16 his hastily raised troops attacked and defeated British and Hessian detachments at the Battle of Bennington, Vt. Stark was thereupon raised to the rank of brigadier general in the Continental Army. He helped force the surrender of Burgoyne at Saratoga, N.Y., in October 1777 and served in Rhode Island (1779) and at the Battle of Springfield, N.J. (1780). The same year, he was a member of the court-martial that condemned Maj. John André, who served as a British spy. In September 1783 Stark was made a major general.

FREDERICK WILLIAM, BARON VON STEUBEN
(b. Sept. 17, 1730, Magdeburg, Prussia [Germany]—d. Nov. 28, 1794, near Remsen, N.Y.)

Prussian officer Baron von Steuben made a huge contribution to the American cause by converting the Revolutionary army into a disciplined fighting force.

Born into a military family, Steuben led a soldier's life from age 16. During the Seven Years' War he rose to the rank of captain in the Prussian army and was for a time attached to the general staff of Frederick II the Great. After the close of the war he was retired from the army and became court chamberlain for the prince of Hohenzollern-Hechingen, and at some unknown date he apparently was created

Major General baron von Steuben, a Prussian officer who became a tactical advisor to George Washington during the American Revolution. Hulton Archive/Getty Images

a baron (*Freiherr*). In 1777 it was rumoured that he had been obliged to leave Hohenzollern-Hechingen for unsavoury conduct.

His availability came to the attention of Benjamin Franklin and Silas Deane—in France as agents of the newly formed U.S. government—and they composed a letter introducing him to George Washington as a "Lieut. Genl. in the King of Prussia's Service," who was fired with "Zeal for our Cause." Thus armed, Steuben arrived in America in December 1777. Impressed by his fictitiously high rank, his pleasing personality, and Washington's favourable comments, Congress appointed him to train the Continental forces stationed at the winter encampment at Valley Forge, Pa.

The model drill company that Steuben formed and commanded was copied throughout the ranks. That winter he wrote *Regulations for the Order and Discipline of the Troops of the United States*, which soon became the "blue book" for the entire army and served as the country's official military guide until 1812. On Washington's recommendation, in May 1778, Steuben was appointed inspector general of the army with the rank of major general. In 1780 he was finally granted a field command; he served as a division commander in Virginia and participated in the Siege of Yorktown (1781), where the British met final defeat.

After the war Steuben settled in New York City, where he lived so extravagantly that, despite large grants of money from Congress and the grant of 16,000 acres (6,000 hectares) of land by New York state, he fell into debt. Finally, after ceaseless importunity, in 1790 he was voted a life pension of $2,500, which sufficed to maintain him on his farm until he died.

JOHN SULLIVAN
(b. Feb. 17, 1740, Somersworth, N.H.—d. Jan. 23, 1795, Durham, N.H.)

American Gen. John Sullivan won distinction during the Revolution for his defeat of the Iroquois Indians and their loyalist allies in western New York (1779).

An attorney, Sullivan was elected to the New Hampshire provincial congress (1774) and served at the First Continental Congress, in Philadelphia, the same year. In June 1775 he was appointed brigadier general in the Continental Army and aided in the Siege of Boston. The following year he was ordered to Canada to command the retreating American troops after the death of their commander at the disastrous Battle of Quebec (Dec. 31, 1775). Sullivan shortly rejoined Gen. George Washington and, after being promoted to major general, participated in the Battle of Long Island (August 1776), where he was taken prisoner. Exchanged in December, he led the right column in Washington's successful attack on Trenton, N.J. (December 1776), but a night attack on Staten Island in August was unsuccessful.

In 1779 Sullivan was commissioned to lead an expedition in retaliation for British-inspired Indian raids in the Mohawk Valley of New York. With 4,000 troops he routed the Iroquois and their loyalist supporters at Newtown, N.Y. (near present Elmira), burning their villages and destroying their crops. He thus earned the thanks of Congress (October 1779), but ill health forced him to resign from military service soon afterward.

Sullivan continued in public service for 15 years, however: as a delegate to the Continental Congress (1780-81), state's attorney general (1782-86), New Hampshire governor (1786-87, 1789), presiding officer of the state convention that ratified the federal Constitution (1788), and U.S. district judge (1789-95).

Thomas Sumter
(b. Aug. 14, 1734, Hanover County, Va.—d. June 1, 1832, South Mount, S.C.)

American officer Thomas Sumter earned the sobriquet "the Carolina Gamecock" for his leadership of troops against British forces in North and South Carolina during the Revolution.

Sumter served in the French and Indian War and later moved to South Carolina. After the fall of Charleston (1780) during the Revolution, he escaped to North Carolina, where he became brigadier general of state troops. After successes over the British at Catawba and at Hanging Rock (Lancaster County), he was defeated the same year at Fishing Creek (Chester County). He defeated Mayor Wemyss at Fishdam Ford and repulsed Col. Banastre Tarleton at Blackstock (both in Union County) in November 1780. After the war Sumter served in the U.S. House of Representatives (1789-93; 1797-1801) and in the U.S. Senate (1801-10). He was the last surviving general officer of the Revolution. Fort Sumter in Charleston Harbor was named for him.

Joseph Warren
(b. June 11, 1741, Roxbury, Mass.—d. June 17, 1775, Bunker Hill, Mass.)

On April 18, 1775, soldier and Revolutionary leader Joseph Warren sent Paul

Revere and William Dawes to Lexington and Concord on their famous ride to warn local patriots that British troops were being sent against them.

Warren graduated from Harvard in 1759, studied medicine in Boston, and soon acquired a high reputation as a physician. The passage of the Stamp Act in 1765 aroused his patriotic sympathies and brought him into close association with other prominent Whigs in Massachusetts. He helped draft a group of protests to Parliament known as the Suffolk Resolves, which were adopted by a convention in Suffolk County, Massachusetts, on Sept. 9, 1774, and endorsed by the Continental Congress in Philadelphia.

Warren was a member of the first three provincial congresses held in Massachusetts (1774–75), president of the third, and an active member of the Massachusetts Committee of Public Safety. On June 14, 1775, he was chosen a major general, but three days later he was killed in the Battle of Bunker Hill.

GEORGE WASHINGTON

(b. Feb. 22, 1732, Westmoreland County, Va.—d. Dec. 14., 1799, Mount Vernon, Va.)

So great were George Washington's contributions to the Revolution, as the commander of the Continental Army, and to the early days of the republic, as its first president, that he has gone down in history as simply the "Father of his country."

EARLY LIFE

Born into a wealthy family, George Washington was educated privately. In 1752 he inherited his brother's estate at Mount Vernon, Va., including 18 slaves; their ranks grew to 49 by 1760, though he disapproved of slavery. In the French and Indian War he was commissioned a colonel and sent to the Ohio Territory. After Edward Braddock was killed, Washington became commander of all Virginia forces, entrusted with defending the western frontier (1755–58). He resigned to manage his estate and in 1759 married Martha Dandridge Custis (1731–1802), a widow. In 1759 he also began serving in Virginia's House of Burgesses.

PREREVOLUTIONARY POLITICS

Washington's contented life was interrupted by the rising storm in imperial affairs. The British ministry, facing a heavy postwar debt, high home taxes, and continued military costs in America, decided in 1764 to obtain revenue from the colonies. Up to that time, Washington, though regarded by associates, in Col. John L. Peyton's words, as "a young man of an extraordinary and exalted character," had shown no signs of personal greatness and few signs of interest in state affairs. The Proclamation of 1763 interdicting settlement beyond the Alleghenies irked him, for he was interested in the Ohio Company, the Mississippi Company, and other speculative western ventures.

He nevertheless played a silent part in the House of Burgesses and was a thoroughly loyal subject.

But he was present when Patrick Henry introduced his resolutions against the Stamp Act in May 1765 and shortly thereafter gave token of his adherence to the cause of the colonial Whigs against the Tory ministries of England. In 1768 he told George Mason at Mount Vernon that he would take his musket on his shoulder whenever his country called him. The next spring, on April 4, 1769, he sent Mason the Philadelphia nonimportation resolutions with a letter declaring that it was necessary to resist the strokes of "our lordly masters" in England; that, courteous remonstrances to Parliament having failed, he wholly endorsed the resort to commercial warfare; and that as a last resort no man should scruple to use arms in defense of liberty. When, the following May, the royal governor dissolved the House of Burgesses, he shared in the gathering at the Raleigh, N.C., tavern that drew up nonimportation resolutions, and he went further than most of his neighbours in adhering to them. At that time and later, he believed with most Americans that peace need not be broken.

Late in 1770 he paid a land-hunting visit to Fort Pitt, where George Croghan was maturing his plans for the proposed 14th colony of Vandalia. Washington directed his agent to locate and survey 10,000 acres adjoining the Vandalia tract, and at one time he wished to share in certain of Croghan's schemes. But the Boston Tea Party of December 1773 and the bursting of the Vandalia bubble at about the same time turned his eyes back to the East and the threatening state of Anglo-American relations. He was not a member of the Virginia committee of correspondence formed in 1773 to communicate with other colonies, but when the Virginia legislators, meeting irregularly again at the Raleigh tavern in May 1774, called for a Continental Congress, he was present and signed the resolutions. Moreover, he was a leading member of the first provincial convention or Revolutionary legislature late that summer, and to that body he made a speech that was much praised for its pithy eloquence, declaring that "I will raise one thousand men, subsist them at my own expense, and march myself at their head for the relief of Boston."

The Virginia provincial convention promptly elected Washington one of the seven delegates to the First Continental Congress. He was by this time known as a radical rather than a moderate, and in several letters of the time he opposed a continuance of petitions to the British crown, declaring that they would inevitably meet with a humiliating rejection. "Shall we after this whine and cry for relief when we have already tried it in vain?" he wrote. When the Congress met in Philadelphia on Sept. 5, 1774, he was in his seat in full uniform, and his participation in its councils marks the beginning of his national career.

His letters of the period show that, while still utterly opposed to the idea of independence, he was determined never to submit "to the loss of those valuable rights and privileges, which are essential to the happiness of every free State, and without which life, liberty, and property are rendered totally insecure." If the ministry pushed matters to an extremity, he wrote, "more blood will be spilled on this occasion than ever before in American history." Though he served on none of the committees, he was a useful member, his advice being sought on military matters and weight being attached to his advocacy of a nonexportation as well as nonimportation agreement. He also helped to secure approval of the Suffolk Resolves, which looked toward armed resistance as a last resort and did much to harden the king's heart against America.

Returning to Virginia in November, he took command of the volunteer companies drilling there and served as chairman of the Committee of Safety in Fairfax County. Although the province contained many experienced officers and Col. William Byrd of Westover had succeeded Washington as commander in chief, the unanimity with which the Virginia troops turned to Washington was a tribute to his reputation and personality; it was understood that Virginia expected him to be its general. He was elected to the Second Continental Congress at the March 1775 session of the legislature and again set out for Philadelphia.

REVOLUTIONARY LEADERSHIP

The choice of Washington as commander in chief of the military forces of all the colonies followed immediately upon the first fighting, though it was by no means inevitable and was the product of partly artificial forces. The Virginia delegates differed upon his appointment. Edmund Pendleton was, according to John Adams, "very full and clear against it," and Washington himself recommended Gen. Andrew Lewis for the post. It was chiefly the fruit of a political bargain by which New England offered Virginia the chief command as its price for the adoption and support of the New England army. This army had gathered hastily and in force about Boston immediately after the clash of British troops and American Minutemen at Lexington and Concord on April 19, 1775. When the Second Continental Congress met in Philadelphia on May 10, one of its first tasks was to find a permanent leadership for this force. On June 15, Washington, whose military counsel had already proved invaluable on two committees, was nominated and chosen by unanimous vote. Beyond the considerations noted, he owed being chosen to the facts that Virginia stood with Massachusetts as one of the most powerful colonies; that his appointment would augment the zeal of the Southern people; that he had gained an enduring reputation in the Braddock campaign; and that his poise, sense, and resolution had impressed all the delegates. The scene of his election, with Washington darting modestly into an adjoining room and John Hancock flushing with jealous mortification, will always impress the historical imagination; so also will the scene of July 3, 1775, when, wheeling his horse under an elm in front of the troops paraded on Cambridge common, he drew his sword and took command of the army investing Boston. News of Bunker Hill had reached him before he was a day's journey from Philadelphia, and he had expressed confidence of victory when told how the militia had fought. In accepting the command, he refused any payment beyond his expenses and called upon "every gentleman in the room" to bear witness that he disclaimed fitness for it. At once he showed characteristic decision and energy in organizing the raw volunteers, collecting provisions and munitions, and rallying Congress and the colonies to his support.

The first phase of Washington's command covered the period from July 1775 to the British evacuation of Boston in March 1776. In those eight months he imparted discipline to the army, which at maximum strength slightly exceeded 20,000; he dealt with subordinates who, as John Adams said, quarrelled "like cats and dogs"; and he kept the siege vigorously alive. Having himself planned an invasion of Canada by Lake Champlain, to be entrusted to Gen. Philip Schuyler, he heartily approved of Benedict Arnold's proposal to march north along the Kennebec River in Maine and take

On Dec. 25, 1776, George Washington crossed the Delaware River to defeat British-employed Hessian soldiers in the Battle of Trenton. This 1856 engraving by Paul Girardet was based on Emanuel Leutze's famous painting, Washington Crossing the Delaware (1850). MPI/Hulton Archive/Getty Images

Quebec. Giving Arnold 1,100 men, he instructed him to do everything possible to conciliate the Canadians. He was equally active in encouraging privateers to attack British commerce. As fast as means offered, he strengthened his army with ammunition and siege guns, having heavy artillery brought from Fort

Ticonderoga, N.Y., over the frozen roads early in 1776. His position was at first precarious, for the Charles River pierced the centre of his lines investing Boston. If the British general, Sir William Howe, had moved his 20 veteran regiments boldly up the stream, he might have pierced Washington's army and rolled either wing back to destruction. But all the generalship was on Washington's side. Seeing that Dorchester Heights, just south of Boston, commanded the city and harbour and that Howe had unaccountably failed to occupy it, he seized it on the night of March 4, 1776, placing his Ticonderoga guns in position. The British naval commander declared that he could not remain if the Americans were not dislodged, and Howe, after a storm disrupted his plans for an assault, evacuated the city on March 17. He left 200 cannons and invaluable stores of small arms and munitions. After collecting his booty, Washington hurried south to take up the defense of New York.

Washington had won the first round, but there remained five years of the war, during which the American cause was repeatedly near complete disaster. It is unquestionable that Washington's strength of character, his ability to hold the confidence of army and people and to diffuse his own courage among them, his unremitting activity, and his strong common sense constituted the chief factors in achieving American victory. He was not a great tactician: as Jefferson said later, he often "failed in the field"; he was sometimes guilty of grave military blunders,

the chief being his assumption of a position on Long Island, N.Y., in 1776 that exposed his entire army to capture the moment it was defeated. At the outset he was painfully inexperienced, the wilderness fighting of the French war having done nothing to teach him the strategy of maneuvering whole armies. One of his chief faults was his tendency to subordinate his own judgment to that of the generals surrounding him; at every critical juncture, before Boston, before New York, before Philadelphia, and in New Jersey, he called a council of war and in almost every instance accepted its decision. Naturally bold and dashing, as he proved at Trenton, Princeton, and Germantown, he repeatedly adopted evasive and delaying tactics on the advice of his associates; however, he did succeed in keeping a strong army in existence and maintaining the flame of national spirit. When the auspicious moment arrived, he planned the rapid movements that ended the war.

One element of Washington's strength was his sternness as a disciplinarian. The army was continually dwindling and refilling, politics largely governed the selection of officers by Congress and the states, and the ill-fed, ill-clothed, ill-paid forces were often half-prostrated by sickness and ripe for mutiny. Troops from each of the three sections, New England, the middle states, and the South, showed a deplorable jealousy of the others. Washington was rigorous in breaking cowardly, inefficient, and dishonest men and boasted in front of

Boston that he had "made a pretty good sort of slam among such kind of officers." Deserters and plunderers were flogged, and Washington once erected a gallows 40 feet (12 metres) high, writing, "I am determined if I can be justified in the proceeding, to hang two or three on it, as an example to others." At the same time, the commander in chief won the devotion of many of his men by his earnestness in demanding better treatment for them from Congress. He complained of their short rations, declaring once that they were forced to "eat every kind of horse food but hay."

The darkest chapter in Washington's military leadership was opened when, reaching New York in April 1776, he placed half his army, about 9,000 men, under Israel Putnam, on the perilous position of Brooklyn Heights, Long Island, where a British fleet in the East River might cut off their retreat. He spent a fortnight in May with the Continental Congress in Philadelphia, then discussing the question of independence; though no record of his utterances exists, there can be no doubt that he advocated complete separation. His return to New York preceded but slightly the arrival of the British army under Howe, which made its main encampment on Staten Island until its whole strength of nearly 30,000 could be mobilized. On Aug. 22, 1776, Howe moved about 20,000 men across to Gravesend Bay on Long Island. Four days later, sending the fleet under command of his brother Adm. Richard Howe to make a feint against New York City, he

thrust a crushing force along feebly protected roads against the American flank. The patriots were outmaneuvered, defeated, and suffered a total loss of 5,000 men, of whom 2,000 were captured. Their whole position might have been carried by storm, but, fortunately for Washington, General Howe delayed. While the enemy lingered, Washington succeeded under cover of a dense fog in ferrying the remaining force across the East River to Manhattan, where he took up a fortified position. The British, suddenly landing on the lower part of the island, drove back the Americans in a clash marked by disgraceful cowardice on the part of troops from Connecticut and others. In a series of actions, Washington was forced northward, more than once in danger of capture, until the loss of his two Hudson River forts, one of them with 2,600 men, compelled him to retreat from White Plains across the river into New Jersey. He retired toward the Delaware River while his army melted away, until it seemed that armed resistance to the British was about to expire.

It was at this darkest hour of the Revolution that Washington struck his brilliant blows at Trenton and Princeton, N.J., reviving the hopes and energies of the nation. Howe, believing that the American army soon would dissolve totally, retired to New York, leaving strong forces in Trenton and Burlington. Washington, at his camp west of the Delaware River, planned a simultaneous attack on both posts, using his whole command of 6,000 men. But his subordinates in charge of both wings failed him, and he was left on the night of Dec. 25, 1776, to march on Trenton with about 2,400 men. With the help of Col. John Glover's regiment, which was comprised of fishermen and sailors from Marblehead, Mass., Washington and his troops were ferried across the Delaware River. In the dead of night and amid a blinding snowstorm, they then marched 10 miles (16 km) downstream and in the early hours of the morning caught the enemy at Trenton unaware. In less than two hours and without the loss of a single man in battle, Washington's troops defeated the Hessians, killed their commander (Johann Rall), and captured nearly 1,000 prisoners and arms and ammunition. This historic Christmas crossing proved to be a turning point in the war, and it was immortalized for posterity by Emanuel Gottlieb Leutze in his famous 1851 painting of the event. (The painting is historically inaccurate: the depicted flag is anachronistic, the boats are the wrong size and shape, and it is questionable whether Washington could have crossed the icy Delaware while standing in the manner depicted.)

The immediate result of this American victory was that Lord Cornwallis hastened with about 8,000 men to Trenton, where he found Washington strongly posted behind the Assunpink Creek, skirmished with him, and decided to wait overnight "to bag the old fox." During the night, the wind shifted, the roads froze hard, and Washington was able to steal away from

camp (leaving his fires deceptively burning), march around Cornwallis's rear, and fall at daybreak upon the three British regiments at Princeton. These were put to flight with a loss of 500 men, and Washington escaped with more captured munitions to a strong position at Morristown, N.J.. The effect of these victories heartened all Americans, brought recruits flocking to camp in the spring, and encouraged foreign sympathizers with the American cause.

Thus far the important successes had been won by Washington; then battlefield success fell to others, while he was left to face popular apathy, military cabals, and the disaffection of Congress. The year 1777 was marked by the British capture of Philadelphia and the surrender of British Gen. John Burgoyne's invading army to Gen. Horatio Gates at Saratoga, N.Y., followed by intrigues to displace Washington from his command. Howe's main British army of 18,000 left New York by sea on July 23, 1777, and landed on August 25 in Maryland, not far below Philadelphia. Washington, despite his inferiority of force—he had only 11,000 men, mostly militia and, in the marquis de Lafayette's words, "badly armed and worse clothed"—risked a pitched battle on September 11 at the fords of Brandywine Creek, about 13 miles (21 km) north of Wilmington, Del. While part of the British force held the Americans engaged, Lord Cornwallis, with the rest, made a secret 17-mile (27-km) detour and fell with crushing effect on the American right and rear, the result being a complete defeat from which Washington was fortunate to extricate his army in fairly good order. For a time he hoped to hold the Schuylkill Fords, but the British passed them and on September 26 triumphantly marched into Philadelphia. Congress fled to the interior of Pennsylvania, and Washington, after an unsuccessful effort to repeat his stroke at Trenton against the British troops posted at Germantown, had to take up winter quarters at Valley Forge. His army, twice beaten, ill housed, and ill fed, with thousands of men "barefoot and otherwise naked," was at the point of exhaustion; it could not keep the field, for inside of a month it would have disappeared. Under these circumstances, there is nothing that better proves the true fibre of Washington's character and the courage of his soul than the unyielding persistence with which he held his strong position at Valley Forge through a winter of semi-starvation, of justified grumbling by his men, of harsh public criticism, and of captious meddling by a Congress that was too weak to help him. In February Martha Washington arrived and helped to organize entertainment for the soldiers.

Washington's enemies seized the moment of his greatest weakness to give vent to an antagonism that had been nourished by sectional jealousies of North against South, by the ambition of small rivals, and by baseless accusations that he showed favouritism to such foreigners as Lafayette. The intrigues of Thomas Conway, an Irish adventurer who had served in the French army and had become an American general, enlisted Thomas Mifflin, Charles Lee, Benjamin Rush, and others in an attempt to displace Washington. General Gates appears to have been a tool of rather than a party to the plot, expecting that the chief command would devolve upon himself. A faction of Congress sympathized with the movement and attempted to paralyze Washington by reorganizing the board of war, a body vested with the general superintendence of operations, of which Gates became the president; his chief of staff, James Wilkinson, the secretary; and Mifflin and Timothy Pickering, members. Washington was well aware of the hostility in congress, of the slanders spread by Rush and James Lovell of Massachusetts, and of the effect of forgeries published in the American press by adroit British agents. He realized the intense jealousy of many New Englanders, which made even John Adams write his wife that he was thankful Burgoyne had not been captured by Washington, who would then "have been deified. It is bad enough as it is." But Washington decisively crushed the cabal: after the loose tongue of Wilkinson disclosed Conway's treachery, Washington sent the general on Nov. 9, 1777, proof of his knowledge of the whole affair.

With the conclusion of the French alliance in the spring of 1778, the aspect of the war was radically altered. The British army in Philadelphia, fearing that a French fleet would blockade the Delaware while the militia of New Jersey and Pennsylvania invested the city, hastily retreated upon New York City. Washington hoped to cut off part of the enemy and by a hurried march with six brigades interposed himself at the end of June between Sir Henry Clinton (who had succeeded Howe) and the New Jersey coast. The result was the Battle of Monmouth on June 28, where a shrewd strategic plan and vigorous assault were brought to naught by the treachery of Charles Lee. When Lee ruined the attack by a sudden order to retreat, Washington hurried forward, fiercely denounced him, and restored the line, but the golden opportunity had been lost. The British made good their march to Sandy Hook, and Washington took up his quarters at New Brunswick. Lee was arrested, court-martialed, and convicted on all three of the charges made against him; but instead of being shot, as he deserved, he was sentenced to a suspension from command for one year. The arrival of the French fleet under Adm. Charles-Hector Estaing on July 1778 completed the isolation of the British, and Clinton was thenceforth held to New York City and the surrounding area. Washington made his headquarters in the highlands of the Hudson and distributed his troops in cantonments around the city and in New Jersey.

The final decisive stroke of the war, the capture of Cornwallis at Yorktown, is to be credited chiefly to Washington's vision. With the domestic situation intensely gloomy early in 1781, he was hampered by the feebleness of Congress, the popular discouragement, and the lack of prompt and strong support by the French fleet. A French army under the comte de Rochambeau had arrived to reinforce him in 1780, and Washington had pressed Admiral de Grasse to assist in an attack upon either Cornwallis in the south or Clinton in New York. In August the French admiral sent definite word that he preferred the Chesapeake, with its large area and deep water, as the scene of his operations; and within a week, on Aug. 19, 1781, Washington marched south with his army, leaving Gen. William Heath with 4,000 men to hold West Point. He hurried his troops through New Jersey, embarked them on transports in Delaware Bay, and landed them at Williamsburg, Va., where he had arrived on September 14. Cornwallis had retreated to Yorktown and entrenched his army of 7,000 British regulars. Their works were completely invested before the end of the month; the siege was pressed with vigour by the allied armies under Washington, consisting of 5,500 Continentals, 3,500 Virginia militia, and 5,000 French regulars, and on October 19 Cornwallis surrendered. By this campaign, probably the finest single display of Washington's generalship, the war was brought to a virtual close.

Washington remained during the winter of 1781–82 with the Continental Congress in Philadelphia, exhorting it to maintain its exertions for liberty and to settle the army's claims for pay. He continued these exhortations after he joined his command at Newburgh on the Hudson in April 1782. He was astounded and angered when some loose camp suggestions found expression in a letter from Col. Lewis Nicola offering a plan by which he should use the army to make himself king. He blasted the proposal with fierce condemnation. When the discontent of his unpaid men came to a head in the circulation of the "Newburgh Address" (an anonymously written grievance) early in 1783, he issued a general order censuring the paper and at a meeting of officers on March 15 read a speech admonishing the army to obey Congress and promising his best efforts for a redress of grievances. He was present at the entrance of the American army into New York on the day of the British evacuation, Nov. 25, 1783, and on December 4 took leave of his closest officers in an affecting scene at Fraunces Tavern. Traveling south, on December 23, in a solemn ceremonial immortalized by the pen of William Makepeace Thackeray, he resigned his commission to the Continental Congress in the state senate chamber of Maryland in Annapolis and received the thanks of the nation. His accounts of personal expenditures during his service, kept with minute exactness in his own handwriting and totalling £24,700 ($40,819), without charge for salary, had been given the controller of the treasury to be discharged. Washington left Annapolis at sunrise of December 24 and before nightfall was at home in Mount Vernon.

POSTREVOLUTIONARY POLITICS

Of course, Washington's service for his country was anything but completed. He was a delegate to and presiding officer of the Constitutional Convention (1787) and helped secure ratification of the Constitution in Virginia. When the state electors met to select the first president (1789), Washington was the unanimous choice. He formed a cabinet to balance sectional and political differences but was committed to a strong central government. Elected to a second term, he followed a middle course between the political factions that later became the Federalist Party and the Democratic Party. He proclaimed a policy of neutrality in the war between Britain and France (1793) and sent troops to suppress the Whiskey Rebellion (1794). He declined to serve a third term (thereby setting a 144-year precedent) and retired in 1797 after delivering his "Farewell Address."

ANTHONY WAYNE
(b. Jan. 1, 1745, near Paoli, Pa.—d. Dec. 15, 1796, Presque Isle, Pa.)

Renowned for his fearlessness, Gen. "Mad Anthony" Wayne was one of the most heralded officers in the Continental Army and his battlefield heroics continued after the Revolution in the service of the young American republic.

The owner of a tannery and extensive property in Pennsylvania, Wayne was commissioned a colonel in the Continental Army in January 1776. That spring his regiment was sent to reinforce American forces retreating from the disastrous Canadian expedition, after which he was put in command of Fort Ticonderoga, N.Y. Promoted to the rank of brigadier general in early 1777, he played a prominent role that fall in the battles of Brandywine,

"Mad" Anthony Wayne, American general during the Revolutionary War. Kean Collection/Hulton Archive/ Getty Images

Paoli, and Germantown, Pa. After spending the winter at the Valley Forge encampment, he led an attack on the British at the indecisive Battle of Monmouth, N.J., the following June.

His most brilliant exploit of the war was the successful storming of the British fort at Stony Point, N.Y. (July 16, 1779). This feat gave a huge boost in morale to the American armies. Wayne earned the name "Mad Anthony" because of his tactical boldness and his personal courage in the field. In 1781 he was sent with 1,000 men to join in the successful Siege of Yorktown, Va. He was then dispatched to join the Continental Army in the South. He served largely in Georgia, recovering that state and defeating the Indians allied to the British. Elected in 1790 to the Georgia House of Representatives, he served nearly two years before his seat was declared vacant because of election frauds.

In 1792 Wayne was appointed by Pres. George Washington to serve as commander in chief of the modest U.S. Army, which had suffered several defeats at the hands of the intertribal Indian Confederation formed to resist the white man's incursions into the Midwest. At the Battle of Fallen Timbers in Ohio (Aug. 20, 1794), Wayne effectively ended Indian resistance when his seasoned force of 1,000 men routed the 2,000 warriors gathered for a final confrontation near Fort Miami on the Maumee River. This victory enabled Wayne to negotiate the Treaty of Greenville (August 1795), by which the Indians ceded most of Ohio and large sections of Indiana, Illinois, and Michigan.

THE BRITISH SIDE

Many in the British military were well-trained officers and enlisted men who came straight from Britain; others were mercenary troops from Germany; still others were American loyalists who wanted the colonies to remain under British control. Though there were among them veterans of the French and Indian War who were thus familiar with America, for many, fighting in America's wild terrain was a new challenge.

John André
(b. May 2, 1750, London, Eng.—d. Oct.2, 1780, Tappan, N.Y.)

British army officer John André negotiated with the treasonous American Gen. Benedict Arnold and was executed as a spy.

Sent to America in 1774, André became chief intelligence officer to the British commander in chief, Gen. Sir Henry Clinton, in New York City. From May 1779 he carried on a secret correspondence with Arnold, who had become disillusioned with the American cause. In August 1780 Arnold was appointed commandant of the fort at West Point, N.Y., which, at a meeting with André on September 21, he agreed to surrender for £20,000 ($33,052).

While returning to New York City, André was captured by three American militiamen; he failed to use the pass that Arnold had given him, and papers concerning West Point were found in one of his boots. A board of officers designated by Gen. George Washington found him guilty of spying and condemned him to death. When General Clinton refused to exchange him for Arnold, who had escaped to British territory, André was hanged. He was mourned on both sides because of his personal charm and literary talent.

John André, copperplate engraving.
Photos.com/Jupiterimages

EDWARD BANCROFT
(b. Jan. 9, 1744, Westfield, Mass.—
d. Sept. 8, 1821, Margate, Kent, Eng.)

While serving as secretary to the American commissioners in France during the Revolution, Edward Bancroft acted as a spy for the British.

Although he had no formal education, Bancroft assumed the title and style of "Doctor." In 1769 he established his credentials as a scientist with the publication of his "Essay on the Natural History of Guiana." About 1770 he went to England, where he became friendly with Benjamin Franklin during one of Franklin's early missions to London. Bancroft became an adherent of the American cause and returned to the colonies. As a result of his friendship with Franklin he accompanied Franklin and the two other American commissioners to France in 1776. In France Bancroft was contacted by Paul Wentworth, an American-born loyalist who headed a ring of loyalist spies for the British. By December of that year Bancroft had begun receiving a salary from the British. Between 1777 and 1783 he reported every movement of Franklin and the other Americans to the British, writing his reports in invisible ink and relaying them by means of a dead drop. Bancroft's information included the details of treaties and the movement of ships and troops from France to America. To avoid suspicion Bancroft made several trips to Britain ostensibly to spy on the British; they provided him with harmless or false information and once pretended to arrest him.

In 1783 Bancroft moved to England, primarily to preserve his British citizenship and the pension due him for his secret service. He continued to correspond with Franklin, who never suspected him. He invented several processes for dyeing textiles and in 1794 wrote a work called "Experimental Researches concerning the Philosophy of Permanent Colors." He gained international fame as a chemist and was made a fellow of the Royal Society. Not until nearly 70 years after his death did his role as a British spy become public knowledge.

JOSEPH BRANT
(b. 1742, on the banks of the Ohio
River—d. Nov. 24, 1807, near
Brantford, Ont., Can.)

Mohawk Indian chief Joseph Brant (original name, Thayendanegea) served not only as a spokesman for his people but also as a Christian missionary and a British military officer during the Revolution.

Brant was converted to the Anglican church after two years (1761–63) at Moor's Charity School for Indians in Lebanon, Conn., where he learned English and became acquainted with Western history and literature. He left school to become an interpreter for an Anglican missionary and later aided in translating the prayer book and the Gospel of Mark into Mohawk (1787).

Brant's sister Molly was the wife of the British superintendent for northern Indian affairs, Sir William Johnson, whom he followed into battle at age 13. He fought for the British in the last French and Indian War, and in 1774 he was appointed secretary to Sir William's successor, Guy Johnson. In 1775 Brant received a captain's commission and was sent to England, where he was presented at court.

On his return, Brant led four of the six Iroquois nations on the British side in the Revolution. He attacked colonial outposts on the New York frontier, skillfully commanding the Indian contingent in the Battle of Oriskany (Aug. 6, 1777) and winning a formidable reputation after the raid on the fortified village of Cherry Valley, N.Y. (Nov. 11, 1778). Cooperating with British regulars and loyalists, Brant brought fear and destruction to the entire Mohawk Valley, southern New York, and northern Pennsylvania. He also thwarted the attempt of a rival chief, Red Jacket, to persuade the Iroquois to conclude a separate peace with the revolutionaries.

After the war, Brant discouraged further Indian warfare on the frontier and aided the U.S. commissioners in securing peace treaties with the Miamis and other western tribes. He retained his commission in the British army and was awarded a grant of land on the Grand River, in Ontario, where he ruled peacefully over his followers who settled there. He continued his missionary work and in 1785 again visited England, where he raised funds for the first Episcopal Church in Upper Canada.

JOHN BURGOYNE
(b. 1722, Sutton, Bedfordshire, Eng.— d. June 4, 1792, London)

British Gen. John Burgoyne is best remembered for his defeat by superior American forces in the Saratoga (New York) campaign of 1777.

After serving with distinction in the Seven Years' War, Burgoyne was elected to the House of Commons in 1761 and again in 1768. Assigned to Canada in 1776 as a major general, he entered into an offensive in which British armies from

Oct. 17, 1777: British Gen. Sir John Burgoyne presents his sword to American Gen. Horatio Gates, signaling the British defeat at the Battle of Saratoga. Popperfoto/Getty Images

the north (Burgoyne's troops), south (Gen. William Howe's), and west (Col. Barry St. Leger's) would unite at Albany, N.Y., isolating New England from the other rebellious colonies. Burgoyne's force captured Fort Ticonderoga, N.Y., on July 6, 1777, but, after reaching the Hudson River, was fought to a standstill by a much larger army commanded successively by Gen. Philip Schuyler and Gen. Horatio Gates, who were brilliantly assisted by Gen. Benedict Arnold. Exhausting his food and ammunition and receiving no aid from Howe (who chose to fight in Pennsylvania) or St. Leger (who was defeated at Oriskany, N.Y., and withdrew westward), Burgoyne had to surrender to Gates north of Saratoga Springs on Oct. 17, 1777. Paroled along with his troops, he returned to England, where he faced severe criticism. For a short time (1782–83) he was commander in chief in Ireland, but he retired increasingly to private life, in which he was a leader of London society and fashion. He also wrote several plays, of which the most successful was *The Heiress* (1786).

SIR HENRY CLINTON
(b. April 16?, 1730?—d. Dec. 23, 1795, Cornwall, Eng.)

Sir Henry Clinton served as the British commander in chief in America during the Revolution.

The son of George Clinton, a naval officer and administrator, Henry joined the New York militia in 1745 as a lieutenant. He went to London in 1749 and was commissioned in the British army in 1751. He was wounded (1762) in the Seven Years' War in Europe and was promoted to major general in 1772. He went to North America in 1775 as second in command to Sir William Howe. He fought with distinction at Bunker Hill and Long Island and was left in command in New York when Howe went south to Pennsylvania. On Howe's retirement (1778), Clinton (knighted 1777) succeeded to the supreme command. He led the main body of his army in an offensive in the Carolinas in 1780. After Charleston fell, he returned to New York, leaving Lord Cornwallis, his second in command, in charge of the subsequent operations that led to the capitulation at Yorktown and the peace treaty recognizing American independence. Clinton resigned his command in 1781 and went back to England, where he found Cornwallis viewed with sympathy and himself blamed for the Yorktown defeat. His *Narrative of the Campaign of 1781 in North America* (1783) provoked an angry reply from Cornwallis.

CHARLES CORNWALLIS, 1ST MARQUESS AND 2ND EARL CORNWALLIS
(b. Dec. 31, 1738, London, Eng.—d. Oct. 5, 1805, Ghazipur, India [now in Uttar Pradesh, India])

British soldier and statesman Lord Charles Cornwallis is probably best known for his defeat at Yorktown, Va., in the last important campaign (Sept. 28–Oct. 19, 1781) of the Revolution. Cornwallis was possibly the most capable British general in that war, but he was more important for his achievements as British governor-general of India (1786–93, 1805) and viceroy of Ireland (1798–1801).

A veteran of the Seven Years' War—during which (1762) he succeeded to his father's earldom and other

Gen. Charles Cornwallis, one of the leading British generals during the American Revolution. MPI/Hulton Archive/Getty Images

titles—Cornwallis, who had opposed the British policies that antagonized the North American colonists, nonetheless fought to suppress the American Revolution. Late in 1776 he drove Gen. George Washington's patriot forces out of New Jersey, but early in 1777 Washington recaptured part of that state. As British commander in the South from June 1780, Cornwallis won a great victory over Gen. Horatio Gates at Camden, S.C., on August 16 of that year. Marching through eastern North Carolina into Virginia, he established his base at the tidewater seaport of Yorktown. Trapped there by American and French ground forces under Washington and the comte de Rochambeau and a French fleet under the comte de Grasse, he surrendered his large army after a siege.

Although the Yorktown capitulation decided the war in favour of the colonists, Cornwallis remained in high esteem at home. On Feb. 23, 1786, he accepted the governor-generalship of India. Before leaving office on Aug. 13, 1793, he brought about a series of legal and administrative reforms, notably the Cornwallis Code (1793). By paying civil servants adequately while forbidding them to engage in private business, he established a tradition of law-abiding, incorruptible British rule in India. He disbelieved, however, in the capacity of Indians for self-government, and some of his measures—the reorganization of the courts in various regions and of the revenue system in Bengal—proved ill-advised. In the third of four Mysore Wars, he inflicted a temporary defeat (1792) on Tippu Sultan, the anti-British ruler of the Mysore state. For his services in India he was created a marquess in 1792.

As viceroy of Ireland (1798–1801), Cornwallis won the confidence of both militant Protestants (Orangemen) and Roman Catholics. After suppressing a serious Irish rebellion in 1798 and defeating a French invasion force on September 9 of that year, he wisely insisted that only the revolutionary leaders be punished. As he had done in India, he worked to eliminate corruption among British officials in Ireland. He also supported the parliamentary union of Great Britain and Ireland (effective Jan. 1, 1801) and the concession of political rights to Roman Catholics (rejected by King George III in 1801, causing Cornwallis to resign).

As British plenipotentiary, Cornwallis negotiated the Treaty of Amiens (March 27, 1802), which established peace in Europe during the Napoleonic Wars. He was reappointed governor-general of India in 1805 but died shortly after his arrival.

SIR JAMES CRAIG
(b. 1748, Gibraltar—d. Jan. 12, 1812, London, Eng.)

Sir James Craig was a British veteran of the American Revolution, but he became better known later as governor-general of Canada (1807–11) and was charged by French-Canadians with conducting a "reign of terror" in Quebec.

Craig entered the British army at the age of 15 and was made captain in 1771. In his Revolutionary War service he was wounded at the Battle of Bunker Hill (June 17, 1775). He helped repel the Continental Army's invasion of Canada (1776) and was noted for distinguished service in the early part of Gen. John Burgoyne's invasion of the Hudson River valley.

After fighting in North Carolina (1781), Craig was promoted to lieutenant colonel. He played a leading role in the capture (1795) of the Dutch colony of the Cape of Good Hope and served as its temporary governor (1795–97). Knighted in 1797, he was given commands in India and in England and saw service in the renewed Napoleonic Wars.

In 1807 Craig was appointed governor-general of Canada, a post to which he was temperamentally unsuited. His cooperation with the governing clique in Quebec and his repressive policy toward the French-Canadians were not popular. He resigned his post in 1811 and returned to England, where he was promoted to general just before his death.

PATRICK FERGUSON
(b. 1744, Pitfours, Aberdeenshire, Scot.—d. Oct. 7, 1780, Kings Mountain, S.C.)

Scottish soldier and marksman Patrick Ferguson, who served in the British army during the American Revolution, was the inventor of the Ferguson flintlock rifle.

Ferguson served in the British army from 1759. In 1776 he patented a rifle—one of the earliest practical breechloaders—that was the best military firearm used in the American Revolution. His breechlock was grooved to prevent the action's being jammed with powder. The rifle could be fired six times a minute, a major advance in firepower for the time, but because of official British conservatism not more than 200 of them were used in the war.

Ferguson led a small force armed with his rifle during the Pennsylvania campaign of 1777. At the Battle of Brandywine, his right arm was permanently crippled. Considered one of the British army's best leaders of light troops, he recruited a corps of New York loyalists in 1779 for service in the American South, using it as a cadre for locally enlisted loyalist militia. All of these men carried muskets at the Battle of Kings Mountain in 1780, when Ferguson was killed and his unit annihilated.

THOMAS GAGE
(b. 1721, Firle, Sussex, Eng.—d. April 2, 1787, Eng.)

British Gen. Thomas Gage successfully commanded all British forces in North America for more than 10 years (1763–74) but failed to stem the tide of rebellion as military governor of Massachusetts (1774–75) at the outbreak of the American Revolution.

Gage's military career in North America began in 1754, when he sailed with his regiment to serve in the last French and Indian War (1756–63). He participated in Gen. Edward Braddock's disastrous campaign in western Pennsylvania (1754) and in the successful operation against Quebec (1759–60). He was thereupon made governor of Montreal (1760) and promoted to major general (1761).

In 1763 Gage was appointed commander in chief of all British forces in North America—the most important and influential post in the colonies. Headquartered in New York, he ran a vast military machine of more than 50

Gen. Thomas Gage, known as "The Lenient Commander," was commander in chief of the British forces in America until he was replaced by Gen. William Howe in 1775. Hulton Archive/ Getty Images

garrisons and stations stretching from Newfoundland to Florida and from Bermuda to the Mississippi. He exhibited both patience and tact in handling matters of diplomacy, trade, communication, Indian relations, and western boundaries. His great failure, however, was in his assessment of the burgeoning independence movement. As the main permanent adviser to the mother country in that period, he sent critical and unsympathetic reports that did much to harden the attitude of successive ministries toward the colonies.

When resistance turned violent at the Boston Tea Party (1773), Gage was instrumental in shaping Parliament's retaliatory Intolerable (Coercive) Acts (1774), by which the port of Boston was closed until the destroyed tea should be paid for. He was largely responsible for inclusion of the inflammatory provision for quartering of soldiers in private homes and of the Massachusetts Government Act, by which colonial democratic institutions were superseded by a British military government. Thus Gage is chiefly remembered in the U.S. as the protagonist of the British cause while he served as military governor in Massachusetts from 1774 to 1775. In this capacity, he ordered the march of the redcoats on Lexington and Concord (April 1775), which was intended to uncover ammunition caches and to capture the leading Revolutionary agitator, Samuel Adams, who escaped. This unfortunate manoeuvre signalled the start of the American Revolution; after the equally disastrous Battle of Bunker Hill in June, Gage was succeeded by Gen. Sir William Howe. He soon returned to England and was commissioned a full general in 1782.

CHARLES GREY, 1ST EARL GREY
(b. 1729, Howick, Northumberland, Eng.—d. Nov. 14, 1807, Howick)

Lord Charles Grey served as a British general during the American Revolution and as a commander was credited with victories in several battles, notably against Gen. Anthony Wayne and at the Battle of Germantown (1777–78).

A member of an old Northumberland family and son of Sir Henry Grey, Baronet, Grey entered the army at age 19 and, by 1755, had become lieutenant colonel, serving with forces in France and Germany in the years 1757–61 and in the capture of Havana (1762). Out of service and on half-pay after the peace of 1763, he returned to service as a colonel in 1772. In 1776 he went to America with Gen. Sir William Howe, receiving the rank of major general. His successes as a commander were remarkable in the northern theatre from Pennsylvania to eastern Massachusetts. His night attack with the bayonet on the American camp at Paoli in 1777, widely denounced as an atrocity, earned him the cognomen "No-Flint Grey." After returning home in 1778, he was promoted to lieutenant general in 1782 and appointed commander in chief in America, though, the war soon ending, he never took command. After the French Revolution he saw service in the West Indies. He retired and was given a barony in 1801; in 1806 he was raised to Viscount Howick and Earl Grey.

WILLIAM HOWE, 5TH VISCOUNT HOWE
(b. Aug. 10, 1729—d. July 12, 1814, Plymouth, Devonshire, Eng.)

Despite several military successes, Gen. Sir William Howe, the commander in chief of the British army in North America from 1776 to 1778, failed to destroy the Continental Army and stem the American Revolution.

Brother of Adm. Richard Lord Howe, William Howe had been active in North America during the last French and Indian War, in which he earned a reputation as one of the army's most brilliant young generals. Sent in 1775 to reinforce Gen. Thomas Gage in the Siege of Boston, he led the left wing in three costly but finally successful assaults in the Battle of Bunker Hill.

Assuming supreme command the following year, Howe transferred his forces southward and captured the strategic port city of New York, severely defeating the Americans at the Battle of Long Island. A competent tactician, he preferred maneuver to battle, partly to conserve scarce British manpower, but also in the hopes of demonstrating British military superiority so convincingly that the Americans would accept negotiation and reconciliation with Britain.

When active operations were resumed in June 1777, Howe moved his troops to the south bank of the Delaware River and won two successive victories over the Americans at the Battle of Brandywine (September) and the Battle of Germantown (October). His next winter was spent in the occupation of Philadelphia. Howe recognized his failure, however, to destroy the modest force of Gen. George Washington, then encamped at nearby Valley Forge. His Pennsylvania campaign had furthermore exposed the troops of Gen. John Burgoyne in upper New York State and led to the disastrous British defeat at the Battle of Saratoga that fall. Under increasing criticism from the British press and government, Howe resigned his command before the start of operations in 1778.

Returning to England, Howe saw no more active service but held a number of important home commands. He succeeded to the viscountcy on the death of his brother in 1799; upon his own death, without issue, the peerage expired.

WILHELM, BARON VON KNYPHAUSEN
(b. Nov. 4, 1716, Luxembourg—d. Dec. 7, 1800, Kassel, Hesse-Kassel [Ger.])

After 1777 German officer Baron von Knyphausen commanded "Hessian" troops who fought on the British side in the American Revolution.

A lieutenant general with 42 years of military service, Knyphausen went to North America in 1776 as second in command (under Gen. Leopold von Heister) of German mercenary troops in the

British service. Following Heister's recall in 1777, Knyphausen became their commander. He took part in the battles of Fort Washington and Brandywine, Pa, and Monmouth, N.J.; Sir Henry Clinton's absence from New York in 1779–80 left the area under the command of Knyphausen. An able soldier, he carried out the difficult task of holding together the mercenary forces under his command. He returned to Germany in 1782 and became military governor of Kassel.

RED JACKET
(b. 1758?, Canoga, N.Y.—d. Jan. 20, 1830, Seneca Village, Buffalo, N.Y.)

Seneca Indian chief Sagoyewatha (birth name, Otetiani) was known as "Red Jacket" for the succession of red coats he wore while fighting on the British side during the American Revolution. He used his gift for oratory to mask his schemes to maintain his position of power despite double-dealing against his people's interests.

Red Jacket retreated at the approach of Gen. John Sullivan's American troops in 1779, and he even attempted to conclude a separate peace with the Americans. For these actions, Red Jacket was considered a coward by many of his own people. But he put his splendid oratorical skills to protesting the inevitable peacemaking with the United States at an Indian council in 1786, and his oratory succeeded in sustaining him as a Seneca chief.

Red Jacket constantly sought to portray himself as a bitter enemy of the whites. Yet, while he publicly opposed land sales in 1787, 1788, and 1790, he secretly signed the property cessions to protect his prestige with the Americans. Later, however, he seems to have become more sincere in protesting white influence on Seneca customs, religion, and language. He vehemently opposed missionaries' living on Indian lands, and he vainly attempted to preserve Indian jurisdiction over criminal acts committed on Indian property.

During the 1820s Red Jacket lost prestige as his drinking and general dissipation became evident. In 1827 he was deposed as chief by a council of tribal leaders—only to be reinstated following a personal effort at reform and the intercession of the U.S. Office of Indian Affairs.

CHAPTER 6

NONMILITARY FIGURES OF THE AMERICAN REVOLUTION

M any of those who made valuable contributions to the American cause did so without ever taking up a weapon in its defense. These leaders included politicians who laid down the framework for the Revolution, writers whose fiery words inspired action, financiers who funded the fight, and diplomats who persuaded other countries to assist the revolutionary cause. Their actions helped pave the way to the American victory.

THE AMERICAN SIDE

JOHN ADAMS
(b. Oct. 30, 1735, Braintree, Mass.—d. July 4, 1826, Quincy, Mass.)

Before becoming the first vice president (1789–97) and second president (1797–1801) of the United States, John Adams played a pivotal role in the Continental Congress and served as a diplomat during the Revolution. After graduating from Harvard College in 1755, he practiced law in Boston. In 1764 he married Abigail Smith. Active in the American independence movement, he was elected to the Massachusetts legislature and served as a delegate to the Continental Congress (1774–78),

John Adams the second president of the United States, helped draft the Declaration of Independence. MPI/ Hulton Archive/Getty Images

where he was appointed to a committee with Thomas Jefferson and others to draft the Declaration of Independence. In 1776–78 he was appointed to many congressional committees, including one to create a navy and another to review foreign affairs. He served as a diplomat in France, the Netherlands, and England (1778–88). In the first U.S. presidential election, he received the second largest number of votes and became vice president under George Washington. Adams's term as president was marked by controversy over his signing of the Alien and Sedition Acts in 1798 and by his alliance with the conservative Federalist Party. In 1800 he was defeated for reelection by Jefferson and retired to live a secluded life in Massachusetts. In 1812 he overcame his bitterness toward Jefferson, with whom he began an illuminating correspondence. Both men died on July 4, 1826, the Declaration's 50th anniversary. John Quincy Adams was his son.

SAMUEL ADAMS
(b. Sept. 27, 1722, Boston, Mass.— d. Oct. 2, 1803, Boston)

Bostonian Samuel Adams was among the most prominent leaders of the Revolution. A cousin of John Adams, he graduated from Harvard College in 1740 and briefly practiced law. He became a strong opponent of British taxation measures and organized resistance to the Stamp Act. He was a member of the state legislature (1765–74), and in 1772 he helped found the Committees of Correspondence. He influenced reaction to the Tea Act of 1773, organized the Boston Tea Party, and led opposition to the Intolerable Acts. A delegate to the Continental Congress (1774–81), he continued to call for separation from Britain and signed the Declaration of Independence. He helped draft the Massachusetts constitution in 1780 and served as the state's governor (1794–97).

CRISPUS ATTUCKS
(b. 1723?—d. March 5, 1770, Boston, Mass.)

Crispus Attucks is remembered as an American hero and martyr of the Boston Massacre.

Attucks's life prior to the day of his death is still shrouded in mystery. Most historians say that he was black; others argue that his ancestry was both African and Natick Indian. In any event, in the fall of 1750, a resident of Framingham, Mass., advertised for the recovery of a runaway slave named Crispus—usually thought to be the Crispus in question. In the 20-year interval between his escape from slavery and his death at the hands of British soldiers, Attucks probably spent a good deal of time aboard whaling ships.

All that is definitely known about him concerns the Boston Massacre on March 5, 1770. Toward evening that day, a crowd of colonists gathered and began taunting a small group of British soldiers. Tension mounted rapidly, and when one of the soldiers was struck the others fired their muskets, killing three of the Americans instantly and mortally wounding two others. Attucks was the first to fall, thus becoming one of the first men to lose his life in the cause of American independence. His body was carried to Faneuil Hall, where it lay in state until March 8, when all five victims were buried in a common grave. Attucks was the only victim of the Boston Massacre whose name was widely remembered. In 1888 the Crispus Attucks monument was unveiled in the Boston Common.

Crispus Attucks, a runaway slave, was killed in 1770 by British troops during the Boston Massacre. Archive Photos/ Getty Images

ANNA WARNER BAILEY
(b. Oct. 11?, 1758, Groton, Conn.— d. Jan. 10, 1851, Groton)

American patriot Anna Warner Bailey's heroic actions during the Revolution are the stuff of legend.

Anna Warner was orphaned and was reared by an uncle. On Sept. 6, 1781, a large British force under the turncoat Gen. Benedict Arnold landed on the coast near Groton and stormed Fort Griswold. American casualties were very high, and among them was Warner's uncle, Edward

Mills. She walked several miles to the scene of battle, found her uncle after much difficulty, and learned that he was mortally wounded. At his request she hurried home, saddled a horse for her aunt, and carried her infant cousin back for a last meeting of the family. This feat soon became a favourite tale of the Revolution. Warner later married Capt. Elijah Bailey, postmaster of Groton. In 1813, during the second war with Great Britain, "Mother Bailey," as she was then known, appeared among the Groton soldiers aiding in the defense of New London against a blockading British fleet. On learning of a shortage, she contributed her flannel petticoat—her "martial petticoat," as it came to be known—for use as cartridge wadding.

ELIAS BOUDINOT
(b. May 2, 1740, Philadelphia, Pa.— d. Oct. 24, 1821, Burlington, N.J.)

Lawyer and public official Elias Boudinot was a party to more than a few important political developments in the Revolution and early days of the republic.

Boudinot became a lawyer and attorney-at-law in 1760. He was a leader in his profession, and, though he was a conservative Whig, he supported the American Revolution. He became a member of the Revolutionary Party at the outbreak of the war, serving first as deputy in the New Jersey provincial assembly and then as one of New Jersey's representatives in the Continental Congress. After the establishment of the government of the United States of America, Boudinot served for

six years (1789–95) as a member of the national House of Representatives. He became director of the U.S. Mint at Philadelphia in 1795 and held that position for 10 years.

JAMES BOWDOIN
(b. Aug. 7, 1726, Boston, Mass.— d. Nov. 6, 1790, Boston)

In addition to being the founder and first president of the American Academy of Arts and Sciences (1780), James Bowdoin was an important political leader in Massachusetts during the era of the Revolution.

Bowdoin graduated from Harvard in 1745. A merchant by profession, he was president of the constitutional convention of Massachusetts (1779–80) and a member of the state convention to ratify the federal Constitution (1788). As governor of Massachusetts (1785–87), he took prompt action to suppress Shays's Rebellion (an uprising among poor and heavily taxed farmers) and was, in general, a stabilizing force in the critical postwar period.

Bowdoin was also a scientist prominent in physics and astronomy. He wrote several papers, including one on electricity with Benjamin Franklin. Bowdoin College, Brunswick, Maine, was named in his honour.

DAVID BUSHNELL
(b. 1742, Saybrook, Conn.—d. 1824, Warrenton, Ga.)

American inventor David Bushnell is renowned as the father of the submarine, which was first tested during the American Revolution.

Graduated from Yale in 1775, at the outbreak of the Revolution, Bushnell went to Saybrook, where he built a unique turtle-shaped vessel designed to be propelled under water by an operator who turned its propeller by hand. The craft was armed with a mine, or a torpedo, to be attached to the hull of an enemy ship. Several attempts were made with Bushnell's "Turtle" against British warships. Though the submarine gave proof of underwater capability, the attacks were failures, partly because Bushnell's physical frailty made it almost impossible for

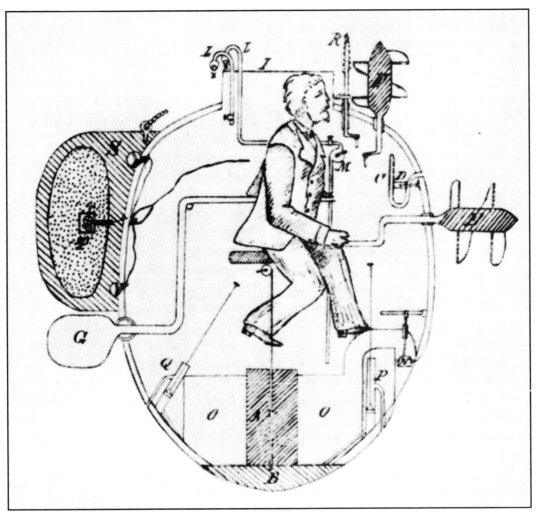

Bushnell's submarine torpedo boat, 1776. Drawing of a cutaway view made by Lt. Cmdr. F.M. Barber in 1885 from a description left by Bushnell. Courtesy of the U.S. Navy

him to perform in person the many demanding functions required to control the craft. Gen. George Washington, however, gave him a commission in the engineers, where he rose to captain and command of the U.S. Army Corps of Engineers stationed at West Point. In his later years he studied medicine and entered practice in Warrenton.

GEORGE CABOT
(b. Jan. 16, 1752, Salem, Mass.—
d. April 18, 1823, Boston, Mass.)

Powerful Federalist Party leader George Cabot exercised considerable influence, especially in New England, during the Revolutionary era and its aftermath.

At age 16, not long after his father's death, Cabot left Harvard after his second year to become a cabin boy. Due to his hard work and family connections—he belonged to one of the earliest families to settle in Massachusetts—he became a ship's captain before he was an adult and soon owned a number of ships. During the war, he was a fervent Patriot, and like many other New England shipowners, engaged in privateering, a practice in which private ships were authorized by the government to attack enemy vessels. At one point, his ships captured two West Indian ships that contained more than 100,000 pounds in British sterling. He also interested himself in government affairs. At 25, he joined Massachusetts's provincial congress, in 1788 he became a member of the state convention that adopted the U.S.

Constitution, and in 1791 he became a U.S. senator.

CHARLES CARROLL
(b. Sept. 19, 1737, Annapolis, Md.—
d. Nov. 14, 1832, Baltimore, Md.)

Patriotic American leader Charles Carroll was the longest surviving signer of the Declaration of Independence and the only Roman Catholic to sign that document.

Until 1765 Carroll attended Jesuit colleges in Maryland and France and studied law in France and England. Before and during the American Revolution, he served on committees of correspondence and in the Continental Congress (1776–78), where he was an important member of the board of war. In 1776, with Benjamin Franklin, Samuel Chase, and his cousin, the Reverend John Carroll, he was sent to Canada in a fruitless effort to persuade Canadians to join the cause of the 13 colonies.

Carroll was a state senator in Maryland (1777–1800) and concurrently a U.S. Senator (1789–92). When political parties were formed in the United States, he became a Federalist.

SOCIETY OF THE CINCINNATI

The hereditary, military, and patriotic organization known as the Society of the Cincinnati was formed in May 1783 by officers who had served in the Revolution. Its objectives were to promote union and national honour, maintain their war-born friendship, perpetuate the rights for which they had fought, and aid members and their families in case of need.

The society took its name from the Roman citizen-soldier Lucius Quinctius Cincinnatus. With membership open to Revolutionary officers and their eldest male descendants, branches of the society were organized in each of the 13 states; Gen. George Washington was elected its first president. Through failure of heirs, most state societies were dormant by 1835, but a revival was effected at the end of the 19th century. The city of Cincinnati, Ohio, was named in honour of the society in 1790.

ABRAHAM CLARK
(b. Feb. 15, 1726, Elizabethtown, N.J.—d. Sept. 15, 1794, Elizabeth, N.J.)

Abraham Clark is remembered as a signer of the Declaration of Independence.

Though he had little formal education, Clark became a surveyor and managed transfers of property. He had a gift for politics and served in many public offices in New Jersey. He championed the cause of the colonies and in 1776 was elected to the Continental Congress, where he voted for separation from Great Britain and signed the Declaration. He was reelected to the Continental Congress several times and was also a delegate to the Annapolis Convention (1786). He was chosen to be a delegate to the federal Constitutional Convention (1787) but was unable to attend because of illness. Clark opposed the adoption of the new U.S.

Constitution until he was assured that a bill of rights would be added to it. He served in the U.S. House of Representatives from 1791 until his death.

MARGARET CORBIN
(b. Nov. 12, 1751, western Pennsylvania [now Franklin County, Pa.]—d. Jan. 16, 1800, Westchester County, N.Y.)

Margaret Corbin was yet another woman whose valour and sacrifice during the Revolution earned her a position of honour in the annals of American history.

Margaret Cochran, having lost both her parents in an Indian raid when she was five, grew up with relatives and, in 1772, married John Corbin. When he enlisted in the First Company of Pennsylvania Artillery for service in the Revolution, she followed him east. (According to some historians, she held a paid position as an enlisted soldier.) On Nov. 16, 1776, Corbin was manning a gun on a ridge near Fort Washington, N.Y., when he was killed during a Hessian advance. Observing from nearby, Margaret immediately leaped to the gun and continued to serve in her husband's stead until she was felled by grapeshot wounds. Upon the surrender of the American position she was not taken among the prisoners. She made her way to Philadelphia and there, completely disabled, came to the attention of the state's Executive Council, by which she was granted temporary relief in June 1779. The next month the Continental

Congress approved the granting of a life-time soldier's half-pay pension to her. She was thereafter included on military rolls and in April 1783 was formally mustered out of the Continental Army. She lived in Westchester County, N.Y., until her death. Her story has sometimes been confused with that of Mary McCauley ("Molly Pitcher").

LYDIA BARRINGTON DARRAGH
(b. 1729, Dublin, Ire.—d. Dec. 28, 1789, Philadelphia, Pa.)

Lydia Barrington Darragh is said to have saved Gen. George Washington's army from a British attack during the Revolution.

Lydia Barrington married William Darragh, a teacher, in 1753. Shortly thereafter she immigrated with her husband to America, settling in Philadelphia. She worked as a nurse and midwife with considerable skill and success. In a story first published in 1827 and later elaborated upon, she was credited with having saved Washington's army in the following manner: During the British occupation of Philadelphia, Gen. William Howe had his headquarters opposite the Darragh house. On the night of Dec. 2, 1777, the adjutant general and other officers commandeered one of her rooms for a secret conference, and, listening at the keyhole, she learned of their plan to attack Washington at Whitemarsh, 8 miles (13 km) away, two nights later. On the morning of the day, December 4, she let it be known that she needed flour from the Frankford mill and obtained a pass to leave the city for that purpose. Once away, she made for Whitemarsh. Encountering Col. Thomas Craig, a friend, on the road, she told him what she had learned and then, securing her flour, hurried home. The British march that night found the Continental Army at arms and ready to repel, and Howe was forced to return to Philadelphia. Darragh lived in Philadelphia until her death.

SILAS DEANE
(b. Dec. 24, 1737, Groton, Conn.— d. Sept. 23, 1789, at sea near Deal, Kent, Eng.)

The first U.S. diplomat sent abroad (1776), Silas Deane helped secure much-needed French aid for the American Revolutionary cause.

Admitted to the bar in 1761, Deane served as a delegate from Connecticut to the Continental Congress in Philadelphia (1774–76). Congress then sent him to France as a secret agent to obtain financial and military assistance and to investigate the possibility of an alliance. He obtained and sent arms valued at more than 6,000,000 livres to America, an important contribution to the decisive victory over the British at Saratoga (October 1777). In November 1777 Congress recalled Deane, but before leaving Paris he signed the treaties of commerce and alliance (Feb. 6, 1778) that he and two other commissioners, Arthur Lee and Benjamin Franklin, had negotiated. Upon his return he was accused of embezzlement and disloyalty on the basis of insinuations by Lee that Deane was charging for supplies that France intended as gifts to America. Although never proved, the accusations led to his ruin.

Deane returned to France in 1780 as a private citizen and prepared letters to old friends in America attacking the French alliance and recommending a reconciliation with England. When the letters were published in *The Royal Gazette*, a Tory paper in New York (1781), he was denounced as a traitor. He began an exile, first in Ghent and then in London, where in 1784 he published his defense in *An Address to the Free and Independent Citizens of the United States*. Five years later Deane set sail for America but died on board under mysterious circumstances. He never admitted doing wrong and in 1842 was finally exonerated by Congress.

JOHN DICKINSON
(b. Nov. 8, 1732, Talbot County, Md.— d. Feb.14, 1808, Wilmington, Del.)

American statesman John Dickinson is often referred to as the "penman of the Revolution."

Dickinson studied law in London at the Middle Temple and practiced law in Philadelphia (1757–60) before entering public life. He represented Pennsylvania in the Stamp Act Congress (1765) and drafted its declaration of rights and grievances. He won fame in 1767–68 as the author of the *Letters from a Farmer in Pennsylvania, to the Inhabitants of the British Colonies*, which appeared in many colonial newspapers. The letters helped turn opinion against the Townshend Acts (1767), under which new duties were collected to pay the salaries of royal officials in the colonies. He also denounced the establishing of the American Board of Customs Commissioners at Boston to enforce the acts.

Dickinson was a delegate from Pennsylvania in the Continental Congress (1774–76) and was the principal author of the *Declaration of the Causes and Necessity of Taking Up Arms*. He helped prepare the first draft of the Articles of Confederation (1776–77) but voted against the Declaration of Independence (1776) because he still hoped for conciliation with the British. Although he was accused of being a loyalist, he later served in the patriot militia.

As a delegate from Delaware to the Federal Constitutional Convention (1787), Dickinson signed the U.S. Constitution and worked for its adoption. He later defended the document in a series of letters signed "Fabius."

Dickinson College at Carlisle, Pa., chartered in 1783, was named in his honour.

BENJAMIN FRANKLIN
(b. Jan. 17, 1706, Boston, Mass.—d. April 17, 1790, Philadelphia, Pa.)

American printer and publisher, author, scientist and inventor, and diplomat Benjamin Franklin is among the mostly highly regarded of the Founding Fathers.

He was apprenticed at age 12 to his brother, a local printer. He taught himself to write effectively, and in 1723 he moved to Philadelphia, where he founded the *Pennsylvania Gazette* (1729–48) and wrote *Poor Richard's almanac* (1732–57), often remembered for its proverbs and aphorisms emphasizing prudence, industry, and honesty. He became prosperous and promoted public services in Philadelphia, including a library, a fire department, a hospital, an insurance company, and an academy that became the University of Pennsylvania. His inventions include the Franklin stove and bifocal spectacles, and his experiments helped pioneer the understanding of electricity. He served as a member of the colonial legislature (1736–51). He was a delegate to the Albany Congress (1754), where he put forth a plan for colonial union. He represented the colony in England in a dispute over land and taxes (1757–62); he returned there in 1764. The issue of taxation gradually caused him to abandon his longtime support for continued American colonial membership in the British Empire. Believing that taxation ought to be the prerogative of the representative legislatures, he opposed the Stamp Act. He served as a delegate to the second Continental Congress and as a member of the committee to draft the Declaration of Independence. In 1776 he went to France to seek aid for the American Revolution. Lionized by the French, he negotiated a treaty that provided loans and military support for the U.S. He also played a crucial role in bringing

Benjamin Franklin, a Renaissance man during the Revolutionary era, was well known as a writer, inventor, diplomat, politician, scientist, and printer. MPI/ Hulton Archive/Getty Images

about the final peace treaty with Britain in 1783. As a member of the 1787 Constitutional Convention, he was instrumental in achieving adoption of the Constitution of the United States. He is regarded as one of the most extraordinary and brilliant public servants in U.S. history.

ALEXANDER HAMILTON
(b. Jan. 11, 1755/57, Nevis, British West Indies—d. July 12, 1804, New York, N.Y.)

The military contributions of Alexander Hamilton to the Revolution are sometimes lost in the shadow of his role in the political events of the young United States.

Hamilton first came to colonial America in 1772, arriving in New Jersey. During the Revolution he joined the Continental Army and showed conspicuous bravery at the Battle of Trenton. He served as aide-de-camp to Gen. George Washington (1777–81); fluent in French, he became a liaison with French commanders. After the war he practiced law in New York. At the Continental Congress, he argued for a strong central government. As a delegate to the Annapolis Convention in 1786, he drafted the address that led to the Constitutional Convention. With James Madison and John Jay, he wrote an influential series of essays, later known as the Federalist Papers, in defense of the new Constitution and republican government. Appointed the first secretary of the Treasury (1789), Hamilton developed fiscal policies designed to strengthen the national government at the expense of the states. His proposal for a Bank of the United States was opposed by Thomas Jefferson but adopted by Congress in 1791. Differences between Hamilton and Jefferson over the powers of the national government and the country's foreign policy led to the rise of political parties; Hamilton became leader of the Federalist Party, and Madison and Jefferson created the Democratic-Republican Party. Hamilton favoured friendship with Britain and influenced Washington to take a neutral stand toward the French Revolution. In 1796 he caused a rift in the Federalist Party by opposing its nomination of John Adams for president. In 1800 he tried to prevent Adams's reelection, circulating a private attack that Aaron Burr, long at odds with Hamilton, obtained and published. When Jefferson and Burr both defeated Adams but received an equal number of electoral votes, Hamilton helped persuade the Federalists in the House of Representatives to choose

Prior to writing the Federalist papers, Alexander Hamilton served under General Washington in the American Revolution. MPI/Hulton Archive/ Getty Images

Jefferson. In 1804 he opposed Burr's candidacy for governor of New York. This affront, coupled with alleged remarks questioning Burr's character, led Burr to challenge Hamilton to a duel, in which Hamilton was mortally wounded.

JOHN HANCOCK
(b. Jan. 12, 1737, Braintree (now in Quincy), Mass.—d. Oct. 8, 1793, Quincy)

American Revolutionary leader John Hancock earned his place in history as the first signer of the Declaration of Independence.

After graduating from Harvard (1754), Hancock entered a mercantile house in Boston owned by his uncle Thomas Hancock, who later left him a large fortune. In 1765 he became a selectman of Boston and from 1769 to 1774 was a member of the Massachusetts General Court. He was chairman of the Boston town committee formed immediately after the Boston Massacre in 1770 to demand the removal of British troops from the city.

In 1774 and 1775 Hancock was president of the first and second provincial congresses, and he shared with Samuel Adams the leadership of the Massachusetts Patriots. With Adams he was forced to flee Lexington for Philadelphia when warned in April 1775 that he was being sought by Gen. Thomas Gage's troops, approaching from Boston. Hancock was a member of the Continental Congress from 1775 to 1780; he served as its president from May 1775 to

October 1777. He hoped to become commander in chief of the Continental Army, but George Washington was selected instead.

Hancock was a member of the Massachusetts Constitutional Convention of 1780 and in the same year was elected governor of the state. He served in Congress under the Articles of Confederation in 1785–86 and then returned to the governorship. He presided over the Mas-

As president of the Continental Congress, John Hancock was the first to put his signature on the Declaration of Independence. MPI/Hulton Archive/ Getty Images

sachusetts Convention of 1788 that ratified the federal Constitution, although he had been unfriendly at first toward the document. Hancock died while serving his ninth term as governor.

PATRICK HENRY
(b. May 29, 1736, Studley, Va.—
d. June 6, 1799, Red Hill, near
Brookneal, Va.)

A brilliant orator and a major figure of the American Revolution, Patrick Henry is perhaps best known for his words "give me liberty or give me death."

Admitted to the bar in 1760, he soon built a large and profitable practice. His skill as an orator was displayed in the Parson's Cause trial (1763). Elected to the Virginia House of Burgesses in 1765, he opposed the Stamp Act; during the next decade he became a leader of the radical opposition to British rule. He was a founding member of the Committees of Correspondence and a delegate to the Continental Congress. At a Virginia assembly in 1775 he delivered his famous speech in defense of liberty, which concluded with the words "Give me liberty or give me death." He helped draft the state's first constitution in 1776 and was elected governor the same year (1776–79, 1784–86). As wartime governor, he ably supported Gen. George Washington; during his second term, he authorized the expedition of George Rogers Clark to invade the Illinois country. In 1788 he opposed ratification of the U.S. Constitution, which he felt did not sufficiently secure the rights of states and individuals. He was later instrumental in the adoption of the Bill of Rights.

THOMAS JEFFERSON
(b. April 13, 1743, Shadwell, Va.—
d. July 4, 1826, Monticello, Va.)

The principal author of the Declaration of Independence (and later the third president of the United States [1801–09]), Thomas Jefferson was the most eloquent American proponent of individual freedom as the core meaning of the American Revolution.

Jefferson was a planter and became a lawyer in 1767. While a member of the House of Burgesses (1769–75), he initiated the Virginia Committee of Correspondence (1773) with Richard Henry Lee and Patrick Henry. In 1774 he wrote the influential *A Summary View of the Rights of British America*, stating that the British Parliament had no authority to legislate for the colonies. A delegate to the Second Continental Congress, he was appointed to the committee to draft the Declaration of Independence and became its primary author. He was elected governor of Virginia (1779–81) but was unable to organize effective opposition when British forces invaded the colony (1780–81). Criticized for his conduct, he retired, vowing to remain a private citizen. Again a member of the Continental Congress (1783–85), he drafted the first of the Northwest Ordinances for dividing and settling the Northwest Territory. In 1785 he succeeded Benjamin

Franklin as U.S. minister to France. Appointed the first secretary of state (1790–93) by George Washington, he soon became embroiled in a bitter conflict with Alexander Hamilton over the country's foreign policy and their opposing interpretations of the Constitution. Their divisions gave rise to political factions and eventually to political parties. Jefferson served as vice president (1797–1801) under John Adams but opposed Adams's signing of the Alien and Sedition Acts (1798); the Virginia and Kentucky Resolutions, adopted by the legislatures of those states in 1798 and 1799 as a protest against the Acts, were written by Jefferson and James Madison. In the presidential election of 1800 Jefferson and Aaron Burr received the same number of votes in the electoral college; the decision was thrown to the U.S. House of Representatives, which chose Jefferson on the 36th ballot. As president, Jefferson attempted to reduce the powers of the embryonic federal government and to eliminate the national debt; he also dispensed with a great deal of the ceremony and formality that had attended the office of president to that time. In 1803 he oversaw the Louisiana Purchase, which doubled the land area of the country, and he authorized the Lewis and Clark Expedition. In an effort to force Britain and France to cease their molestation of U.S. merchant ships during the Napoleonic Wars, he signed the Embargo Act. In 1809 he retired to his plantation, Monticello, where he pursued his interests in science, philosophy, and architecture. He served

as president of the American Philosophical Society (1797–1815), and in 1819 he founded and designed the University of Virginia. In 1812, after a long estrangement, he and Adams were reconciled and began a lengthy correspondence that illuminated their opposing political philosophies. They died within hours of each other on July 4, 1826, the 50th anniversary of the signing of the Declaration of Independence. Though a lifelong slaveholder, Jefferson was an anomaly among the Virginia planter class for his support of gradual emancipation.

SAMUEL KIRKLAND
(b. Dec. 1, 1741, Norwich, Conn.— d. Feb. 28, 1808, Clinton, N.Y.)

A Congregational minister, Samuel Kirkland played a vital role during the Revolution as a negotiator with the Oneida Alliance.

While still a student at Princeton, Kirkland began his wilderness treks on snowshoes to preach to the Indians. Gradually he mastered several Indian languages and became a trusted friend of the Tuscarora and the Oneida Indians. During the war he served as chaplain to colonial troops and was commended by Gen. George Washington for his diplomacy with the Indians. He was rewarded for these services by a congressional land grant (1785), augmented in 1788 by a joint grant from the Indians and the state of New York, where he founded the Hamilton Oneida Academy for young Indian and white men in the new town of

Kirkland. (In 1812 the school became Hamilton College.)

JOHN LANGDON
(b. June 26, 1741, Portsmouth, N.H.—
d. Sept. 18, 1819, Portsmouth)

A state legislator, governor, and U.S. senator during the Revolution and early national period, John Langdon organized and financed John Stark's expedition against British Gen. John Burgoyne (1777).

After an apprenticeship in a Portsmouth countinghouse and several years at sea, he became a prosperous shipowner and merchant. He was a member of the Continental Congress (1775-76, 1783-84), of the New Hampshire legislature (1777-82, 1801-15), and of the state senate (1784-85). He was president of New Hampshire (1785-86, 1788-89), a delegate to the Federal Constitutional Convention of 1787, and a U.S. senator (1789-1801). In the Senate he identified himself with the followers of Thomas Jefferson but declined any national office. Later he served as governor of New Hampshire (1805-09, 1810-12).

HENRY LAURENS
(b. March 6, 1724, Charleston, S.C.—
d. Dec. 8, 1792, near Charleston, S.C.)

South Carolinian Henry Laurens served as president of the Continental Congress (1777-78) and later was entrusted with an important wartime diplomatic mission.

After pursuing a profitable career as a merchant and planter, Laurens espoused the patriot cause in the disputes with Great Britain preceding the American Revolution. He was made president of the South Carolina Council of Safety and vice president of the state in 1776. Sent as a delegate to the Continental Congress meeting at Philadelphia, he was soon elected chief officer of that body.

In August 1780 Laurens embarked on a mission to Holland to negotiate on behalf of Congress a $10,000,000 loan, but he was captured off Newfoundland and imprisoned in the Tower of London. When his papers were found to contain a draft of a proposed treaty between the Americans and the Dutch, war broke out between Great Britain and Holland. On Dec. 31, 1781, he was released on parole and finally exchanged for the British general Charles Cornwallis. The following June he was appointed one of the U.S. commissioners for negotiating peace with the British, but, because of failing health, he was absent from the signing of the final peace treaty and retired to his plantation.

ARTHUR LEE
(b. Dec. 21, 1740, Westmoreland County, Va.—d. Dec. 12, 1792, Middlesex County, Va.)

As a diplomat Arthur Lee sought recognition and aid in Europe for the Continental Congress during the American Revolution.

Lee gave up a medical practice for the study of law and then became interested in colonial politics. He wrote political tracts, among them a series of 10 essays called "The Monitor's Letters" in the *Virginia Gazette* in 1768. In 1770 he became an agent for the colony of Massachusetts, and in 1776 he, Benjamin Franklin, and Silas Deane were appointed by the Continental Congress as commissioners to negotiate an alliance with France and to solicit aid from other European governments. Important treaties of commerce were signed with France in 1778; however, Lee's quarrels with his associates led to the recall of Lee and Deane to the United States. He was elected to the Virginia House of Delegates in 1781 and served as a delegate to the Continental Congress (1782–84). He was on the U.S. Treasury Board (1785–89). After the adoption (1789) of the federal Constitution, which he opposed, he retired to Landsdowne, his Virginia estate.

RICHARD HENRY LEE
(b. Jan. 20, 1732, Stratford, Va.—
d. June 19, 1794, Chantilly, Va.)

Richard Henry Lee was among the earliest and most adamant colonial critics of British imperial policy in North America.

Educated in England, Lee served in the Virginia House of Burgesses (1758–75). He opposed arbitrary British policies at the time of the Stamp Act and the Townshend Acts, and, with Patrick Henry and Thomas Jefferson, he originated a plan for intercolonial committees of correspondence (March 1777).

Lee was an active member of the First Continental Congress, where admirers of his oratory compared him with Cicero. In the Second Continental Congress he introduced three resolutions: (1) for declaring independence; (2) for forming foreign alliances; and (3) for preparing a plan of confederation. His first resolution was adopted on July 2, and the Declaration of Independence followed two days later. He remained active in Congress until forced to resign in 1779 because of poor health. In 1777, 1780, and 1785 he served in the Virginia House of Delegates and in 1784 was back in Congress, where he remained until 1787, acting as its president in 1784. He opposed ratification of the federal Constitution because it created a "consolidated" government and lacked a bill of rights. He served, nonetheless, as senator from Virginia in the first Congress from 1789 to 1792, when he retired from public life.

WILLIAM LIVINGSTON
(b. Nov. 30, 1723, Albany, N.Y.—
d. July 25, 1790, Elizabeth, N.J.)

William Livingston was the first Revolutionary governor of New Jersey.

A graduate of Yale, Livingston was admitted to the New York bar in 1748 and served briefly in the New York legislature (1759–60). His chief political influence was exerted through pamphlets and newspaper articles, first in the short-lived *Independent Reflector* (1752–53), which he founded, and later in the *New*

York Mercury. With the historian William Smith, he prepared a digest of the laws of New York for the period 1691–1756 (2 vol., 1752–62).

Moving to New Jersey in 1772, he represented that colony in the First and Second Continental Congresses (1774–76) but left Philadelphia in June 1776 to command the New Jersey troops. Chosen in 1776 as the state's first governor, he was regularly reelected to that office until his death. He was a delegate to the federal Constitutional Convention of 1787, and the following year led his state to an early ratification of the new constitution.

Livingston's brother Philip (1716–78) was a member of the First Continental Congress and a signer of the Declaration of Independence.

GEORGE MASON
(b. 1725, Fairfax County, Va.— d. Oct. 7, 1792, Fairfax County)

American patriot George Mason insisted on the protection of individual liberties in the composition of both the Virginia and U.S. Constitutions (1776, 1787); he was ahead of his time in opposing slavery and in rejecting the constitutional compromise that perpetuated it.

As a landowner and near neighbour of George Washington, Mason took a leading part in local affairs. He also became deeply interested in Western expansion and was active in the Ohio Company, organized in 1749 to develop trade and sell land on the upper Ohio River. At about the

same time, Mason helped to found the town of Alexandria, Va. Because of ill health and family problems, he generally eschewed public office, though he accepted election to the House of Burgesses in 1759. Except for his membership in the Constitutional Convention at Philadelphia, this was the highest office he ever held—yet few men did more to shape U.S. political institutions.

A leader of the Virginia patriots on the eve of the Revolution, Mason served on the Committee of Safety and in 1776 drafted the state constitution, his declaration of rights being the first authoritative formulation of the doctrine of inalienable rights. Mason's work was known to Thomas Jefferson and influenced his drafting of the Declaration of Independence. The model was soon followed by most of the states and was also incorporated in diluted form in the federal Constitution. He served as a member of the Virginia House of Delegates from 1776 to 1788.

As a member of the Constitutional Convention, Mason strenuously opposed the compromise permitting the continuation of the slave trade until 1808. Although he was a Southerner, Mason castigated the trade as "disgraceful to mankind"; he favoured manumission and education for bondsmen and supported a system of free labour. Because he also objected to the large and indefinite powers vested in the new government, he joined several other Virginians in opposing adoption of the new document. A

Jeffersonian Republican, he believed that local government should be kept strong and central government weak. His criticism helped bring about the adoption of the Bill of Rights to the Constitution.

Soon after the Convention, Mason retired to his home, Gunston Hall.

PHILIP MAZZEI
(b. Dec. 25, 1730, Poggio a Caiano, Tuscany [Italy]—d. March 19, 1816, Pisa, Italy)

Italian physician, merchant, and author Philip Mazzei was an ardent supporter of the American Revolution and corresponded with Thomas Jefferson.

Mazzei studied medicine in Florence and practiced in Turkey before moving in 1755 to London, where he became a wine merchant. In 1773 Mazzei set sail for the American colonies, intending to launch the development of olive and grape growing in Virginia. He established an experimental farm next to Jefferson's Monticello. Mazzei soon became enveloped in the independence movement, and he strongly favoured Virginia's strides toward religious and political freedom. In 1779 he accepted a commission from Patrick Henry, the Virginia governor, to seek a loan from the grand duke of Tuscany. After being captured by the British and imprisoned for three months, Mazzei arrived in Europe—only to find his every effort blocked by Benjamin Franklin, who

believed that the national government alone could contract foreign debts.

Mazzei remained in Europe until late 1783, collecting political and military information for Jefferson. He returned to the United States briefly in quest of a foreign service post, but when that effort failed he went back to Europe. In 1788 his four volumes on America, *Recherches historiques et politiques sur les États-Unis de l'Amérique septentrionale* ("Historical and Political Studies of the Northern United States of America"), were published in Paris.

In 1789 Mazzei became an adviser to Stanisław II August Poniatowski, last king of an independent Poland, and in 1802 he began to receive a pension from Russia. He continued for many years to correspond with Jefferson and other Virginians. One of Jefferson's letters to him—criticizing the Federalists and, by implication, George Washington—created a storm of controversy when it fell into the hands of political opponents and American newspapers reprinted it.

Three years before his death, Mazzei completed an account in Italian of his remarkable life and travels; it was published in two volumes in 1845–46.

JANE MCCREA
(b. c. 1752, Bedminster [now Lamington], N.J.—d. July 27, 1777, Fort Edward, N.Y.)

Among the more sensational stories connected with the Revolution was that of the death of American colonist Jane McCrea, which aroused anti-British feeling and helped sway opinion and stir action in the colonies toward independence.

McCrea, a tall, attractive woman, was courted by David Jones. In 1776 Jones was one of several Tories in the area to join the British army. In the summer of 1777 the approach of a large British force under Gen. John Burgoyne down Lake Champlain and the Hudson River valley and the consequent abandonment of Fort Ticonderoga and Fort Edward by colonial defenders caused a panic among the remaining settlers, who quickly began to evacuate southward. McCrea declined to leave, however, because she had received a letter from Jones, by then a lieutenant with Burgoyne, saying that he hoped soon to see her at Fort Edward. Later legend has it that they were to be married at that time.

On the morning of July 27, 1777, McCrea visited a friend, Sarah McNeil, who was preparing to leave Fort Edward for safety. About noon the two women were captured by some Native American scouts whom Burgoyne had employed as an advance force. McNeil was delivered safely to British hands, but McCrea was later discovered dead, several bullet wounds in her body, and scalped. Her captors claimed she had been killed by a stray bullet from a colonial detachment, but it was generally accepted that one of the scouts had killed her. The murder and scalping sent a shock of horror

through the colonies; it was even felt in England, where in the House of Commons Edmund Burke denounced the use of Indian allies. In America the deed galvanized patriotic sentiment, swung waverers against the British, and encouraged a tide of enlistments that helped end Burgoyne's invasion three months later. The tale of Jane McCrea became a favourite and was much romanticized in popular versions by such authors as Philip Freneau, Joel Barlow, and Delia S. Bacon.

ARTHUR MIDDLETON
(b. June 26, 1742, near Charleston, S.C.—d. Jan. 1, 1787, Goose Creek, S.C.)

Arthur Middleton, a signer of the Declaration of Independence, spent time as a prisoner of war during the Revolution.

After completing his education in England, Middleton returned to South Carolina in 1763 and was elected to the colonial legislature. In 1775–76 he was a member of the Council of Safety, a committee that directed leadership for the colony's preparations for revolution. He served on the legislative committee that drafted the South Carolina state constitution and was a delegate to the Continental Congress (1776–78).

At the Siege of Charleston (1780) he served in the militia, was taken prisoner when the city fell to the British, and was sent to St. Augustine, Fla., as a prisoner of war. After being exchanged in July 1781, he was a member of the Continental

Congress (1781–83), the South Carolina legislature (1785–86), and on the original board of trustees of the College of Charleston.

ROBERT MORRIS
(b. Jan. 31, 1734, Liverpool, Merseyside, Eng.—d. May 8, 1806, Philadelphia, Pa.)

Merchant and banker Robert Morris came to be known as the financier of the American Revolution.

Morris left England to join his father in Maryland in 1747 and then entered a mercantile house in Philadelphia. During the war, Morris was vice president of the Pennsylvania Committee of Safety (1775–76) and was a member of both the Continental Congress (1775–78) and the Pennsylvania legislature (1778–79, 1780–81, 1785–86). Because he was hoping for reconciliation with Britain, he did not sign the Declaration of Independence until several weeks after its adoption.

As chairman or member of various committees of the Continental Congress, Morris practically controlled the financial operations of the war from 1776 to 1778. He raised the funds that made it possible for Gen. George Washington to move his army from the New York area to Yorktown, where Lord Cornwallis surrendered (1781). Morris had borrowed from the French, requisitioned from the states, and also advanced money from his own pocket. That same year, in Philadelphia, Morris established the

Bank of North America. After the war he served as superintendent of finance under the Articles of Confederation (1781–84). He was a delegate to the Constitutional Convention (1787) and served in the U.S. Senate (1789–95). Meanwhile, he had disposed of his mercantile and banking investments and had plunged heavily into land speculation. When returns from his lands slowed, he fell into bankruptcy and was confined

Robert Morris, engraving, late 19th or early 20th century. Library of Congress, Washington, D.C. (photo no. LC-USZ62-48942)

in a debtors' prison for more than three years before his release in 1801.

JAMES OTIS
(b. Feb. 5, 1725, West Barnstable, Mass.—d. May 23, 1783, Andover, Mass.)

A political activist during the period leading up to the Revolution, James Otis helped formulate the colonists' grievances against the British government in the 1760s.

Son of the elder James Otis, who was already prominent in Massachusetts politics, the younger Otis graduated from Harvard College in 1743 and was admitted to the bar in 1748. He moved his law practice from Plymouth to Boston in 1750. His reputation was built mainly upon his famous challenge in 1761 to the British-imposed writs of assistance—general search warrants designed to enforce more strictly the trade and navigation laws in North America. These search warrants authorized customhouse officers to search any house for smuggled goods; neither the house nor the goods had to be specifically mentioned in the writs. Arguing before the Superior Court in Boston, Otis raised the doctrine of natural law underlying the rights of citizens and argued that such writs, even if authorized by Parliament, were null and void. In harking back to fundamental English constitutional law, Otis offered the colonists a basic doctrine upon which their publicists could draw for decades to come. At this time he also reportedly coined the oft-quoted phrase "Taxation without representation is tyranny."

Otis was elected in May 1761 to the General Court (provincial legislature) of Massachusetts and was reelected nearly every year thereafter during his active life. In 1766 he was chosen speaker of the house, though this choice was negated by the royal governor of the province.

In September 1762 Otis published *A Vindication of the Conduct of the House of Representatives of the Province of Massachusetts Bay* in defense of that body's rebuke of the governor for asking the assembly to pay for ships not authorized by them—though sent to protect New England fisheries against French privateers. Otis also wrote various state papers addressed to the colonies to enlist them in the common cause, and he also sent such papers to the government in England to uphold the rights or set forth the grievances of the colonists. His influence at home in controlling and directing the movement of events toward freedom was universally felt and acknowledged, and few Americans were so frequently quoted, denounced, or applauded in Parliament and the British press before 1769. In 1765 he was a delegate to the Stamp Act Congress in New York City, and there he was a conspicuous figure, serving on the committee that prepared the address sent to the House of Commons.

Already prone to fits of insanity, Otis was struck on the head during an altercation with a crown officer in 1769 and was rendered harmlessly insane, with only occasional lucid intervals, until his death. He died in 1783 after being struck by lightning.

ROBERT TREAT PAINE
(b. March 11, 1731, Boston, Mass.— d. May 11, 1814, Boston)

Robert Treat Paine was both a member of the Continental Congress and a signer of the Declaration of Independence.

Paine graduated from Harvard in 1749 and, after trying teaching and the ministry, turned to the study of law and was admitted to the Massachusetts bar in 1757. An early champion of the patriot cause, he gained recognition throughout the colonies in 1770 when he was chosen as a prosecuting attorney in the murder trial of British soldiers involved in the Boston Massacre of March 5, 1770. His opponent in the case was John Adams. He was elected several times to the Massachusetts legislature in the 1770s and became the state's first attorney general in 1777. He helped draft the state constitution in 1780 and from 1790 to 1804 served as a judge of the state supreme court. Long interested in astronomy, Paine was a founder of the American Academy of Arts and Sciences in 1780.

THOMAS PAINE
(b. Jan. 29, 1737, Thetford, Norfolk, Eng.—d. June 8, 1809, New York, N.Y.)

English-American writer and political pamphleteer Thomas Paine is best remembered as the author of *Common Sense*, a political treatise that helped spark the Revolution.

After a series of professional failures in England, he met Benjamin Franklin, who advised him to immigrate to America. He arrived in Philadelphia in 1774 and helped edit the *Pennsylvania Magazine*. In January 1776 he wrote *Common Sense*, a 50-page pamphlet eloquently

Writer and propagandist Thomas Paine helped shape the course of both the American and French Revolutions. Hulton Archive/Getty Images

advocating independence; more than 500,000 copies were quickly sold, and it greatly strengthened the colonists' resolve. As a volunteer aide to Gen. Nathanael Greene during the American Revolution he wrote his 16 *Crisis* papers (1776–83), each signed "Common Sense"; the first, beginning "These are the times that try men's souls," was read to the troops at Valley Forge on George Washington's order. In 1787 Paine traveled to England and became involved in debate over the French Revolution; his *The Rights of Man* (1791–92) defended the revolution and espoused republicanism. Viewed as an attack on the monarchy, it was banned, and Paine was declared an outlaw in England. He then went to France, where he was elected to the National Convention (1792–93). After he criticized the Reign of Terror, he was imprisoned by Maximilien Robespierre (1793–94). His *The Age of Reason* (1794, 1796), the first part of which was published while he was still in prison, earned him a reputation as an atheist, though it in fact espouses Deism. He returned to the U.S. in 1802; criticized for his Deist writings and little remembered for his service to the Revolution, he died in poverty.

EDMUND PENDLETON

(b. Sept. 9, 1721, Caroline County, Va.—d. Oct. 26, 1803, Caroline County)

Although he often found himself at odds with fellow Virginian Patrick Henry, Edmund Pendleton was nevertheless very much an American patriot and supporter of the Revolution.

Pendleton's father and grandfather died the year of his birth, and the young man grew up without paternal care. Apprenticed at the age of 14 to the clerk of the Caroline county court, Pendleton acquired a legal education, and in 1741 he was admitted to the bar.

In 1751 Pendleton became a justice of the peace, and the following year he was elected to the House of Burgesses. A conservative, he clashed repeatedly with Patrick Henry (whom Pendleton considered a demagogue) over Henry's radical opposition to the Stamp Act and other divisive issues between Britain and the American colonies. Pendleton did charge that Parliament had exceeded its authority in passing the Stamp Act, and he soon emerged as a leader among the patriots.

Selected in 1773 as a member of Virginia's Committee of Correspondence, Pendleton represented the colony at the first Continental Congress in 1774. In 1775 he served as president of the Virginia Committee of Public Safety, which acted as a temporary government during the critical period just prior to independence. At the Virginia convention of 1776, Pendleton drew up the instructions to Virginia's representatives in Congress, directing them to propose a declaration of independence. He later helped revise the laws of Virginia and helped draft the state's first constitution.

Under the new constitution, Pendleton served as first speaker of Virginia's House of Delegates. In 1779 he became president of the supreme court of appeals, but except for trips to Richmond in order to preside, he spent much of the remainder of his life at his estate, "Edmunsbury," in Caroline county. He nonetheless exerted influence over national affairs by corresponding regularly with his friends in Congress, especially James Madison. Elected president of Virginia's ratifying convention in 1788, Pendleton vigorously supported acceptance of the new federal Constitution. He thereafter refused several positions in the national government offered by his long-time friend George Washington and spent his final years at his Virginia estate.

PEYTON RANDOLPH
(b. 1721, Williamsburg, Va.—d. Oct. 22, 1775, Philadelphia, Pa.)

Virginian Peyton Randolph served as the first president of the Continental Congress.

Randolph was educated at the College of William and Mary, Williamsburg, Va., and became a member of the Virginia bar in 1744. Four years later, in recognition of his stature as a lawyer, he was appointed king's attorney for Virginia. The same year, he was elected to Virginia's House of Burgesses, where he served almost continuously until the time of his death. A member of the colonial aristocracy, he regarded himself as a spokesman for both the crown and his fellow Virginians.

Randolph was opposed to the colonists' radical response to the Stamp Act.

Looked to for leadership during the pre-Revolutionary disputes with England, he played a moderating and cautious role. But his patriotism was never in question, and he became more radical over time. By 1773 he was serving as chairman of the Virginia Committee of Correspondence.

In 1774 Randolph led the seven Virginia delegates to the first session of the Continental Congress. There he was elected president of the Congress, but in 1775 he suffered a stroke while in Philadelphia and died. John Hancock, whose views were far more radical, succeeded him as president.

PAUL REVERE
(b. Jan. 1, 1735, Boston, Mass.— d. May 10, 1818, Boston)

Perhaps the most famous folk hero of the American Revolution was Paul Revere, whose dramatic horseback ride on the night of April 18, 1775, warning Boston-area residents that the British were coming, was immortalized in a ballad by Henry Wadsworth Longfellow.

His father, Apollos De Revoire (later changed to Revere), was a Huguenot refugee who had come to Boston as a child and had been apprenticed to a silversmith. This craft he taught his son Paul Revere, who became one of America's greatest artists in silver. As a boy Revere received sufficient education to enable him later to read the difficult metallurgical books of his period. Although it was in metal that Revere did most of his work, his energy and skill (and the necessity of

Paul Revere, most famous for his "midnight ride," was a silversmith and engraver by trade. Hulton Archive/ Getty Images

he provided an invaluable link between artisans and intellectuals. In 1773 he donned Indian garb and joined 50 other patriots in the Boston Tea Party protest against parliamentary taxation without representation. Although many have questioned the historical liberties taken in Longfellow's narrative poem "Paul Revere's Ride" (1863), the fact is that Revere served for years as the principal rider for Boston's Committee of Safety, making journeys to New York and Philadelphia in its service. On April 16, 1775, he rode to nearby Concord to urge the patriots to move their military stores, which were endangered by pending British troop movements. At this time he arranged to signal the patriots of the British approach by having lanterns placed in Boston's Old North Church steeple: "One if by land, and two if by sea." Two days later he set out from Boston on his most famous journey to alert his countrymen that British troops were on the march, particularly in search of Revolutionary leaders John Hancock and Samuel Adams. Both he and his compatriot, William Dawes, reached Lexington separately and were able to warn Hancock and Adams to flee. The two men together with Samuel Prescott then started for Concord, but they were soon stopped by a British patrol, and only Prescott got through. Revere was released by the British and returned on foot to Lexington. Because of Revere's warning, the Minutemen were ready the next morning on Lexington green for the historic battle that launched the American Revolution.

supporting an ever-growing family) turned him in many directions. He not only made silver articles but also crafted surgical instruments, sold spectacles, replaced missing teeth, and engraved copper plates, the most famous of which portrayed his version of the Boston Massacre.

In the 1770s Revere enthusiastically supported the patriot cause; as acknowledged leader of Boston's mechanic class,

With the outbreak of hostilities, Revere turned industrialist and constructed a much-needed powder mill to supply colonial arms. In 1776 he was put in command of Boston Harbor's principal defense at Castle William, but his war record as a lieutenant colonel was largely undistinguished. He resumed his stride as a successful industrialist after the war, however, and set up a rolling mill for the manufacture of sheet copper at Canton, Mass. From this factory came sheathing for many U.S. ships, including the *Constitution*, and for the dome of the Massachusetts statehouse.

BETSY ROSS
(b. Jan. 1, 1752, Philadelphia, Pa.— d. Jan. 30, 1836, Philadelphia)

According to legend, seamstress Betsy Ross (née Elizabeth Griscom) fashioned the first flag of the United States.

Elizabeth Griscom was brought up a Quaker and educated in Quaker schools. On her marriage to John Ross, an Episcopalian, in 1773, she was disowned by the Society of Friends. Her husband was killed in 1776 while serving in the militia, and Ross took over the upholstering

Members of Congress consult with Betsy Ross at 239 Arch Street in Philadelphia, where the first American flag was reputedly made. Three Lions/Hulton Archive/Getty Images

business he had founded. According to her grandson, William Canby, in a paper presented before the Historical Society of Pennsylvania in 1870, Ross was visited in June 1776 by George Washington, Robert Morris, and George Ross, her late husband's uncle. The story is that they asked her to make a flag for the new nation that would declare its independence the following month. A rough sketch presented to her was redrawn by Washington incorporating her suggestions. Betsy Ross then fashioned the flag in her back parlor—again, according to the legend. She is supposed also to have suggested the use of the five-pointed star rather than the six-pointed one chosen by Washington. On June 14, 1777, the Continental Congress adopted the Stars and Stripes as the national flag of the United States. It is known that Ross made flags for the navy of Pennsylvania, but there is no firm evidence in support of the popular story about the national flag. There is, however, no conflicting testimony or evidence, either, and the story is now indelibly a part of American legend. Ross married Joseph Ashburn in 1777, and, after his death in a British prison in 1782, she was married for a third time, in 1783, to John Claypoole. She continued the upholstering business, which became very profitable, until 1827, when she turned it over to her daughter. The Philadelphia house in which Betsy Ross lived and from which she ran her upholstery business still stands; it has been restored and is open to the public.

HAYM SALOMON
(b. 1740, Lissa, Pol.—d. Jan. 6, 1785, Philadelphia, Pa.)

Haym Salomon, a Polish Jewish émigré, was one of the principal financiers of the fledgling American republic.

In 1772, probably because of his revolutionary activities for Polish liberty, Salomon fled to New York City, where he established himself as a commission merchant. He soon became a successful financier and supported the patriotic cause on the outbreak of the American Revolution. In 1776 the British, who controlled New York City, arrested Salomon; exposure suffered in prison later contributed to his early death. He was paroled but was arrested again in 1778 on more serious charges; he escaped and went to Philadelphia. There he established a brokerage office and acted without salary as the financial agent of the French, doing all in his power to facilitate the Franco-American Alliance.

Among his many other contributions to the colonies, Salomon subscribed heavily to government loans, endorsed notes, gave generously to soldiers, and equipped several military units with his own money. Robert Morris, the superintendent of finance from 1781 to 1784, appointed Salomon as broker to his office. Morris records in his diary that between 1781 and 1784 Salomon lent more than $200,000. In addition, he made private loans to prominent statesmen such as James Madison, Thomas Jefferson, and

James Monroe, from whom he would not take interest. In all, the government owed Salomon more than $600,000. Generations of his descendants tried in vain to collect some portion of these loans, which had helped to impoverish Salomon in his last years.

A statue in Chicago of Washington, Morris, and Salomon commemorates the financial contributions of the latter two to the Revolution and acknowledges Salomon's Jewish heritage by quoting Washington's statement that the government of the United States gives "to bigotry no sanction" and "to persecution no assistance."

ISAAC SEARS
(b. July 1?, 1730, West Brewster, Mass.—d. Oct. 28, 1786, Canton, China)

A patriot leader in New York City before the American Revolution, Issac Sears earned the nickname "King Sears" by virtue of his prominent role in inciting and commanding anti-British demonstrations.

A merchant whose shipping activities included privateering, Sears first exhibited his patriot leanings when the Stamp Act crisis erupted in 1765. He became a mob leader during the anti-British riots in New York City, and he belonged to the newly formed patriot organization the Sons of Liberty.

Sears led the boycott of British goods during colonial protests of the Townshend Acts. Repeal of the Townshend Acts produced a period of calm in the colonies

from 1770 to 1773, but imposition of the Tea Act in 1773 gave new life to the Sons of Liberty. In 1774 Sears led a New York version of the Boston Tea Party, and he signed the call for a meeting of representatives from the colonies.

Sears was arrested in April 1775 for his activities, but his admirers rescued him at the jailhouse door. Later that month—after the bloodshed at Lexington and Concord—he and his followers drove the loyalist officials out of New York City and seized control of the municipal government. His subsequent attacks on loyalist businessmen elicited official disapproval from patriot committees, but they earned Sears the backing of the New York citizenry.

The capture of New York City by the British compelled Sears to move to Boston from 1777 to 1783, during which time Sears spent time at sea as a privateer. In 1784 and again in 1786 he was elected to the New York state legislature. He was in China on a trading venture when he died there in 1786.

ROBERT SMITH
(b. Nov. 3, 1757, Lancaster, Pa.—d. Nov. 26, 1842, Baltimore, Md.)

Robert Smith, who was secretary of state under Pres. James Madison, first served the United States as a private in the Continental Army during the Revolution.

Smith grew up in Baltimore. He graduated in 1781 from the College of New Jersey (now Princeton University), studied law, and became a prominent and prosperous Baltimore attorney. From 1793 to 1801 Smith was active in Maryland politics, serving in both the state senate and house of delegates and in the Baltimore City Council. Following Thomas Jefferson's election to the presidency, Smith was appointed secretary of the navy, largely owing to the influence of his brother.

During the Jefferson administrations, Smith successfully prosecuted the naval war against the Barbary States, and he conscientiously enforced Jefferson's embargo despite his personal opposition to the policy. It was during those years (1801–09), however, that Smith and Albert Gallatin, secretary of the Treasury, became foes.

When James Madison became president, he wanted Gallatin to be secretary of state. But Samuel Smith and other prominent senators opposed Gallatin, and Robert Smith ultimately gained the post. Smith and Madison frequently disagreed—Smith objecting to the president's commercial restrictions, Madison unable to tolerate Smith's incoherent diplomatic communications.

In 1811, in a face-to-face confrontation, Madison accused Smith of inefficiency and of creating discord among members of the administration. The president offered Smith the position of minister to Russia in exchange for resigning. Smith hesitated, then refused, resigned, and retired. He spent the final 30 years of his life in Baltimore.

JAMES WILSON
(b. Sept. 14, 1742, Fife, Scot.—d. Aug. 21, 1798, Edenton, N.C.)

Lawyer and political theorist James Wilson was both a signer of the Declaration of Independence and member of the Constitutional Convention of 1787.

Immigrating to North America from Scotland in 1765, Wilson taught Greek and rhetoric in the College of Philadelphia and then studied law under John Dickinson, statesman and delegate to the First Continental Congress. Wilson's fame spread with publication in 1774 of his treatise *Considerations on the Nature and Extent of the Legislative Authority of the British Parliament.* In this work he set out a scheme of empire in which the British colonies would have the equivalent of dominion status. In 1774 he became a member of the Committee of Correspondence in Cumberland County, Pa., and he served as a delegate to the Second Continental Congress. In 1779 he was appointed advocate general for France and represented that country in cases rising out of its alliance with the American colonies. He became a champion of the Bank of North America and an associate of merchant-banker Robert Morris in his struggle for currency reform after 1781. As a member of the federal Congress (1783; 1785–86), he pressed for an amendment to the Articles of Confederation to permit Congress to levy a general tax.

During the Constitutional Convention in 1787, Wilson helped to draft the

U.S. Constitution; he then led the fight for ratification in Pennsylvania. In 1790 he engineered the drafting of Pennsylvania's new constitution and delivered a series of lectures that are landmarks in the evolution of American jurisprudence. He was appointed an associate justice of the U.S. Supreme Court (1789–98), where his most notable decision was that on *Chisholm v. Georgia*. In the winter of 1796–97 financial ruin brought on by unwise land speculation shattered his health and ended his career.

JOHN WITHERSPOON
(b. Feb. 15, 1723, Gifford, East Lothian, Scot.—d. Nov. 15, 1794, Tusculum, N.J.)

A Scottish-American Presbyterian minister and the president of the College of New Jersey (now Princeton University), John Witherspoon was the only clergyman to sign the Declaration of Independence.

After completing his theological studies at the University of Edinburgh (1743), he was called to the parish of Beith in 1745 and in 1757 became pastor at Paisley. A conservative churchman, he frequently involved himself in ecclesiastical controversies, in which he proved himself a keen dialectician and an effective speaker. In 1768 he left Paisley to assume the presidency of the College of New Jersey. He was warmly received by the American Presbyterian Church and contributed significantly to its revitalization and growth. He was a vigorous college president, expanding the curriculum, providing scientific equipment, and working to increase the endowment and enrollment.

From his arrival, Witherspoon was an enthusiast about America, and in the dispute with the mother country he ranged himself uncompromisingly on the side of the colonists. He presided over the Somerset County Committee of Correspondence (1775–76), was a member of two provincial congresses, and was a delegate to the Continental Congress (1776–79, 1780–82), where in 1776 he was a persuasive advocate of adopting a resolution of independence.

Witherspoon wrote extensively on religious and political topics. His works include *Ecclesiastical Characteristics* (1753), *Considerations on the Nature and Extent of the Legislative Authority of the British Parliament* (1774), as well as numerous essays, sermons, and pamphlets.

OLIVER WOLCOTT
(b. Nov. 20, 1726, Windsor, Conn.— d. Dec. 1, 1797, Litchfield, Conn.)

Oliver Wolcott was a signer of the Declaration of Independence and a military veteran of the Revolution, but perhaps his greatest contribution to the new republic was his negotiation of a settlement with the Iroquois in 1784.

Descended from an old Connecticut family long active in public affairs, he was the son of Roger Wolcott, who was the colonial governor in 1750–54. Settling in Litchfield County, where he practiced law and was made sheriff (1751), he became a member of the Connecticut council (1771–86) and a delegate to the Continental Congress in Philadelphia. At the beginning of the Revolution, Wolcott signed the Declaration of Independence, then returned home to raise a state militia, which he commanded in defense of New York City (August 1776). The following year he organized more Connecticut volunteers and took part in the successful campaign against Gen. John Burgoyne. In 1779 he commanded Continental troops during the British invasion of his home state.

Wolcott had been appointed a commissioner for northern Indian affairs in 1775. After the war he helped negotiate the Second Treaty of Fort Stanwix, which redrew the western boundaries of the Six (Iroquois) Nations. He went on to serve as Connecticut's lieutenant governor (1787–96) and governor (1796–97), as well as a member of the Connecticut convention that ratified the new federal Constitution.

His son, Oliver Wolcott (1760–1833), continued the family tradition of public service as U.S. secretary of the treasury (1795–1800) and governor of Connecticut (1817–27).

THE BRITISH SIDE

Many civilians played a strong role in making the case for maintaining British sovereignty in the New World, and for creating policies and economic support that aided in the British war effort. Among them were important leaders, both in North America and in Britain.

JONATHAN BOUCHER
(b. March 12, 1738, Cumberland [now Cumbria], Eng.—d. April 27, 1804, Epsom, Surrey)

English clergyman Jonathan Boucher won fame as a loyalist in America.

In 1759 Boucher went to Virginia as a private tutor. After a visit to London in 1762 for his ordination, he became rector of Annapolis, Md., and tutored George Washington's stepson, thus becoming a family friend of the Washingtons. His loyalist views cost him his position: by 1775 he was keeping pistols on his pulpit cushion while conducting services, and he was forced to return to England. He nevertheless dedicated to Washington *A View of the Causes and Consequences of the American Revolution* (1797), consisting of 13 of the eloquent sermons that he had preached in America urging loyalty to England, and he received a friendly acknowledgment.

Having obtained a pension and the living of Epsom, Surrey, Boucher devoted his leisure to writing and to philology. He contributed to William Hutchinson's *The History of the County of Cumberland*, 2 vol. (1794), and spent 14 years compiling a "Glossary of Archaic and Provincial Words," intended to supplement Samuel

Johnson's *Dictionary of the English Language*. It was published only in part but was later used for Noah Webster's *American Dictionary of the English Language*.

WILLIAM LEGGE, 2ND EARL OF DARTMOUTH
(b. June 20, 1731—d. July 15, 1801, Blackheath, Kent, Eng.)

British statesman Lord Dartmouth played a significant role in the events leading to the American Revolution.

Legge was educated at Westminster School and Trinity College, Oxford. In 1750 he succeeded his grandfather as earl of Dartmouth and later entered on a political career, taking his seat in the House of Lords in May 1754. In the marquess of Rockingham's first administration, Dartmouth was appointed president of the Board of Trade and a member of the Privy Council (July 1765). During his tenure (1765–66) he opposed the Stamp Act and worked for the act's repeal.

In 1772 Dartmouth became secretary of state for the colonies in the ministry of his stepbrother, Lord North. Faced with mounting hostility in the British North American colonies, he adopted a policy of conciliation to allow tensions to abate. When this policy was rendered ineffective by the Boston Tea Party, Dartmouth sought to reimpose strict British control over the colonies. The Intolerable Acts, which he supported, only exacerbated tensions, as did the Quebec Act (1774), which he defended from attempts at repeal. He rejected further proposals for conciliation with the colonies and in 1776 called for the use of overwhelming force to suppress the growing rebellion. Unwilling, however, to direct a war against the colonists, he resigned his offices in November 1775 but remained in the cabinet as Lord Privy Seal until 1782 in order to support Lord North.

Dartmouth, a devout evangelical Anglican, befriended the Methodist John Wesley and the Quaker John Fothergill. He supported the work of Eleazar Wheelock, a Congregationalist minister, in establishing a school for the education of Native Americans. This school developed into Dartmouth College of Hanover, N.H., which was named in Dartmouth's honour.

DANIEL DULANY
(b. June 28, 1722, Annapolis, Md.—d. March 17, 1797, Baltimore, Md.)

Maryland lawyer Daniel Dulany, an influential political figure in the period just before the Revolution, opposed the Stamp Act but remained a loyalist.

The son of the Maryland official of the same name, Daniel Dulany was educated in England and became a lawyer after returning to Maryland. He was a member of the Maryland legislative assembly from 1751 to 1754, and he was appointed to the Governor's Council in 1757 in recognition of his support for the colony's proprietary government. In the following years he held other high offices and also became known as one of the best lawyers in the American colonies. Though his sympathies were those of a loyal British subject, Dulany was critical of some policies of the British government, and, during the crisis over the Stamp Act of 1765, he wrote *Considerations on the Propriety of Imposing Taxes in the British Colonies* (1765), which was the most influential pamphlet that appeared in opposition to the Stamp Act. He opposed Revolutionary action against British rule, however, and, during the American Revolution, he remained a loyalist, being deprived of his property in 1781 on account of this.

JOHN MURRAY,
4TH EARL OF DUNMORE
(b. 1730?–d. Feb. 25 or March 5, 1809, Ramsgate, Kent, Eng.)

Lord Dunmore served as the British royal governor of Virginia on the eve of the American Revolution.

A descendant of the Scottish house of Stuart, he was the eldest son of William Murray, the 3rd earl, whom he succeeded in 1756. He sat in the House of Lords from 1761 to 1770 and then was appointed governor first of New York in 1770 and then of Virginia in 1771. Personally interested in western lands as well as officially concerned with protection of the Virginia frontier to the west, he raised 3,000 militiamen to subdue the Shawnee Indians in the upper Ohio River valley in 1774, an action known as Lord Dunmore's War.

As the revolution approached, Dunmore's power declined rapidly, especially through his own rashness. He dissolved the Virginia Assembly in 1772, 1773, and 1774 on account of its Revolutionary sentiments. In April 1775 he seized the colony's store of powder, thereby bringing about an armed uprising. Taking refuge aboard an English warship, he shortly declared martial law, proclaimed freedom to slaves who would join the British, and proposed to Lord Dartmouth the use of Indians against the rebels. Defeated at Great Bridge near Norfolk on Jan. 1, 1776, he ordered his ships to bombard Norfolk, thereby setting it afire. He returned to England in July 1776. After serving again in the House of Lords, he was royal governor of the Bahamas from 1787 to 1796.

JOSEPH GALLOWAY
(b. c. 1731, West River, Md. [U.S.]–
d. Aug. 29, 1803, Watford,
Hertfordshire, Eng.)

Distinguished American colonial attorney and legislator Joseph Galloway remained loyal to Great Britain at the time of the American Revolution. His effort in 1774 to settle differences peacefully narrowly missed adoption by the Continental Congress. He was, perhaps, the greatest of the colonial loyalists.

Entering law practice in Philadelphia in 1747, Galloway won a reputation by pleading cases before the Supreme Court of Pennsylvania before he was 20. Elected to the provincial assembly in 1756, he occupied the powerful post of speaker from 1766 to 1775. His "A plan of a proposed Union between Great Britain and the Colonies" in 1774 provided for a president general to be appointed by the king and a colonial legislature to have rights and duties similar to the House of Commons. After a day's debate his plan was rejected by the Continental Congress by only one vote and was later expunged from the record.

In the belief that the Revolution was unreasonable and unjust, Galloway left Philadelphia and joined Gen. Sir William Howe's British army. He returned to the city as a civil administrator during the British occupation and drew up several plans of union after the Declaration of Independence with the hope that they might be used when the rebels had been defeated. With the reentry of the Continentals into Philadelphia in 1778 he fled to England, where he remained until his death.

GEORGE III
(b. June 4, 1738, London, Eng.—d. Jan. 29, 1820, Windsor Castle, near London)

The king of Great Britain and Ireland from 1760 to 1820, George III was the ruler of Britain during the American Revolution.

EARLY RULE AND POLITICAL INSTABILITY, 1760–70

The grandson of George II, he ascended the throne during the Seven Years' War.

His chief minister, Lord Bute, forced William Pitt's resignation and caused intrigue rather than stability within the government. Bute resigned in 1763, but George's political overtures to others were snubbed, until Lord North became prime minister in 1770. England was in financial distress caused by the war, and George supported attempts to raise funds through taxation of the American colonies, which led to the American Revolution. With North, he was blamed for prolonging the war and losing the colonies. He reasserted his power when North and Charles James Fox planned to take control of the East India Company; he forced them to resign and reaffirmed his control through a new "patriotic" prime minister, William Pitt, the Younger. George supported him until the war with revolutionary France (1793) and fears of related uprisings in Ireland caused Pitt to propose political emancipation of the Roman Catholics. George's vehement opposition led to Pitt's resignation in 1801. In 1811 George's ill health and a return of the madness that had afflicted him for short periods earlier in his life caused Parliament to enact the regency of his son, the future George IV.

Politically, Bute encouraged the most disastrous of George's delusions. The government of England at the time lacked effective executive machinery, and members of Parliament were always more ready to criticize than to cooperate with it. Moreover, the ministers were, for the most part, quarrelsome and difficult

Serving as king between 1760 and 1820, George III ruled England during the American Revolution. Kean Collection/Hulton Archive/Getty Images

to drive as a team. The king's first responsibility was to hold coalitions of great peers together. But under Bute's influence he imagined that his duty was to purify public life and to substitute duty to himself for personal intrigue. The two great men in office at the accession were the elder Pitt and Thomas Pelham-Holles, duke of Newcastle. Bute and George III disliked both. Pitt was allowed to resign (October 1761) over the question of war against Spain. Newcastle followed into retirement when his control of treasury matters seemed to be challenged. The two former ministers were each dangerous as a focal point for criticism of the new government under the touchy captaincy of Bute. The government had two principal problems: to make peace and to restore peacetime finance.

Peace was made but in such a way as to isolate Britain in Europe, and for almost 30 years the country suffered from the new alignments of the European powers. Nor was George III happy in his attempt to express the agreed purposes of the country that to Bute had seemed so clear. George III might "glory in the name of Briton," but his attempts to speak out for his country were ill-received. In 1765 he was being vilified by the gutter press organized by the parliamentary radical John Wilkes, while "patriotic" gentlemen, moved by Pitt or Newcastle, suspected that the peace had been botched and that the king was conspiring with Bute against their liberties. For Bute the way out was easy—he resigned (April 1763).

George realized too late that his clumsiness had destroyed one political combination and made any other difficult to assemble. He turned to George Grenville, to his uncle, William Augustus, duke of Cumberland, to Pitt, and to the 3rd duke of Grafton for help. All failed him. The first decade of the reign was one of such ministerial instability that little was done to solve the basic financial difficulties of the crown, made serious by the expense of the Seven Years' War. Overseas trade expanded, but the riches of the East India Company made no significant contribution to the state. The attempt to make the American colonists meet their own administrative costs only aroused them to resistance. Nor was there consistency in British colonial policy. The Stamp Act (1765) passed by Grenville was repealed by Lord Rockingham in 1766. Indirect taxes, in the form of the Townshend Acts (1767), were imposed without calculation of their probable yield and then repealed (except for that on tea) as a maneuver in home politics.

George III was personally blamed for this instability. According to the Whig statesman Edmund Burke and his friends, the king could not keep a ministry because he was faithless and intrigued with friends "behind the curtain." Burke's remedy was to urge that solidity should be given to a cabinet by the building up of party loyalty: the king as a binding agent was to be replaced by the organization of groups upon agreed principles. Thus the early years of George III produced, inadvertently, the germ of modern party politics. In truth, however, the king was not guilty of causing chaos by intrigue. He had no political contact with Bute after 1766; the so-called king's friends were not his agents but rather those who looked to him for leadership such as his predecessors had given. The king's failure lay in his tactlessness and inexperience, and it was not his fault that no one group was strong enough to control the Commons.

By 1770, however, George III had learned a good deal. He was still as obstinate as ever and still felt an intense duty to guide the country, but now he reckoned with political reality. He no longer scorned to make use of executive power for winning elections nor did he withhold his official blessing from those of whose characters he disapproved.

NORTH'S MINISTRY, 1770–82

In 1770 the king was lucky in finding a minister, Lord North, with the power to cajole the Commons. North's policy of letting sleeping dogs lie lulled the suspicions of independent rural members who were always ready to imagine that the executive was growing too strong. As a result, 12 years of stable government followed a decade of disturbance.

Unfortunately, issues and prejudices survived from the earlier period that North could only muffle. America was the greatest and the fatal issue, and North could not avoid it because the English squires in Parliament agreed with their king that America must pay for its own defense and for its share of the debt remaining from the war that had given it security. George III's personal responsibility for the loss of America lies not in any assertion of his royal prerogative. Americans, rather, were disposed to admit his personal supremacy. Their quarrel was with the assertion of the sovereignty of Parliament, and George III was eventually hated in America because he insisted upon linking himself with that Parliament. North would have had difficulty in ignoring the colonists' insults in any case; with the king and the House of Commons watching to see that he was not weak, he inevitably took the steps that led to war in 1775.

By 1779 the typical English squires in Parliament had sickened of the war, but the king argued that though the war was indefensible on economic grounds it still had to be fought, that if disobedience were seen to prosper, Ireland would follow suit. He argued also, after the French had joined the Americans in 1778, that French finances would collapse before those of Britain. So the king prolonged the war, possibly by two years, by his desperate determination. The period from 1779 to 1782 left a further black mark upon the king's reputation. By 1780 a majority in Parliament blamed North's government for the calamities that had befallen the country, yet there was no responsible or acceptable alternative, for the opposition was reputed to be both unpatriotic and divided. At the time people believed that corruption alone supported an administration that was equally incapable of waging war or ending it. This supposed increase in corruption was laid directly at the king's door, for North wearily repeated his wish to resign, thus appearing to be a mere puppet of George III. When North fell at last in 1782, George III's prestige was at a low ebb. The failure of Shelburne's ministry (1782–83) reduced George to the lowest point of all. North joined with the liberal Whig Charles James Fox to form a coalition government, and George even contemplated abdication.

With North, he was blamed for prolonging the war and losing the colonies. He reasserted his power when North and Charles James Fox planned to take control of the East India Company; he forced them to resign and reaffirmed his control through a new "patriotic" prime minister, William Pitt, the Younger. George supported him until the war with Revolutionary France (1793) and fears of related uprisings in Ireland caused Pitt to propose political emancipation of the Roman Catholics. George's vehement opposition led to Pitt's resignation in 1801. In 1811 the king's ill health and a return of the madness that had afflicted him for short periods earlier in his life caused Parliament to enact the regency of his son, the future George IV.

GEORGE GRENVILLE
(b. Oct. 14, 1712—d. Nov. 13, 1770, London, Eng.)

While serving as first lord of the treasury of Britain, George Grenville formulated the policy of taxing the American colonies, initiated by his Revenue Act of 1764 and the Stamp Act of 1765, thus starting the train of events leading to the American Revolution.

He entered Parliament in 1741, one of the "cousinhood" of men interrelated by blood or marriage and further united in their opposition to Sir Robert Walpole, who held power from 1721 to 1742. After holding a number of ministerial appointments, Grenville was recommended to George III by Lord Bute to be his successor as first lord of the Treasury (prime minister). Grenville's ministry (1763–65) was unhappy and disastrous, largely because of his lack of finesse, eloquence, and imagination and his determination to control all crown patronage. His relationship with the king suffered from George III's habit of continual consultation with Bute. Apart from American taxation, other notable incidents during the Grenville administration included the prosecution of John Wilkes for seditious libel and the clumsy handling of the Regency Act of 1765 that had been introduced as a result of a severe illness the king had suffered. This bumbling finally alienated the king and led to the fall of the ministry. In opposition after 1765, Grenville castigated politicians opposed to American taxation and helped to bring about the passage of Townshend's Revenue Act of 1767, which renewed tension between Britain and the colonies.

THOMAS HUTCHINSON
(b. Sept. 9, 1711, Boston, Mass.— d. June 3, 1780, London, Eng.)

As the royal governor of the British North American Province of Massachusetts Bay (1771–74), Thomas Hutchinson introduced stringent measures that helped precipitate colonial unrest and eventually the American Revolution.

The son of a wealthy merchant, Hutchinson devoted himself to business ventures before beginning his public career (1737) as a member of the Boston Board of Selectmen and then the General Court (legislature) of Massachusetts Bay, where he served almost continuously until 1749. He continued to rise in politics by serving as a member of the state council (1749-66), chief justice of the Superior Court (1760-69), and lieutenant governor (1758-71).

Hutchinson was originally in harmony with his colleagues, even attending the Albany Congress of 1754, which projected a plan of union among the colonies. But he was deeply loyalist and resisted the gradual movement toward independence from the British crown. He was convinced that the rebellious spirit was only the work of such patriot hotheads as Samuel Adams, for whom he developed a deep enmity. Because many Bostonians considered

that he had instigated the repugnant Stamp Act of 1765, a mob sacked his splendid Boston residence that year, destroying a number of valuable documents and manuscripts. Barely escaping with his life, the embittered Hutchinson from that time on increasingly distrusted the "common sort" and secretly advised Parliament to pass repressive measures that would emphasize that body's supremacy over the colonies.

Hutchinson was acting governor at the time of the Boston Massacre in 1770; he felt impelled to administer the letter of the British law and thus became more and more unpopular. Against the advice of both houses of the legislature, in 1773 he insisted that a shipment of imported tea be landed before being given clearance papers; this resulted in the Boston Tea Party, in which dissidents dumped the import into the harbour.

As the tension worsened, Hutchinson was replaced by Gen. Thomas Gage as military governor (1774). He sailed to England and acted as an adviser to George III and to the British ministry on North American affairs; at that time he counseled moderation. He wrote *History of the Colony and Province of Massachusetts Bay*, 3 vol. (1764–1828).

ALEXANDER MCGILLIVRAY
(b. c. 1759—d. Feb. 17, 1793, Pensacola, Fla.)

Of Scots–French–Indian heritage, Alexander McGillivray became the principal chief of the Creek Indians in the years following the American Revolution. During the Revolution, he played a principal role in keeping most Creeks on the loyalist side of the conflict. He was largely responsible for the Creeks' retention of their tribal identity and the major part of their homeland for another generation.

In a letter to the Spanish commandant at Pensacola in 1783, McGillivray identified himself as "a Native of and a chief of the Creek Nation." The penmanship and the name made that statement seem improbable, but it was correct. McGillivray was, in fact, of mixed Indian and European blood. His father was Lachlan McGillivray, a Scottish trader. His mother was Sehoy Marchand, a French-Creek woman. By blood McGillivray was thus only one-quarter Indian. But the Creeks, with whom descent was matrilineal, had no difficulty in claiming McGillivray as Creek. As was the custom, his early upbringing was primarily by his mother and, though bilingual, was in the ways of her people.

At 14 McGillivray was sent to Charleston, S.C., for tutoring and served a short apprenticeship in a countinghouse in Savannah, Ga. He might have stayed on, but the American Revolution intervened. His father was proscribed as a loyalist, and his properties were confiscated. Father and son decided to go home, Lachlan to Scotland and Alexander to the Creek Nation, where he was given status as a chief and where

the British commissioned him colonel and Indian agent. During the American Revolution the Creeks were opportunists. Some of them fought alongside the Revolutionaries, while McGillivray contributed toward keeping a larger number on the loyalist side.

By 1782 British military defeats made it clear that the Creeks would lose their British connection. Deeply distrusting American land speculators and encroaching settlers, McGillivray put out feelers for Spanish support and suggested a council at Pensacola, West Florida. There, on June 1, 1784, he and governors Esteban Miró and Arturo O'Neill signed a treaty headed "Articles of Agreement, Trade, and Peace." Spain would extend a protectorate over the Creeks within Spanish territorial limits and would supply an adequate trade. McGillivray's more remarkable success was in persuading the Spanish that the trade should be in English goods and that a contract for the purpose should go to a British merchant, William Panton.

Over the next several years, McGillivray staunchly resisted overtures from Georgia and the United States to concede lands and trading privileges. On occasion he sent raiding parties to clear the Indian hunting grounds. Then, in 1788, Miró gave notice that Spanish support would be reduced. McGillivray indicated that in the circumstances he could not refuse discussions with commissioners sent by Georgia and the U.S. Congress.

In 1789 Pres. George Washington sent distinguished commissioners to negotiate with the Creeks. The commissioners proposed a boundary well into the Creek hunting lands and recognition of U.S. sovereignty over the entire Creek area. Bolstered by reactivated Spanish support, McGillivray objected. Obtaining no concession, he and his companions decamped. Washington then sent another commissioner to invite McGillivray and a delegation of chiefs to come to New York City to make a treaty "as strong as the hills and as lasting as the rivers."

With the commissioner, the delegation members traveled overland to New York City, where they were welcomed by the newly formed political Society of St. Tammany. Secretary of War Henry Knox and McGillivray worked out the terms of a treaty specifying American sovereignty over Creek lands within the limits of United States territory and setting a line near the Altamaha River separating Georgian and Creek lands. McGillivray accepted a U.S. Army commission as a brigadier general and a salary of $100 a month, but he did not promise U.S. trade except in the event of war between Britain and Spain, at the time a possibility.

In 1792 McGillivray went to New Orleans, La., to establish a better understanding with the Spanish. The new treaty specified that the Creeks would order Americans off their lands and that Spain would guarantee territorial integrity within Spanish limits and provide sufficient arms and ammunition. Although

the Spanish urged that the Americans be driven back, McGillivray wisely pursued a much less aggressive course.

En route home, McGillivray contracted a violent fever that immobilized him for months. He had never been robust and was sickly, plagued by severe headaches and afflicted by gout, rheumatism, and the symptoms of venereal disease. He died at Pensacola in his 34th year. Panton, in whose garden he was buried, attributed his death to "gout of the stomach" and "perepneumonia." Neither Panton nor the Spaniards found a suitable replacement for him, nor did his tribesmen the Creeks, though the policies he had put into effect carried on and served the Creek nation well.

Frederick North, Lord North (of Kirtling)
(b. April 13, 1732, London, Eng.— d. Aug. 5, 1792, London)

Lord North served as the prime minister of Great Britain from 1770 to 1782, and his vacillating leadership contributed to Britain's loss of its American colonies in the Revolution.

The son of a Tory nobleman, the 1st earl of Guilford, Lord North was educated at Eton and Trinity College, Oxford. Elected member of Parliament for Banbury at the age of 22, he represented the town (of which his father was high steward) for nearly 40 years. The Duke of Newcastle, when prime minister, made him a lord of the treasury in 1759, and

North held this office under the succeeding prime ministers, the earl of Bute and George Grenville, until 1765. On the fall of the Marquess of Rockingham's first ministry in 1766, North was sworn a member of the Privy Council and made paymaster general by the next prime minister, the Duke of Grafton. On the death of Charles Townshend in September 1767 North became chancellor of the exchequer.

North succeeded Grafton as prime minister in February 1770 and continued in office for 12 of the most eventful years in English history. George III had at last clinched the defeat of the Whiggish Newcastle-Rockingham connection and found in North a congenial Tory and chief minister. The path of the minister in Parliament was a hard one; he was popular and an able debater, but at times he had to defend measures which he had not designed and of which he had not approved, and this too in the House of Commons in which the oratorical ability of Edmund Burke and Charles James Fox was ranged against him.

During peacetime North's financial administration was sound, but he lacked the initiative to introduce radical fiscal reforms. The most important events of his ministry were those concerned with the American Revolution. He cannot be accused of causing it, but one of the first acts of his ministry was the retention of the tea duty, and his ministry responded to the Boston Tea Party with the Coercive Acts of 1774. Underestimating the colonists' powers of resistance, he attempted to combine severity and conciliation. He faced war halfheartedly and was easily depressed by reverses; after 1777 it was only George III's repeated entreaties not to abandon his sovereign to the mercy of the Rockingham Whigs that induced North to defend a war that at times he felt to be hopeless and impolitic. In March 1782 he insisted on resigning, after the news of Cornwallis' surrender at Yorktown made defeat in the House of Commons imminent.

North had been rewarded for his assistance to the king by honours for himself and sinecures for his relatives, but in April 1783 he formed a famous coalition with the prominent Whig Fox (much to George III's disgust) and became secretary of state with Fox under the nominal premiership of the duke of Portland. The coalition went out of office on Fox's India bill in December 1783. For about three years North continued to act with Fox in opposition, but failing eyesight then caused his retirement from politics. He succeeded to the earldom of Guilford on his father's death in 1790.

CHARLES TOWNSHEND
(b. Aug. 27, 1725—d. Sept. 4, 1767, London, Eng.)

As the British chancellor of the Exchequer, Charles Townshend introduced measures for the taxation of the American colonies that intensified the hostilities that eventually led to the American Revolution.

He was the second son of the 3rd Viscount Townshend. As a member of the Board of Trade from 1749 to 1754, he showed an interest in increasing British powers of taxation and control over the colonies. In 1754 and 1755 he served on the Board of Admiralty. He was secretary at war in 1761–62 and paymaster general from May 1765 to July 1766, when he became chancellor of the Exchequer in the ministry of William Pitt, the Elder. Soon Pitt became severely ill, and Townshend assumed effective control of the administration.

Townshend proved to be financially brilliant and determined but devoid of sound political judgment. In his last official act before his death, he obtained passage (June–July 1767) of four resolutions that threatened American colonial traditions of self-government and imposed revenue duties on a number of items necessary to the colonies. The provision that customs revenue would be used to pay officials caused concern among the colonists because it reduced the dependence of such officials on the colonial assemblies. Townshend estimated that the acts would produce the insignificant sum of £40,000 ($66,104) for the British Treasury; shrewder observers correctly prophesied that they would lead to the loss of the colonies.

AFTERMATH

The Peace of Paris (Sept. 3, 1783) ended the American Revolution. Great Britain recognized the independence of the United States (with western boundaries to the Mississippi River) and ceded Florida to Spain. Other provisions called for payment of U.S. private debts to British citizens, American use of the Newfoundland fisheries, and fair treatment for American colonials loyal to Britain.

In explaining the outcome of the war, scholars have pointed out that the British never contrived an overall general strategy for winning it. Also, even if the war could have been terminated by British power in the early stages, the generals during that period, notably Howe, declined to make a prompt, vigorous, intelligent application of that power. They acted, to be sure, within the conventions of their age, but in choosing to take minimal risks (for example, Carleton at Ticonderoga and Howe at Brooklyn Heights and later in New Jersey and Pennsylvania) they lost the opportunity to deal potentially mortal blows to the rebellion. There was also a grave lack of understanding and cooperation at crucial moments (as with Burgoyne and Howe in 1777). Finally, the British counted too strongly on loyalist support they did not receive.

But British mistakes alone could not account for the success of the United States. Feeble as their war effort occasionally became, the Americans were able generally to take advantage of their enemies' mistakes. The Continental Army, moreover, was by no means an inept force even before Steuben's reforms.

The militias, while usually unreliable, could perform admirably under the leadership of men who understood them, and often reinforced the Continentals in crises.

The militias also drew upon an American tradition of guerrilla warfare that been pioneered by Robert Rogers' Rangers during the French and Indian War. Rogers' Rangers had conducted scouting, reconnaissance, and screening missions that made it possible for the British army to know what was happening in vast ranges of American territory without having to occupy that territory with regular soldiers. The Rangers thus allowed the British to mass their regular forces on critical objectives and use minimal forces in areas of secondary importance. And the techniques and methods Rogers' Rangers learned from fighting with and against Indians in the rugged virgin forest of the New World were further developed during the Revolution.

Col. Daniel Morgan organized a ranger unit known as Morgan's Riflemen. Using highly accurate rifles instead of the smoothbore musket employed by regular infantry, Morgan's men could engage targets accurately from safe distances while remaining hidden. This capability allowed the Americans to wear down British forces on the march. Morgan's Riflemen fought

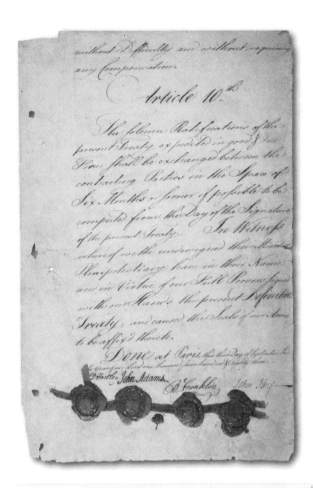

The Treaty of Paris, signed on Sept. 3, 1783, formally ended the American Revolutionary War. National Archives and Records Administration

in the Battle of Freeman's Farm in the Saratoga Campaign, in the Battle of Cowpens, and in numerous other engagements.

In the southern states, ranger-type units were organized by Francis ("Swamp Fox") Marion. Based in the

IN FOCUS: THE PEACE OF PARIS

The Peace of Paris was actually a collection of treaties signed by representatives of Great Britain on one side and the United States, France, and Spain on the other. Preliminary articles (often called the Preliminary Treaty of Paris) were signed at Paris between Britain and the United States on Nov. 30, 1782. On Sept. 3, 1783, three definitive treaties were signed—between Britain and the United States in Paris (the Treaty of Paris) and between Britain and France and Spain, respectively, at Versailles. The Netherlands and Britain also signed a preliminary treaty on Sept. 2, 1783, and a final separate peace on May 20, 1784.

By the terms of the U.S.-Britain treaty, Britain recognized the independence of the United States with generous boundaries to the Mississippi River but retained Canada. Access to the Newfoundland fisheries was guaranteed to Americans, and navigation of the Mississippi was to be open to both Great Britain and the United States. Creditors of neither country were to be impeded in the collection of their debts, and Congress was to recommend to the states that American loyalists be treated fairly and their confiscated property restored. (Some of these provisions were to cause later difficulties and disputes.)

To France, Britain surrendered Tobago and Senegal. Spain retained Minorca and East and West Florida. The Netherlands came off poorly, ceding the port city of Nagappattinam in India to Britain and allowing the British free navigation rights in the Dutch-held Moluccas.

swamps of South Carolina (which were impassable to British regulars and thus offered security), Marion's units operated in the rear of British forces, conducting raids, ambushes, and harassment. They also fought as part of Washington's army, taking part in the capture of Fort Johnson and Fort Watson, the Battle of Eutaw, and numerous other engagements.

Furthermore, Washington himself was a rock in adversity, who learned slowly but reasonably well the art of generalship. The supplies and funds furnished by France from 1776 to 1778 were invaluable, while French military and naval support after 1778 was essential. The outcome, therefore, resulted from a combination of British blunders, American efforts, and French assistance.

CHAPTER 7

THE WAR OF 1812: MAJOR CAUSES

The problem of financing and organizing the Revolutionary War sometimes overlapped with Congress's other major problem, that of defining its relations with the states. The Congress, being only an association of states, had no power to tax individuals. The Articles of Confederation, a plan of government organization adopted and put into practice by Congress in 1777, although not officially ratified by all the states until 1781, gave Congress the right to make requisitions on the states proportionate to their ability to pay. The states in turn had to raise these sums by their own domestic powers to tax, a method that state legislators looking for reelection were reluctant to employ. The result was that many states were constantly in heavy arrears, and, particularly after the urgency of the war years had subsided, the Congress's ability to meet expenses and repay its war debts was crippled.

Ultimately the Articles of Confederation provided a weak central government and proved inadequate to govern the growing nation. A new constitution was created in 1787, ratified in 1788, and took effect in 1789. George Washington was the first president, and his sober and reasoned judgments were instrumental in establishing both the tenor of the country and the precedents of the executive office. Under the new Constitution, the country began to grow almost immediately. By the Louisiana Purchase of 1803, during the administration of Thomas Jefferson, the third president (1801–09), the

United States acquired from France the entire western half of the Mississippi River basin, thereby nearly doubling the size of the national territory. The movement into the lands west of the Appalachians thenceforth became a flood.

The tensions that caused the War of 1812 arose from the French revolutionary and Napoleonic Wars (1792–1815). During this nearly constant conflict between France and Britain, American interests were injured by each of the two countries' endeavours to block the United States from trading with the other.

American shipping initially prospered from trade with the French and Spanish empires, although the British countered the U.S. claim that "free ships make free goods" with the belated enforcement of the so-called Rule of 1756 (trade not permitted in peacetime would not be allowed in wartime). The Royal Navy did enforce the act from 1793 to 1794, especially in the Caribbean Sea, before the signing of the Jay Treaty (Nov. 19, 1794). Under the primary terms of the treaty, American maritime commerce was given trading privileges in England and the British East Indies, Britain agreed to evacuate forts still held in the Northwest Territory by June 1, 1796, and the Mississippi River was declared freely open to both countries. Although the treaty was ratified by both countries, it was highly unpopular in the United States and was one of the rallying points used by the pro-French Republicans, led by Jefferson and Madison, in wresting power from the pro-British Federalists, led by George Washington and John Adams, the second president (1797–1801).

After Jefferson became president in 1801, relations with Britain slowly deteriorated, and systematic enforcement of the Rule of 1756 resumed after 1805. Compounding this troubling development, the decisive British naval victory at the Battle of Trafalgar (Oct. 21, 1805) and efforts by the British to blockade French ports prompted the French emperor, Napoleon, to cut off Britain from European and American trade. The Berlin Decree (Nov. 21, 1806) established Napoleon's Continental System, which impinged on U.S. neutral rights by designating ships that visited British ports as enemy vessels. The British responded with Orders in Council (Nov. 11, 1807) that required neutral ships to obtain licenses at English ports before trading with France or French colonies. In turn, France announced the Milan Decree (Dec. 17, 1807), which strengthened the Berlin Decree by authorizing the capture of any neutral vessel that had submitted to search by the British. Consequently, American ships that obeyed Britain faced capture by the French in European ports, and if they complied with Napoleon's Continental System, they could fall prey to the Royal Navy.

IMPRESSMENTS

The Royal Navy's use of impressment to keep its ships fully crewed also provoked Americans. Also called crimping, impressment was the enforcement of military or naval service on able-bodied but unwilling men through crude and violent methods. Until the early 19th century this practice flourished in port towns throughout the world. Generally impressment could provide effective crews only when patriotism was not an essential of military success. Impressed men were held to their duty by uncompromising and brutal discipline, although in war they seem to have fought with no less spirit and courage than those who served voluntarily. The "recruiters" preyed to a great extent upon men from the lower classes who were, more often than not, vagabonds or even prisoners. Sources of supply were waterfront boardinghouses, brothels, and taverns whose owners victimized their own clientele. In the early 19th century the Royal Navy would halt U.S. vessels to search for British deserters and in the process would not infrequently impress naturalized American citizens who were on board. In 1807 the frigate H.M.S. *Leopard* fired on the U.S. Navy frigate *Chesapeake* and seized four sailors, three of them U.S. citizens. London eventually apologized for this incident, but it came close to causing war at the time. Jefferson, however, chose to exert economic pressure against Britain and France by pushing Congress in December 1807 to pass the Embargo Act, which forbade all export shipping from U.S. ports and most imports from Britain.

The results were catastrophic for American commerce and produced bitter alienation in New England, where the embargo (ridiculed in a famous cartoon of the day with the backwards spelling "O grab me") was held to be a Southern plot to destroy New England's wealth. Indeed, the Embargo Act hurt Americans more than the British or French, and many Americans simply chose to defy it. Just before Jefferson left office in 1809, Congress replaced the Embargo Act with

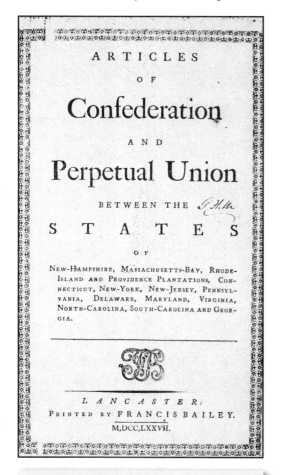

The Articles of Confederation served as the first constitution of the 13 United States of America. MPI/Hulton Archive/ Getty Images

IN FOCUS: THE JAY TREATY

Signed on Nov. 19, 1794, the Jay Treaty assuaged antagonisms between the United States and Great Britain, established a base upon which America could build a sound national economy, and assured its commercial prosperity.

Negotiations were undertaken because of the fears of Federalist leaders that disputes with Great Britain would lead to war. In the treaty Britain, conceding to primary American grievances, agreed to evacuate the Northwest Territory by June 1, 1796; to compensate for its depredations against American shipping; to end discrimination against American commerce; and to grant the United States. trading privileges in England and the British East Indies. Signed in London by Lord Grenville, the British foreign minister, and John Jay, U.S. chief justice and envoy extraordinary, the treaty also declared the Mississippi River open to both countries; prohibited the outfitting of privateers by Britain's enemies in U.S. ports; provided for payment of debts incurred by Americans to British merchants before the American Revolution; and established joint commissions to determine the boundaries between the United States and British North America in the Northwest and Northeast.

By February 1796 the treaty, with the exception of an article dealing with West Indian trade, had been ratified by the United States and Great Britain. France, then at war with England, interpreted the treaty as a violation of its own commercial treaty of 1778 with the United States. This resentment led to French maritime attacks on the United States and between 1798 and 1800 to an undeclared naval war. Finally, the commissions provided for by the Jay Treaty gave such an impetus to the principle of arbitration that modern international arbitration has been generally dated from the treaty's ratification.

John Jay, the first chief justice of the United States. Library of Congress Prints and Photographs Division

the Non-Intercourse Act, which exclusively forbade trade with Great Britain and France. This measure also proved ineffective, and it was replaced by Macon's Bill No. 2 (May 1, 1810) that resumed trade with all nations but stipulated that if either Britain or France dropped commercial restrictions, the United States would revive nonintercourse against the other. In August, Napoleon insinuated that he would exempt American shipping from the Berlin and Milan decrees. Although the British demonstrated that French restrictions continued, the new American president, Pres. James Madison, reinstated nonintercourse against Britain in November 1810, thereby moving one step closer to war.

Britain's refusal to yield on neutral rights derived from more than the emergency of the European war. British manufacturing and shipping interests demanded that the Royal Navy promote and sustain British trade against Yankee competitors. The policy born of that attitude convinced many Americans that they were being consigned to a de facto colonial status. Britons, on the other hand, denounced American actions that effectively made the United States a participant in Napoleon's Continental System.

Events on the U.S. northwestern frontier fostered additional friction. Indian fears over American encroachment coincidentally became conspicuous as Anglo-American tensions grew. Shawnee brothers Tecumseh and Tenskwatawa (The Prophet) attracted followers arising from this discontent and attempted to form an Indian confederation to counteract American expansion. Although Maj. Gen. Isaac Brock, the British commander of Upper Canada (modern Ontario), had orders to avoid worsening American frontier problems, American settlers blamed British intrigue for heightened tensions with Indians in the Northwest Territory. As war loomed, Brock sought to augment his meagre regular and Canadian militia forces with Indian allies, which was enough to confirm the worst fears of American settlers. Brock's efforts were aided in the fall of 1811, when Indiana territorial governor William Henry Harrison fought the Battle of Tippecanoe and destroyed the Indian settlement at Prophet's Town (near modern Battle Ground, Ind.). Harrison's foray convinced most Indians in the Northwest Territory that their only hope of stemming further encroachments by American settlers lay with the British. American settlers, in turn, believed that Britain's removal from Canada would end their Indian problems. Meanwhile, Canadians suspected that American expansionists were using Indian unrest as an excuse for a war of conquest.

Under increasing pressure, Madison summoned the U.S. Congress into session in November 1811. Pro-war western and southern Republicans (War Hawks) assumed a vocal role, especially after Kentucky War Hawk Henry Clay was elected speaker of the House of Representatives. Madison sent a war message to the U.S. Congress on June 1, 1812, and signed the declaration of war on June 18, 1812. The vote seriously divided the House (79–49) and was gravely close in the Senate (19–13). Because seafaring New Englanders opposed the war, while westerners and southerners supported it, Federalists accused war advocates of expansionism under the ruse of protecting American maritime rights. Expansionism, however, was not as much a motive as was the desire to defend American honour. The United States attacked Canada because it was British, but no widespread aspiration existed to incorporate the region. The prospect of taking East and West Florida from Spain encouraged southern support for the war, but southerners, like westerners, were sensitive about the United States's reputation in the world. Furthermore, British commercial restrictions hurt American farmers by barring their produce from Europe. Regions seemingly removed from maritime concerns held a material interest in protecting neutral shipping. "Free trade and sailors' rights" was not an empty phrase for those Americans.

The onset of war both surprised and chagrined the British government, especially because it was preoccupied with the fight against France. In addition, political changes in Britain had already moved the government to assume a conciliatory posture toward the United States. Prime Minister Spencer Perceval's assassination on May 11, 1812, brought to power a more moderate Tory government under Lord Liverpool. British West Indies planters had been complaining for years about the interdiction of U.S. trade, and their growing influence, along with a deepening recession in Great Britain, convinced the Liverpool ministry that the Orders in Council were averse to British interests. On June 16, two days before the United States declared war, the Orders were suspended.

Some have viewed the timing of this concession as a lost opportunity for peace because slow transatlantic communication meant a month's delay in delivering the news to Washington. Yet, because Britain's impressment policy remained in place and frontier Indian wars continued, in all likelihood the repeal of the Orders alone would not have prevented war.

CHAPTER 8

THE WAR OF 1812: AN OVERVIEW

Neither the British in Canada nor the United States were prepared for war. Americans were inordinately optimistic in 1812. William Eustis, the U.S. secretary of war, stated, "We can take the Canadas without soldiers, we have only to send officers into the province and the people . . . will rally round our standard." Henry Clay said that "the militia of Kentucky are alone competent to place Montreal and Upper Canada at your feet." And Thomas Jefferson famously wrote

> *The acquisition of Canada this year, as far as the neighborhood of Quebec, will be a mere matter of marching, and will give us experience for the attack of Halifax the next, and the final expulsion of England from the American continent.*

The British government, preoccupied with the European conflict, saw American hostilities as a bothersome distraction, resulting in a paucity of resources in men, supplies, and naval presence until late in the event. As the British in Canada conducted operations under the shadow of scarcity, their only consolation was an American military malaise. Michigan territorial governor William Hull led U.S. forces into Canada from Detroit, but Isaac Brock and Tecumseh's warriors chased Hull back across the border and frightened him into surrendering Detroit on Aug. 16, 1812, without firing a shot—behaviour that Americans and even Brock's officers found disgraceful.

The Northwest subsequently fell prey to Indian raids and British incursions led by Maj. Gen. Henry Procter. Hull's replacement, William Henry Harrison, could barely defend a few scattered outposts. On the northeastern border, U.S. Brig. Gen. Henry Dearborn could not attack Montreal because of uncooperative New England militias. U.S. forces under Stephen Van Rensselaer crossed the Niagara River to attack Queenston on Oct. 13, 1812, but ultimately were defeated by a stiff British defense organized by Brock, who was killed during the fight. U.S. Gen. Alexander Smyth's subsequent invasion attempts on the Niagara were abortive fiascoes.

In 1813, Madison replaced Dearborn with Maj. Gens. James Wilkinson and Wade Hampton, an awkward arrangement made worse by a complicated invasion plan against Montreal. The generals refused to coordinate their efforts, and neither came close to Montreal. To the west, however, American Oliver Hazard Perry's Lake Erie squadron won a great victory off Put-in-Bay on Sept. 10, 1813, against Capt. Robert Barclay. The battle opened the way for Harrison to retake Detroit and defeat Procter's British and Indian forces at the Battle of the Thames (Oct. 5). Tecumseh was killed during the battle, shattering his confederation and the Anglo-Indian alliance. Indian anger continued elsewhere, however, especially in the southeast where the Creek War erupted in 1813 between Creek Indian nativists (known as Red Sticks) and U.S. forces. The war also took an ugly turn late in the year, when U.S. forces evacuating the Niagara Peninsula razed the Canadian village of Newark, prompting the British commander, Gordon Drummond, to retaliate along the New York frontier, leaving communities such as Buffalo in smoldering ruins.

Early in the war, the small U.S. navy boosted sagging American morale as officers such as Isaac Hull, Stephen Decatur, and William Bainbridge commanded heavy frigates in impressive single-ship actions. The British Admiralty responded by instructing captains to avoid individual contests with Americans, and within a year the Royal Navy had blockaded important American ports, bottling up U.S. frigates. British Adm. George Cockburn also conducted raids on the shores of Chesapeake Bay. In 1814, Britain extended its blockade from New England to Georgia, and forces under John Sherbrooke occupied parts of Maine.

By 1814, capable American officers, such as Jacob Brown, Winfield Scott, and Andrew Jackson, had replaced ineffective veterans from the American Revolution. On March 27, 1814, Jackson defeated the Red Stick Creeks at the Battle of Horseshoe Bend in Alabama, ending the Creek War. That spring, after Brown crossed the Niagara River and took Fort Erie, Brig. Gen. Phineas Riall advanced to challenge the American invasion, but American regulars commanded by Scott repulsed him at the Battle of Chippewa (July 5, 1814). In turn, Brown retreated when Cdre Isaac Chauncey's Lake Ontario squadron failed to rendezvous

PRIMARY SOURCE: JAMES MADISON'S WAR MESSAGE

It is one of the perversities of American history that while Pres. James Madison's message to Congress urging the commencement of hostilities against Great Britain in 1812 listed only maritime grievances as the cause and said nothing about expansionist aims in the Ohio Valley, the Treaty of Ghent, which in 1814 ended the war, dealt only with those expansionist aims and said nothing about maritime grievances. But this was only one of many contradictions in a conflict that began in confusion and unreadiness, was fought amid disagreements that all but tore the country to pieces, and then ended in triumph. What Madison really did was take a long chance. Bedeviled by a tangle of diplomatic and political problems he could not otherwise solve, and largely unprepared for war, he later admitted that he had "thrown forward the flag of the country, sure that the people would press forward." The president gave the following message to Congress on June 1, 1812. Source: A Compilation of the Messages and Papers of the Presidents 1789–1897, James D. Richardson, ed., Washington, 1896–1899, Vol. I, pp. 499–505.

I communicate to Congress certain documents, being a continuation of those heretofore laid before them on the subject of our affairs with Great Britain. Without going back beyond the renewal in 1803 of the war in which Great Britain is engaged, and omitting unrepaired wrongs of inferior magnitude, the conduct of her government presents a series of acts hostile to the United States as an independent and neutral nation.

British cruisers have been in the continued practice of violating the American flag on the great highway of nations, and of seizing and carrying off persons sailing under it, not in the exercise of a belligerent right founded on the law of nations against an enemy but of a municipal prerogative over British subjects. British jurisdiction is thus extended to neutral vessels in a situation where no laws can operate but the law of nations and the laws of the country to which the vessels belong; and a self-redress is assumed which, if British subjects were wrongfully detained and alone concerned, is that substitution of force for a resort to the responsible sovereign which falls within the definition of war. Could the seizure of British subjects in such cases be regarded as within the exercise of a belligerent right, the acknowledged laws of war, which forbid an article of captured property to be adjudged without a regular investigation before a competent tribunal, would imperiously demand the fairest trial where the sacred rights of persons were at issue. In place of such a trial, these rights are subjected to the will of every petty commander.

The practice, hence, is so far from affecting British subjects alone that, under the pretext of searching for these, thousands of American citizens, under the safeguard of public law and of their national flag, have been torn from their country and from everything dear to them; have been dragged on board ships of war of a foreign nation and exposed, under the severities of their discipline, to be exiled to the most distant and deadly climes, to risk their lives in the battles of their oppressors, and to be the melancholy instruments of taking away those of their own brethren.

Against this crying enormity, which Great Britain would be so prompt to avenge if committed against herself, the United States have in vain exhausted remonstrances and expostulations; and that no proof might be wanting of their conciliatory dispositions, and no pretext left for a continuance of the practice, the British government was formally assured of the readiness of the United States to enter into arrangements such as could not be rejected if the recovery of British subjects were the real and the sole object. The communication passed without effect.

British cruisers have been in the practice, also, of violating the rights and the peace of our coasts. They hover over and harass our entering and departing commerce. To the most insulting pretensions they have added the most lawless proceedings in our very harbors, and have wantonly spilled American blood within the sanctuary of our territorial

In this artist's interpretation of Britain's naval losses early in the War of 1812, a bloodied King George III stands to the left of his victorious opponent, Pres. James Madison. The John Bull referred to in the caption represents the personification of England. Library of Congress Prints and Photographs Division

jurisdiction. The principles and rules enforced by that nation, when a neutral nation, against armed vessels of belligerents hovering near her coasts and disturbing her commerce are well known. When called on, nevertheless, by the United States to punish the greater offenses committed by her own vessels, her government has bestowed on their commanders additional marks of honor and confidence.

Under pretended blockades, without the presence of an adequate force and sometimes without the practicability of applying one, our commerce has been plundered in every sea, the great staples of our country have been cut off from their legitimate markets, and a destructive blow aimed at our agricultural and maritime interests. In aggravation of these predatory measures, they have been considered as in force from the dates of their notification, a retrospective effect being thus added, as has been done in other important cases, to the unlawfulness of the course pursued. And to render the outrage the more signal, these mock blockades have been reiterated and enforced in the face of official communications from the British government declaring as the true definition of a legal blockade "that particular ports must be actually invested and previous warning given to vessels bound to them not to enter."

Not content with these occasional expedients for laying waste our neutral trade, the cabinet of Britain resorted at length to the sweeping system of blockades, under the name of orders in council, which has been molded and managed as might best suit its political views, its commercial jealousies, or the avidity of British cruisers.

To our remonstrances against the complicated and transcendent injustice of this innovation, the first reply was that the orders were reluctantly adopted by Great Britain as a necessary retaliation on decrees of her enemy proclaiming a general blockade of the British Isles at a time when the naval force of that enemy dared not issue from his own ports. She was reminded, without effect, that her own prior blockades, unsupported by an adequate naval force actually applied and continued, were a bar to this plea; that executed edicts against millions of our property could not be retaliation on edicts confessedly impossible to be executed; that retaliation, to be just, should fall on the party setting the guilty example, not on an innocent party which was not even chargeable with an acquiescence in it.

When deprived of this flimsy veil for a prohibition of our trade with her enemy by the repeal of his prohibition of our trade with Great Britain, her cabinet, instead of a corresponding repeal or a practical discontinuance of its orders, formally avowed a determination to persist in them against the United States until the markets of her enemy should be laid open to British products; thus asserting an obligation on a neutral power to require one belligerent to encourage, by its internal regulations, the trade of another belligerent, contradicting her own practice toward all nations, in peace as well as in war, and betraying the insincerity of those professions which inculcated a belief that, having resorted to her orders with regret, she was anxious to find an occasion for putting an end to them.

Abandoning still more all respect for the neutral rights of the United States and for its own consistency, the British government now demands, as prerequisites to a repeal of its orders as they relate to the United States, that a formality should be observed in the repeal of the French decrees, nowise necessary to their termination nor exemplified by British usage, and that the French repeal, besides including that portion of the decrees which operates within a territorial jurisdiction as well as that which operates on the high seas against the commerce of the United States should not be a single and special repeal in relation to the United States but should be extended to whatever other neutral nations unconnected with them may be affected by those decrees. And as an additional insult, they are called on for a formal disavowal of conditions and pretensions advanced by the French government, for which the United States are, so far from having made themselves responsible that, in official explanations which have been published to the world and in a correspondence of the American minister at London with the British minister for foreign affairs, such a responsibility was explicitly and emphatically disclaimed.

It has become, indeed, sufficiently certain that the commerce of the United States is to be sacrificed, not as interfering with the belligerent rights of Great Britain; not as supplying the wants of her enemies, which she herself supplies; but as interfering with the monopoly which she covets for her own commerce and navigation. She carries on a war against the lawful commerce of a friend that she may the better carry on a commerce with an enemy — a commerce polluted by the forgeries and perjuries which are for the most part the only passports by which it can succeed.

Anxious to make every experiment short of the last resort of injured nations, the United States have withheld from Great Britain, under successive modifications, the benefits of a free intercourse with their market, the loss of which could not but outweigh the profits accruing from her restrictions of our commerce with other nations. And to entitle these experiments to the more favorable consideration, they were so framed as to enable her to place her adversary under the exclusive operation of them. To these appeals her government has been equally inflexible, as if willing to make sacrifices of every sort rather than yield to the claims of justice or renounce the errors of a false pride. Nay, so far were the attempts carried to overcome the attachment of the British cabinet to its unjust edicts that it received every encouragement within the competency of the executive branch of our government to expect that a repeal of them would be followed by a war between the United States and France, unless the French edicts should also be repealed. Even this communication, although silencing forever the plea of a disposition in the United States to acquiesce in those edicts originally the sole plea for them, received no attention.

If no other proof existed of a predetermination of the British government against a repeal of its orders, it might be found in the correspondence of the minister plenipotentiary of the United States at London and the British secretary for foreign affairs, in 1810, on the question whether the blockade of May 1806 was considered as in force or as not in force. It had been ascertained that the French government, which urged this blockade as the ground of its Berlin Decree, was willing, in the event of its removal, to repeal that decree, which, being followed by alternate repeals of the other offensive edicts, might abolish the whole system on both sides.

This inviting opportunity for accomplishing an object so important to the United States, and professed so often to be the desire of both the belligerents, was made known to the British government. As that government admits that an actual application of an adequate force is necessary to the existence of a legal blockade, and it was notorious that if such a force had ever been applied its long discontinuance had annulled the blockade in question, there could be no sufficient objection on the part of Great Britain to a formal revocation of it, and no imaginable objection to a declaration of the fact that the blockade did not exist. The declaration would have been consistent with her avowed principles of blockade, and would have enabled the United States to demand from France the pledged repeal of her decrees, either with success; in which case the way would have been opened for a general repeal of the belligerent edicts; or without success, in which case the United States would have been justified in turning their measures exclusively against France.

The British government would, however, neither rescind the blockade nor declare its nonexistence, nor permit its nonexistence to be inferred and affirmed by the American plenipotentiary. On the contrary, by representing the blockade to be comprehended in the orders in council, the United States were compelled so to regard it in their subsequent proceedings.

There was a period when a favorable change in the policy of the British cabinet was justly considered as established. The minister plenipotentiary of His Britannic Majesty here proposed an adjustment of the differences more immediately endangering the harmony of the two countries. The proposition was accepted with the promptitude and cordiality corresponding with the invariable professions of this government. A foundation appeared to be laid for a sincere and lasting reconciliation. The prospect, however, quickly vanished. The whole proceeding was disavowed by the British government without any explanations which could at that time repress the belief that the disavowal proceeded from a spirit of hostility to the commercial rights and prosperity of the United States; and it has since come into proof that at the very moment when the public minister was holding the language of friendship and inspiring confidence in the sincerity of the negotiation with which he was charged, a secret agent of his government was employed in intrigues having for their object a subversion of our government and a dismemberment of our happy Union.

In reviewing the conduct of Great Britain toward the United States, our attention is necessarily drawn to the warfare just renewed by the savages on one of our extensive frontiers — a warfare which is known to spare neither age nor sex and to be distinguished by features peculiarly shocking to humanity. It is difficult to account for the activity and combinations which have for some time been developing themselves among tribes in constant intercourse with British traders and garrisons, without connecting their hostility with that influence and without recollecting the authenticated examples of such interpositions heretofore furnished by the officers and agents of that government.

Such is the spectacle of injuries and indignities which have been heaped on our country, and such the crisis which its unexampled forbearance and conciliatory efforts have not been able to avert. It might at least have been expected that an enlightened nation, if less urged by moral obligations or invited by friendly dispositions on the part of the United States, would have found in its true interest alone a sufficient motive to respect their rights and their tranquillity on the high seas; that an enlarged policy would have favored that free and general circulation of commerce in which the British nation is at all times interested, and which in times of war is the best alleviation of its calamities to herself as well as to other belligerents; and more especially that the British cabinet would not, for the sake of a precarious and surreptitious intercourse with hostile markets, have persevered in a course of measures which necessarily put at hazard the invaluable market of a great and growing country, disposed to cultivate the mutual advantages of an active commerce.

Other counsels have prevailed. Our moderation and conciliation have had no other effect than to encourage perseverance and to enlarge pretensions. We behold our seafaring citizens still the daily victims of lawless violence, committed on the great common and highway of nations, even within sight of the country which owes them protection. We behold our vessels, freighted with the products of our soil and industry, or returning with the honest proceeds of them, wrested from their lawful destinations, confiscated by prize courts no longer the organs of public law but the instruments of arbitrary edicts, and their unfortunate crews dispersed and lost, or forced or inveigled in British ports into British fleets, whilst arguments are employed in support of these aggressions which have no foundation but in a principle, equally supporting a claim to regulate our external commerce in all cases whatsoever.

We behold, in fine, on the side of Great Britain, a state of war against the United States, and, on the side of the United States, a state of peace toward Great Britain.

Whether the United States shall continue passive under these progressive usurpations and these accumulating wrongs, or, opposing force to force in defense of their national rights, shall commit a just cause into the hands of the Almighty Disposer of Events, avoiding all connections which might entangle it in the contest or views of other powers, and preserving a constant readiness to concur in an honorable reestablishment of peace and friendship, is a solemn question which the Constitution wisely confides to the Legislative Department of the government. In recommending it to their early deliberations, I am happy in the assurance that the decision will be worthy the enlightened and patriotic councils of a virtuous, a free, and a powerful nation.

Having presented this view of the relations of the United States with Great Britain and of the solemn alternative growing out of them, I proceed to remark that the communications last made to Congress on the subject of our relations with France will have shown that since the revocation of her decrees, as they violated the neutral rights of the United States, her government has authorized illegal captures by its privateers and public ships, and that other outrages have been practised on our vessels and our citizens. It will have been seen, also, that no indemnity had been provided or satisfactorily pledged for the extensive spoliations committed under the violent and retrospective orders of the French government against the property of our citizens seized within the jurisdiction of France. I abstain at this time from recommending to the consideration of Congress definitive measures with respect to that nation, in the expectation that the result of unclosed discussions between our minister plenipotentiary at Paris and the French government will speedily enable Congress to decide with greater advantage on the course due to the rights, the interests, and the honor of our country.

with the army, and during this retrograde the war's costliest engagement occurred at the Battle of Lundy's Lane (July 25). Riall, reinforced by Drummond, fought the Americans to a bloody stalemate in which each side suffered more than 800 casualties before Brown's army withdrew to Fort Erie.

U.S. frigate United States *capturing the British frigate* Macedonian, *Oct. 25, 1812. Colour lithograph by Currier & Ives.* Currier & Ives/Library of Congress, Washington, D.C. (neg. no. LC-USZC2-3120)

THE CONTINUING STRUGGLE

In 1814, Napoleon's defeat allowed sizable British forces to come to America. That summer, veterans under Canadian Governor-general George Prevost marched south along the shores of Lake Champlain into New York, but they returned to Canada after Thomas Macdonough defeated a British squadron under Capt. George Downie at the Battle of Plattsburgh Bay, N.Y. (Sept. 11, 1814). British raids in Chesapeake Bay directed by Adm. Alexander Cochrane were more successful.

On August 24 British troops under the command of Gen. Robert Ross advanced from their landing on the Patuxent River in Maryland and were engaged at Bladensburg by American forces made

IN FOCUS: THE CREEK WAR

An ancillary conflict of the War of 1812, the Creek War (1813–14) was fought between the United States and the Creek Indians, who were allies of the British. The Shawnee leader Tecumseh, who expected British help in recovering hunting grounds lost to settlers, traveled to the south to warn of dangers to native cultures posed by whites. Factions arose among the Creeks, and a group known as the Red Sticks preyed upon white settlements and fought with those Creeks who opposed them. On Aug. 30, 1813, when the Red Sticks swept down upon 553 surprised frontiersmen at a crude fortification at Lake Tensaw, north of Mobile (now in Alabama) the resulting Fort Mims Massacre stirred the Southern states into a vigorous response. The main army of 5,000 militiamen was

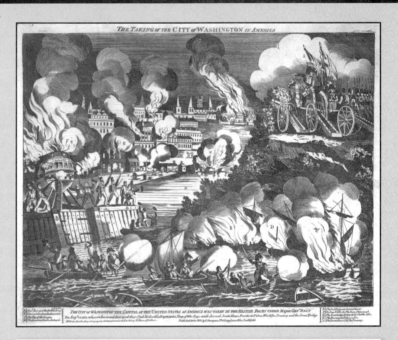

G. Thompson's wood engraving of The Burning of the City of Washington *during the War of 1812. At about 8 PM on the evening of Aug. 24, 1814, British troops under the command of Gen. Robert Ross marched into Washington, D.C., after routing hastily assembled American forces at Bladensburg, Md., earlier in the day. Encountering neither resistance nor any U.S. government officials—President Madison and his cabinet had fled to safety—the British quickly torched government buildings, including the Capitol and the Executive Mansion (now known as the White House).* Library of Congress, Washington, D.C. (neg. no. LC-USZ62-1939)

led by Gen. Andrew Jackson, who succeeded in wiping out two Indian villages that fall: Talla-sahatchee and Talladega.

The following spring hundreds of Creeks gathered at what seemed an impenetrable village fortress on a peninsula on the Tallapoosa River, awaiting the Americans' attack. On March 27, 1814, at the Battle of Horseshoe Bend (Tohopeka, Ala.), Jackson's superior numbers (3,000 to 1,000) and armaments (including cannon) demolished the Creek defenses, slaughtering more than 800 warriors and imprisoning 500 women and children. The power of the Indians of the Old Southwest was broken.

At the Treaty of Fort Jackson (August 9) the Creeks were required to cede 23,000,000 acres of land, comprising more than half of Alabama and part of southern Georgia. Much of that territory belonged to Indians who had earlier been Jackson's allies.

up primarily of militiamen under the command of Gen. William Winder. Prior to the battle the American troops received unauthorized orders to redeploy from Secretary of State (later Pres.) James Monroe, who was on the scene and who had served as a cavalry officer during the Revolution. In relatively short order, the American defense collapsed, the Battle of Bladensburg was over, and the British continued on to capture Washington (August 24) and burn government buildings, including the United States Capitol and the Executive Mansion (now known as the White House). The British justified this action as retaliation for the American destruction of York (modern Toronto), the capital of Upper Canada, the previous year. The British assault on Baltimore (September 12–14) foundered when Americans fended off an attack at Northpoint and withstood the naval bombardment of Fort McHenry, an action that inspired Francis Scott Key's "Star-Spangled Banner." Ross was killed at Baltimore, and

the British left Chesapeake Bay to plan an offensive against New Orleans.

Immediately after the war started, the tsar of Russia offered to mediate. London refused, but early British efforts for an armistice revealed a willingness to negotiate so that Britain could turn its full attention to Napoleon. Talks began at Ghent (in modern Belgium) in August 1814, but, with France defeated, the British stalled while waiting for news of a decisive victory in America. Most Britons were angry that the United States had become an unwitting ally of Napoleon, but even that sentiment was half-hearted among a people who had been at war in Europe for more than 20 years. Consequently, after learning of Plattsburgh and Baltimore and upon the advice of the Duke of Wellington, commander of the British army at the Battle of Waterloo, the British government moved to make peace. Americans abandoned demands about ending impressment (the end of the European war meant its cessation anyway), and

PRIMARY SOURCE: HARTFORD CONVENTION RESOLUTIONS

Dissatisfied with the progress of the war with England, and long resentful over the balance of political power that gave the South, and particularly Virginia, effective control of the national government, federalist delegates from Connecticut, Rhode Island, Massachusetts, New Hampshire, and Vermont called a secret convention at Hartford in the winter of 1814. The more extreme among them were for considering secession, but others sought only to dictate amendments to the Constitution that would protect their interests. The latter course was decided upon, and the proposed amendments, along with some stringent criticisms of Pres. James Madison's administration, were agreed to by the convention on Jan. 4, 1815. The secrecy of the Hartford proceedings, however, discredited the convention and its work, and prompted other parts of the country to question New England's patriotism and Federalist loyalty. Indeed, its unpopularity was a factor in the ultimate demise of the Federalist Party. Source: Theodore Dwight, History of the Hartford Convention, etc., etc., *New York, 1833, pp. 352–379.*

If the Union be destined to dissolution by reason of the multiplied abuses of bad administrations, it should, if possible, be the work of peaceable times and deliberate consent. Some new form of confederacy should be substituted among those states which shall intend to maintain a federal relation to each other. Events may prove that the causes of our calamities are deep and permanent. They may be found to proceed, not merely from the blindness of prejudice, pride of opinion, violence of party spirit, or the confusion of the times but they may be traced to implacable combinations of individuals, or of states, to monopolize power and office, and to trample without remorse upon the rights and interests of commercial sections of the Union. Whenever it shall appear that these causes are radical and permanent, a separation, by equitable arrangement, will be preferable to an alliance by constraint, among nominal friends but real enemies, inflamed by mutual hatred and jealousy, and inviting, by intestine divisions, contempt and aggression from abroad.

But a severance of the Union by one or more states, against the will of the rest, and especially in a time of war, can be justified only by absolute necessity. These are among the principal objections against precipitate measures tending to disunite the states; and when examined in connection with the farewell address of the father of his country, they must, it is believed, be deemed conclusive.

Under these impressions, the Convention have proceeded to confer and deliberate upon the alarming state of public affairs, especially as affecting the interests of the people who have appointed them for this purpose. And they are naturally led to a consideration, in the first place, of the dangers and grievances which menace an immediate or speedy pressure, with a view of suggesting means of present relief; in the next place, of such as are of a more remote and general description, in the hope of attaining future security...

In the catalogue of blessings which have fallen to the lot of the most favored nations, none could be enumerated from which our country was excluded— a free Constitution, administered by great and incorruptible statesmen, realized the fondest hopes of liberty and independence; the progress of agriculture was stimulated by the certainty of value in the harvest; and commerce, after traversing every sea, returned with the riches of every clime. A revenue, secured by a sense of honor, collected without oppression, and paid without murmurs, melted away the national debt; and the chief concern of the public creditor arose from its too rapid diminution. The wars and commotions of the European nations and their interruptions of the commercial intercourse afforded to those who had not promoted but who would have rejoiced to alleviate their calamities, a fair and golden opportunity, by combining themselves to lay a broad foundation for national wealth. Although occasional vexations to commerce arose from the furious collisions of the powers at war, yet the great and good men of that time conformed to the force of circumstances which they could not control, and preserved their country in security from the tempests which overwhelmed the Old World, and threw the wreck of their fortunes on these shores.

Respect abroad, prosperity at home, wise laws made by honored legislators, and prompt obedience yielded by a contented people had silenced the enemies of republican institutions. The arts flourished; the sciences were cultivated; the comforts and conveniences of life were universally diffused; and nothing remained for succeeding administrations but to reap the advantages and cherish the resources flowing from the policy of their predecessors.

But no sooner was a new administration established in the hands of the party opposed to the Washington policy than a fixed determination was perceived and avowed of changing a system which had already produced these substantial fruits. The consequences of this change, for a few years after its commencement, were not sufficient to counteract the prodigious impulse toward prosperity which had been given to the nation. But a steady perseverance in the new plans of administration at length developed their weakness and deformity, but not until a majority of the people had been deceived by flattery, and inflamed by passion, into blindness to their defects. Under the withering influence of this new system, the declension of the nation has been uniform and rapid. The richest advantages for securing the great objects of the Constitution have been wantonly rejected. While Europe reposes from the convulsions that had shaken down her ancient institutions, she beholds with amazement this remote country, once so happy and so envied, involved in a ruinous war and excluded from intercourse with the rest of the world.

To investigate and explain the means whereby this fatal reverse has been effected would require a voluminous discussion. Nothing more can be attempted in this report than a general allusion to the principal outlines of the policy which has produced this vicissitude. Among these may be enumerated:

First, a deliberate and extensive system for effecting a combination among certain states, by exciting local jealousies and ambition, so as to secure to popular leaders in one section of the Union the control of public affairs in perpetual succession; to which primary object most other characteristics of the system may be reconciled.

Second, the political intolerance displayed and avowed in excluding from office men of unexceptable merit for want of adherence to the executive creed.

Third, the infraction of the judiciary authority and rights by depriving judges of their offices in violation of the Constitution.

Fourth, the abolition of existing taxes, requisite to prepare the country for those changes to which nations are always exposed, with a view to the acquisition of popular favor.

Fifth, the influence of patronage in the distribution of offices, which in these states has been almost invariably made among men the least entitled to such distinction, and who have sold themselves as ready instruments for distracting public opinion, and encouraging administration to hold in contempt the wishes and remonstrances of a people thus apparently divided.

Sixth, the admission of new states into the Union, formed at pleasure in the Western region, has destroyed the balance of power which existed among the original states and deeply affected their interest.

Seventh, the easy admission of naturalized foreigners to places of trust, honor, or profit, operating as an inducement to the malcontent subjects of the Old World to come to these states in quest of executive patronage, and to repay it by an abject devotion to executive measures.

Eighth, hostility to Great Britain and partiality to the late government of France, adopted as coincident with popular prejudice and subservient to the main object, party power. Connected with these must be ranked erroneous and distorted estimates of the power and resources of those nations, of the probable results of their controversies, and of our political relations to them respectively.

Last and principally, a visionary and superficial theory in regard to commerce, accompanied by a real hatred but a feigned regard to its interests, and a ruinous perseverance in efforts to render it an instrument of coercion and war.

But it is not conceivable that the obliquity of any administration could, in so short a period, have so nearly consummated the work of national ruin, unless favored by defects in the Constitution. . . .

Therefore resolved: that it be and hereby is recommended to the legislatures of the several states represented in this Convention to adopt all such measures as may be necessary, effectually, to protect the citizens of said states from the operation and effects of all acts which have been or may be passed by the Congress of the United States which shall contain provisions subjecting the militia or other citizens to forcible drafts, conscriptions, or impressments not authorized by the Constitution of the United States.

Resolved, that it be, and hereby is, recommended to the said legislatures to authorize an immediate and earnest application to be made to the government of the United States requesting their consent to some arrangement whereby the said states may, separately or in concert, be empowered to assume upon themselves the defense of their territory against the enemy; and a reasonable portion of the taxes collected within said states may be paid into the respective treasuries thereof, and appropriated to the payment of the balance due said states, and to the future defense of the same. The amount so paid into the said treasuries to be credited, and the disbursements made as aforesaid to be charged to the United States.

Resolved, that it be, and hereby is, recommended to the legislatures of the aforesaid states to pass laws (where it has not already been done) authorizing the governors or commanders in chief of their militia to make detachments from the same, or to form voluntary corps, as shall be most convenient and conformable to their constitutions, and to cause the same to be well armed, equipped, and disciplined, and held in readiness for service; and, upon the request of the governor of either of the other states, to employ the whole of such detachment or corps, as well as the regular forces of the state, or such part thereof as may be required and can be spared consistently with the safety of the state, in assisting the state making such request to repel any invasion thereof which shall be made or attempted by the public enemy.

Resolved, that the following amendments of the Constitution of the United States be recommended to the states represented as aforesaid, to be proposed by them for adoption by the state legislatures, and, in such cases as may be deemed expedient, by a convention chosen by the people of each state.

And it is further recommended that the said states shall persevere in their efforts to obtain such amendments until the same shall be effected.

First, representatives and direct taxes shall be apportioned among the several states which may be included within this Union according to their respective numbers of free persons, including those bound to serve for a term of years, and excluding Indians not taxed and all other persons.

Second, no new state shall be admitted into the Union by Congress, in virtue of the power granted by the Constitution, without the concurrence of two-thirds of both houses.

Third, Congress shall not have power to lay any embargo on the ships or vessels of the citizens of the United States, in the ports or harbors thereof, for more than sixty days.

Fourth, Congress shall not have power, without the concurrence of two-thirds of both houses, to interdict the commercial intercourse between the United States and any foreign nation or the dependencies thereof.

Fifth, Congress shall not make or declare war, or authorize acts of hostility against any foreign nation, without the concurrence of two-thirds of both houses, except such acts of hostility be in defense of the territories of the United States when actually invaded.

Sixth, no person who shall hereafter be naturalized shall be eligible as a member of the Senate or House of Representatives of the United States, nor capable of holding any civil office under the authority of the United States.

Seventh, the same person shall not be elected President of the United States a second time; nor shall the President be elected from the same state two terms in succession.

Resolved, that if the application of these states to the government of the United States, recommended in a foregoing resolution, should be unsuccessful and peace should not be concluded, and the defense of these states should be neglected, as it has been since the commencement of the war, it will, in the opinion of this Convention, be expedient for the legislatures of the several states to appoint delegates to another convention, to meet at Boston . . . with such powers and instructions as the exigency of a crisis so momentous may require.

the British dropped attempts to change the Canadian boundary and establish an Indian barrier state in the Northwest. The commissioners signed a treaty on Dec. 24, 1814. Based on the situation before the war, the Treaty of Ghent did not resolve the issues that had caused the war, but at that point Britain was too weary to win it, and the U.S. government deemed not losing it a tolerable substitute for victory. Nevertheless, many Americans became convinced that they had won the contest.

Unaware of the treaty, British forces under Edward Pakenham assaulted New Orleans on Jan. 8, 1815, and were soundly defeated by Andrew Jackson's ragtag army, an event that contributed to the notion of a U.S. triumph. The unanimous ratification by the U.S. Senate of the Treaty of Ghent and the celebrations that followed cloaked the fact that the United States had achieved none of its objectives.

Contention in the United States had hobbled the war effort, and domestic disaffection had menaced the Union, but after the war a surge of patriotism inspired Americans to pursue national goals. Contrary to American expectations, Canada remained British and eventually developed its own national identity, partly from pride over repulsing U.S. invasions. Meanwhile, Britain's influence among the northwestern Indians was forever ended, and American expansion in that region proceeded unchecked. In the South, the Creek War opened a large part of that region for settlement and led to the events that persuaded Spain to cede Florida to the United States in 1821.

The most enduring international consequence of the war was in the arbitration clauses of Ghent, perhaps the treaty's most important feature. Its arrangements to settle outstanding disagreements established methods that could adapt to changing U.S. administrations, British ministries, and world events. There lay the seeds of an Anglo-American comity that would weather future disagreements to sustain the longest unfortified border in the world.

CHAPTER 9

THE BATTLES OF THE WAR OF 1812

In many ways the course of the War of 1812 unfolded oddly. Initially the British, distracted by their fight with Napoleonic France, devoted few resources to fight in North America, while the Americans began the conflict with grandiose visions of their own abilities, which were quickly belied by incompetence on the battlefield. However, as the list of battles below shows, over time the Americans showed an increased ability to win battles. By the end of 1814, after notching several major victories, the Americans had fought the British to a draw despite the latter's clearly superior naval power.

BATTLE OF QUEENSTON HEIGHTS

On Oct. 13, 1812, Gen. Stephen Van Rensselaer, commanding a force of about 3,100 U.S. militia, sent advance units across the Niagara River. They established themselves on the steep escarpment above Queenston (Queenstown) and at first successfully defended their position. The main body of U.S. troops, however, refused to cross the river in support. The advance party was then surrounded by the British, who captured 925 Americans, thereby temporarily stopping a U.S. invasion into Canada.

BATTLE OF LAKE ERIE

On Sept. 10, 1813, Master Commandant Oliver Hazard Perry's fleet of nine ships engaged six British warships under Capt.

The heroic U.S. Admiral Oliver Hazard Perry in a rowboat on his way to the U.S. Brig Niagara *during the Battle of Lake Erie.* Library of Congress Prints and Photographs Division

Robert Heriot Barclay in Lake Erie. After Perry's flagship, *Lawrence*, had suffered heavy casualties and had been reduced to a defenseless wreck, he transferred to a sister ship, the *Niagara*, and sailed directly into the British line, firing broadsides and forcing its surrender. The British lost 40 men, with 94 wounded; the Americans, 27 killed and 96 wounded. The destruction of the British squadron on Lake Erie ensured American control of the lake, reversed the course of the Northwest campaign, and forced the British to abandon Detroit, precluding any territorial cession in the Northwest to Great Britain in the peace settlement.

BATTLE OF THE THAMES

Fought on Oct. 5, 1813, the Battle of the Thames (also known as the Battle of Moraviantown) was a decisive American victory over British and Indian forces in Ontario, Can., enabling the United States to consolidate its control over the Northwest.

After the U.S. naval triumph in the Battle of Lake Erie in September 1813, the British commander at Detroit, Brig. Gen. Henry A. Procter, found his position untenable and began a hasty retreat across the Ontario peninsula. He was pursued by about 3,500 U.S. troops under Gen. William Henry Harrison, who was supported by the U.S. fleet in command of Lake Erie. The forces met near Moraviantown on the Thames River, a few miles east of what is now Thamesville. The British, with about 600 regulars and 1,000 Indian allies under Tecumseh, the Shawnee intertribal leader, were greatly outnumbered and quickly defeated. Many British troops were captured and Tecumseh was killed, destroying his Indian alliance and breaking the Indian power in the Ohio and Indiana territories. After this battle, most of the tribes abandoned their association with the British.

After destroying Moraviantown, a village of Christian Indians, the U.S. troops returned to Detroit. The U.S. victory helped catapult Harrison into the national limelight and eventually the presidency.

BATTLE OF CHÂTEAUGUAY

In the autumn of 1813, an invading American force of about 4,000 troops under Gen. Wade Hampton marched toward Montreal through the Châteauguay River valley. An American advance party of 1,500 under Col. Robert Purdy and some 460 British troops under Col. Charles de Salaberry met at Châteauguay on October 26. The British had taken up a good defensive position in the woods along the riverbank and, despite their inferior numbers, managed to stop Purdy's advance. After this setback, Hampton withdrew back across the border. (At least 90 percent of the British troops at Châteauguay were French Canadians.) By forcing the Americans to abandon their projected attack on Montreal, the Battle of Châteauguay thus exerted a decisive influence on U.S. strategy during the 1813 campaign.

BATTLE OF CRYSLER'S FARM

In October 1813 a U.S. force of more than 7,000 men set out in ships from Sackets Harbor, N.Y., to attack Montreal. On November 11, the Americans, encountering rapids on the St. Lawrence River at the Long Sault, now in Ontario, disembarked on the Canadian shore at that point. They divided into a main body, under Gen. James Wilkinson, which advanced toward Cornwall, and a rear guard of approximately 1,600 troops commanded by Gen. John Boyd. The rear guard made contact with the British force of about 600 troops under Col. J. W. Morrison, and Wilkinson ordered Boyd to attack.

The resulting action was fought on farmlands beside the river. British casualties numbered 200; American losses were more than 400, including 100 taken prisoner. The battle ended with the withdrawal of the Americans. Learning that another U.S. force, under Gen. Wade Hampton, had been turned back at Châteauguay on October 26, Wilkinson retreated across the river to St. Regis, N.Y.

Crysler's Farm Battlefield Memorial Park was officially opened in 1961.

BATTLE OF CHIPPEWA

At the beginning of July 1814, an American army of more than 4,000 men under Generals Jacob Brown and Winfield Scott crossed the Niagara River and took Fort Erie. The Americans intended to push northward toward Lake Ontario and on to Burlington and York (modern Toronto). About 2,000 British regulars and Canadian militia from Fort George and along the lower Niagara, under Gen. Phineas Riall, rushed southward to stem the U.S. advance. On July 5 Riall launched an attack at Chippewa upon the more numerous U.S. forces and was badly beaten. British casualties numbered 604; the Americans, 335. Although the victory restored American military prestige, it accomplished little else, largely because the expected naval support needed for a U.S. advance to the north and west failed to materialize.

BATTLE OF LUNDY'S LANE

Fought on July 25, 1814, a mile west of Niagara Falls, the Battle of Lundy's Lane ended a U.S. invasion of Canada. After defeating the British in the Battle of Chippewa on July 5, 1814, American troops under Gen. Jacob Brown

established themselves at Queenston. On the night of July 24–25, a British force under Gen. Phineas Riall moved forward to Lundy's Lane. On the 25th he was reinforced by troops from Kingston under the British commander in chief, Gen. Gordon Drummond. The U.S. troops advanced, and the battle began at 6 PM. For hours on end, each side hurled desperate charges against the other in the dusk and darkness. The losses on both sides were the heaviest in the entire war. With fewer than 3,000 men, the British had 878 casualties, 84 of whom were killed; the Americans suffered 853 casualties, with 171 killed. Drummond, Riall, Brown, and the American general Winfield Scott were all severely wounded, and Riall was taken prisoner.

By midnight, the U.S. troops, too exhausted to attack again, fell back, leaving Drummond's men in possession of the field. The British troops, in turn, were too exhausted to pursue. Neither side won a decisive victory, but the action stopped the advance of the Americans, who withdrew to Fort Erie the next day.

BATTLE OF PLATTSBURGH

The Battle of Plattsburgh resulted in an important American victory on Lake Champlain that saved New York from possible British invasion via the Hudson River valley. A British army of some 14,000 troops under Sir George Prevost reached Plattsburgh in a joint land and sea operation. The American defenders

Gen. Andrew Jackson (on the white horse) leading his troops in battle against Gen. Edward Pakenham's vanquished British troops in the Battle of New Orleans, Jan. 8, 1815. Library of Congress Prints and Photographs Division

included 1,500 regulars and about 2,500 militia commanded by Gen. Alexander Macomb, supported by a 14-ship American naval squadron under Commodore Thomas Macdonough. The outcome of the battle was determined on water when the British fleet was decisively defeated on Sept. 11, 1814. Deprived of naval support, the invading army was forced to retreat. The victory at Plattsburgh influenced the terms of peace drawn at the Treaty of Ghent the following December.

BATTLE OF NEW ORLEANS

In the autumn of 1814 a British fleet of more than 50 ships commanded by Gen. Edward Pakenham sailed into the Gulf of Mexico and prepared to attack New Orleans, which is strategically located at the mouth of the Mississippi River. On December 1, Gen. Andrew Jackson, commander of the U.S. Army of the Southwest, hastened to the defense of the city. Jackson's army of between 6,000 and

7,000 troops consisted chiefly of militiamen and volunteers from southern states. Because of slow communications, news of the peace treaty between Britain and the United States that had been signed at Ghent (Dec. 24, 1814) did not reach the United States in time to avert the battle, in which Jackson's troops fought against 7,500 British regulars who stormed their position on Jan. 8, 1815. So effective were the earthworks and the barricades of cotton bales with which the Americans had fortified their position that the fighting lasted only half an hour, ending in a decisive U.S. victory and a British withdrawal. British casualties numbered more than 2,000 (289 killed); American, only 71 (31 killed). News of the victory reached Washington, D.C., at the same time as that of the Treaty of Ghent and did much to raise the low morale of the capital. The Battle of New Orleans greatly enhanced the reputation of Jackson as a national hero.

CHAPTER 10

MILITARY FIGURES OF THE WAR OF 1812

"D on't give up the ship," said Capt. James Lawrence as he lay dying during a sea battle near Boston. The speaker of this much-quoted rallying cry was just one of the important American military leaders of the War of 1812. Others included a "fighting Quaker," an infamous pirate, and several future presidents who would influence events in the United States long after the war was over.

THE AMERICAN SIDE

WILLIAM BAINBRIDGE
(b. May 7, 1774, Princeton, N.J.—d. July 27, 1833, Philadelphia, Pa.)

American naval officer William Bainbridge distinguished himself during the War of 1812 by capturing the British frigate *Java*.

Bainbridge commanded merchant vessels from 1793 to 1798, when he became an officer in the newly organized U.S. Navy. He served in the war with the Barbary States (1801–05) and was in command of the frigate *Philadelphia* when it was captured by the Tripolitans (1803). Imprisoned for a time, he returned to the merchant marine upon his release (1805). At the outbreak of the War of 1812 he was again commissioned in the U.S. Navy and was given command of the frigate *Constitution*. His capture of the *Java* off the Brazilian coast was one of the notable American naval victories of the war and, according to some, helped his ship earn the sobriquet "Old Ironsides."

Jacob Jennings Brown
(b. May 9, 1775, Bucks County, Pa.— d. Feb. 24, 1828, Washington, D.C.)

American Gen. Jacob Jennings Brown made his mark in the War of 1812 as "the fighting Quaker."

Of Pennsylvania Quaker heritage and upbringing, Brown established himself as a prominent New York citizen and rose to brigadier general in the state militia before the War of 1812. His successful defense of Sackets Harbor, N.Y., on May 29, 1813, brought him national recognition and a general's commission in the regular army. He commanded a brigade under Gen. James Wilkinson in the abortive campaign against Montreal, and he succeeded to the command of the Army of the North in January 1814.

After supervising the further training of his still-raw troops, Brown crossed the Niagara River on July 3, 1814. On July 5, he defeated a British force under Gen. Phineas Riall at the Battle of Chippewa, but expected naval support failed to appear and the British brought up reserves. Threatened with being cut off from his base at Fort Erie, on July 25 Brown engaged a slightly larger British force at the Battle of Lundy's Lane. A long day of fierce fighting ended in a draw, with Brown badly wounded.

The Americans retreated to Fort Erie, where they were besieged by the British. Brown, resuming command, launched a sortie on September 17 that destroyed so much of the enemy artillery that the British abandoned the siege a few days later. Though the Americans were in no shape to pursue, Brown's hard fighting solidified his position as a national hero: a fighting Quaker and the ideal model of a citizen soldier. As the army's senior ranking officer, he became its commanding

Gen. Jacob Jennings Brown. Engraving created from the original painting by Alonzo Chappel. Hulton Archive/ Getty Images

general in 1821 and held the appointment uneventfully until his death.

HENRY DEARBORN
(b. Feb. 23, 1751, Hampton, N.H.— d. June 6, 1829, Roxbury, Mass.)

Continental Army officer Henry Dearborn abandoned the practice of medicine to fight in the Revolution and served in the War of 1812, too, though somewhat ignominiously.

He fought at the Battle of Bunker Hill and was captured during the failed expedition against Quebec. Subsequently exchanged, Dearborn served in the Saratoga campaign (1777), at Valley Forge (1778), and in the Battle of Monmouth. He played a prominent role in the 1779 expedition against the Iroquois Confederacy.

Dearborn's success in raising men, supplies, and money for the New Hampshire Continentals led in 1781 to an appointment as deputy quartermaster general. He served on George Washington's staff at Yorktown, and he returned to civilian life in 1783 after eight years of service that established him as one of the best citizen officers developed by the revolution.

On the organization of the U.S. government, Dearborn was appointed marshal for the District of Maine (1789–93). He represented Massachusetts in Congress (1793–97) and was secretary of war under Pres. Thomas Jefferson. As secretary of war he issued an order in 1803 "for erecting barracks and a strong stockade" at "Chikago with a view to the establishment of a Post." Fort Dearborn—whose site is located in what is now the heart of Chicago—was named for him. When the War of 1812 began, Dearborn, then senior major general of the U.S. Army, attempted to invade Canada at several points. After a long succession of delays and reverses, he was removed from command by Pres. James Madison on July 6, 1813. Dearborn ended his public career as U.S. minister to Portugal (1822–24).

STEPHEN DECATUR
(b. Jan. 5, 1779, Sinepuxent, Md.— d. March 22, 1820, Bladensburg, Md.)

American officer Stephen Decatur held a number of important commands during the War of 1812. Replying to a toast after returning from successful engagements abroad (1815), he said the famous words: "Our country! In her intercourse with foreign nations may she always be in the right; but our country, right or wrong."

Decatur entered the navy in 1798 and saw service in the quasi-war with France (1798–1800). In 1804 he led an expedition into the harbour of Tripoli to burn the U.S. frigate *Philadelphia*, which had fallen into Tripolitan hands. He succeeded in this objective and made his escape under fire with only one man wounded. This exploit earned him his captain's commission and a sword of honour from Congress.

In the War of 1812, his ship, the *United States*, captured the British vessel HMS

Macedonian. In 1813 he was appointed commodore to command a squadron in New York Harbor, which was soon blockaded by the British. In an attempt to break out (January 1815), his flagship, the *President*, was forced to surrender to a superior force. Subsequently, he commanded in the Mediterranean area against the corsairs of Algiers, Tunis, and Tripoli with great success. He was made a navy commissioner in November 1815—an office he held until killed in a duel.

WILLIAM HENRY HARRISON
(b. Feb. 9, 1773, Charles City County, Va.—d. April 4, 1841, Washington, D.C.)

Before becoming the ninth president of the United States (1841), William Henry Harrison won fame as a soldier, first in fighting Native Americans, then as a victorious general during the War of 1812.

Born into a politically prominent family, he enlisted in the army at age 18 and served under Anthony Wayne at the Battle of Fallen Timbers. In 1798 he became secretary of the Northwest Territories and in 1800 governor of the new Indiana Territory. In May 1800 Harrison was appointed governor of the newly created Indiana Territory, where, succumbing to the demands of land-hungry whites, he negotiated between 1802 and 1809 a number of treaties that stripped the Indians of that region of millions of acres. Resisting this expansionism, the Shawnee intertribal leader Tecumseh organized an Indian uprising. Harrison,

leading a force of seasoned regulars and militia, defeated the Indians at the Battle of Tippecanoe (Nov. 7, 1811), near present-day Lafayette, Ind., a victory that largely established his military reputation in the public mind. A few months after the War of 1812 broke out with Great Britain, Harrison was made a brigadier general and placed in command of all federal forces in the Northwest Territory. On Oct. 5, 1813, troops under his command decisively defeated the British and their Indian allies at the Battle of the Thames, in Ontario, Can. Tecumseh was killed in the battle, and the British-Indian alliance was permanently destroyed, thus ending resistance in the Northwest. After the war he moved to Ohio, where he became prominent in the Whig Party. He served in the U.S. House of Representatives (1816–19) and Senate (1825–28). As the Whig candidate in the 1836 presidential election, he lost narrowly. In 1840 he and his running mate, John Tyler, won election with a slogan emphasizing Harrison's frontier triumph: "Tippecanoe and Tyler too." The 68-year-old Harrison delivered his inaugural speech without a hat or overcoat in a cold drizzle, contracted pneumonia, and died one month later; he was the first U.S. president to die in office.

ISAAC HULL
(b. March 9, 1773, Derby, Conn.—d. Feb. 13, 1843, Philadelphia, Pa.)

American naval officer Isaac Hull is noted for the victory of his ship the

Constitution over the British frigate *Guerrière* in the War of 1812. The victory united the country behind the war effort and destroyed the legend of British naval invincibility.

Already having been master of a ship at age 19, Hull was commissioned a lieutenant aboard the *Constitution* in 1798. He distinguished himself in the undeclared naval war with France at that time and in the Tripolitan War (1801–05); he was promoted to captain in 1806 and became commander of the *Constitution* four years later.

Encountering a British squadron in July 1812 off Egg Harbor, N.J., Hull escaped through consummate seamanship after three days and nights in one of the most remarkable chases in naval history. Sailing eastward of Boston, the *Constitution* met the *Guerrière* on August 19. After considerable maneuvering, under fire from the British ship, the American man-of-war delivered its first broadside, within pistol shot range. In fewer than 30 minutes of close and violent action, the *Guerrière* was demasted and rendered a total wreck. The helpless hulk was burned, and Hull returned to the mainland a hero. He was recognized as one of the navy's ablest commanders, and his ship became known as "Old Ironsides."

Relieved of his command at his own request, Hull commanded harbour defenses at New York City and at three navy yards. He was one of the first three members of the Board of Naval Commissioners and commanded the U.S. squadron in the Pacific (1824–27) and the Mediterranean (1839–41).

WILLIAM HULL
(b. June 24, 1753, Derby, Conn.—
d. Nov. 29, 1825, Newton, Mass.)

American soldier and civil governor William Hull is ingloriously remembered for failures in command during the early stages of the War of 1812 that resulted in the loss of Detroit to the British and for his celebrated court martial.

A graduate of Yale College, Hull joined the American army during the Revolution, serving in campaigns in Connecticut, New York, and New Jersey. Both before and after the war he practiced law, and in 1805 Pres. Thomas Jefferson named him governor of Michigan Territory (including present-day Michigan, Wisconsin, and part of Minnesota). In 1812, at the outset of the war with Great Britain, he accepted a commission as brigadier general, in command of an army intended to defend Michigan and attack Canada. His invasion of Canada was clumsy and poorly planned; he retreated to Detroit and eventually, on Aug. 16, 1812, without a fight, surrendered his army and Fort Shelby to the British.

A court martial later convicted him of cowardice and neglect of duty and sentenced him to death. Pres. James Madison approved the findings but remitted the sentence. Hull's surrender was a severe blow to American morale during the remaining two years of war.

ANDREW JACKSON

(b. March 15, 1767, Waxhaws region,
S.C.—d. June 8, 1845, the Hermitage,
near Nashville, Tenn.)

Andrew Jackson's assured command of the American forces during the Battle of New Orleans made him one of the biggest heroes of the War of 1812 and a national figure, no doubt contributing greatly to his eventual ascendance as the seventh president of the United States (1829–37).

EARLY LIFE

He had fought briefly in the American Revolution near his frontier home, where his family was killed in the conflict. In 1788 he was appointed prosecuting attorney for western North Carolina. When the region became the state of Tennessee, he was elected to the U.S. House of Representatives (1796–97) and the Senate (1797–98). He served on the state supreme court (1798–1804) and in Tennessee politics. In 1802 Jackson had also been elected major general of the Tennessee militia, a position he still held when the War of 1812 opened the door to a command in the field and a hero's role.

MILITARY FEATS

In March 1812, when it appeared that war with Great Britain was imminent, Jackson issued a call for 50,000 volunteers to be ready for an invasion of Canada. After the declaration of war, in June 1812, Jackson offered his services and those of

his militia to the United States. The government was slow to accept this offer, and, when Jackson finally was given a command in the field, it was to fight against the Creek Indians, who were allied with the British and who were threatening the southern frontier. In a campaign of about five months, in 1813–14, Jackson crushed the Creeks, the final victory coming in the Battle of Tohopeka (or Horseshoe Bend) in Alabama. The

A Nathaniel Currier lithograph of Gen. Andrew Jackson following his suppression of the Creeks during the War of 1812. MPI/Hulton Archive/Getty Images

victory was so decisive that the Creeks never again menaced the frontier, and Jackson was established as the hero of the West.

In August 1814, Jackson moved his army south to Mobile. Though he was without specific instructions, his real objective was the Spanish post at Pensacola. The motive was to prepare the way for U.S. occupation of Florida, then a Spanish possession. Jackson's justification for this bold move was that Spain and Great Britain were allies in the wars in Europe. At Mobile, Jackson learned that an army of British regulars had landed at Pensacola. In the first week in November, he led his army into Florida and, on November 7, occupied that city just as the British evacuated it to go by sea to Louisiana. Jackson then marched his army overland to New Orleans, where he arrived early in December. A series of small skirmishes between detachments of the two armies culminated in the Battle of New Orleans on Jan. 8, 1815, in which Jackson's forces inflicted a decisive defeat upon the British army and forced it to withdraw. The news of this victory reached Washington at a time when morale was at a low point. A few days later, news of the signing of the Treaty of Ghent (Belgium) between the United States and Great Britain on Dec. 24, 1814, reached the capital. The twin tidings brought joy and relief to the American people and made Jackson the hero not only of the West but of a substantial part of the country as well. The decisive victory at the Battle of New

Orleans made him a national hero; he was dubbed "Old Hickory" by the press.

POSTWAR POLITICAL CAREER

After the United States acquired Florida, Jackson was named governor of the territory (1821). One of four candidates in the 1824 presidential election, he won an electoral-vote plurality, but the House of Representatives instead selected John Quincy Adams as president. Jackson's victory over Adams in the 1828 presidential election is commonly regarded as a turning point in U.S. history. Jackson was the first president from west of the Appalachian Mountains, the first to be born into poverty, and the first to be elected through a direct appeal to the mass of voters rather than through the support of a recognized political organization.

The era of his presidency has come to be known as "Jacksonian Democracy." Upon taking office he replaced many federal officials with his political supporters, a practice that became known as the spoils system. His administration acquiesced in the illegal seizure of Cherokee land in Georgia and then forcibly expelled the Indians who refused to leave. When South Carolina claimed a right to nullify a federally imposed tariff, Jackson asked for and received Congressional authority to use the military to enforce federal laws in the state. His reelection in 1832 was partially the result of his controversial veto of a bill to recharter the Bank of the United States, which was unpopular with many of his supporters. The intensity of the political struggles during his tenure led to the strengthening of the Democratic Party and to the further development of the two-party system.

JACOB JONES
(b. March 1768, Smyrna, Del.—d. Aug. 3, 1850, Philadelphia, Pa.)

U.S. naval officer Jacob Jones had the distinction of becoming a British prisoner of war almost immediately after leading the ship he commanded to a victory early in the War of 1812.

After trying medicine and politics, Jones served in the undeclared U.S. naval war against France (1798–1800), as a midshipman, and in the Tripolitan War (1801–05), as a lieutenant. In the War of 1812 Jones was commander of the sloop of war *Wasp*, which took the British sloop of war *Frolic* off Cape Hatteras (Oct. 18, 1812). Just as the battle ended, the British 74-gun *Poictiers* happened upon the scene and took both ships. When prisoners were exchanged a year later, Jones received a gold medal from Congress.

After the war Jones commanded the former British frigate *Macedonian* in the U.S. squadron that overawed the Barbary States at Algiers (1815). Later he commanded the Mediterranean Squadron (1821–23) and the Pacific Squadron (1826–29); stationed at Baltimore (1829–39) and at New York (1842–45), he was governor of the United States Naval Asylum in Philadelphia when he died.

JEAN LAFFITE
(b. 1780?, France—d. 1825?)

Privateer and smuggler Jean Laffite interrupted his illicit adventures to fight heroically for the United States in defense of New Orleans in the War of 1812.

Little is known of Laffite's early life, but by 1809 he and his brother Pierre apparently had established in New Orleans a blacksmith shop that reportedly served as a depot for smuggled goods and slaves brought ashore by a band of privateers. From 1810 to 1814 this group probably formed the nucleus for Laffite's illicit colony on the secluded islands of Barataria Bay south of the city. Holding privateer commissions from the republic of Cartagena (in modern Colombia), Laffite's group preyed on Spanish commerce, illegally disposing of its plunder through merchant connections on the mainland.

Because Barataria Bay was an important approach to New Orleans, the British during the War of 1812 offered Laffite $30,000 and a captaincy in the Royal Navy for his allegiance. Laffite pretended to cooperate, then warned Louisiana officials of New Orleans' peril. Instead of believing him, Gov. W.C.C. Claiborne summoned the U.S. Army and Navy to wipe out the colony. Some of Laffite's ships were captured, but his business was not destroyed. Still protesting his loyalty to the United States, Laffite next offered aid to the hard-pressed forces of Gen. Andrew Jackson in defense of New

Orleans if he and his men could be granted a full pardon. Jackson accepted, and in the Battle of New Orleans (December 1814–January 1815) the Baratarians, as Laffite and his men came to be known, fought with distinction. Jackson personally commended Laffite as "one of the ablest men" of the battle, and Pres. James Madison issued a public proclamation of pardon for the group.

Nevertheless, after the war the pirate chief returned to his old ways, and in 1817, with nearly 1,000 followers, he organized a commune called Campeche on the island site of the future city of Galveston, Texas, where he served briefly as governor in 1819. From this depot he continued his privateering against the Spanish, and his men were commonly acknowledged as pirates. When several of his lieutenants attacked U.S. ships in 1820, official pressure was brought to bear on the operation. As a consequence, the following year Laffite suddenly picked a crew to man his favourite vessel, *The Pride*, burned the town, and sailed away— apparently continuing his depredations along the coast of Spanish America (the Spanish Main) for several more years.

JAMES LAWRENCE
(b. Oct. 1, 1781, Burlington, N.J.—d. June 1, 1813, in a sea battle off Boston, Mass.)

The dying words of American naval officer James Lawrence, "Don't give up the ship," uttered during a sea battle in the War of 1812, became one of the U.S. Navy's most cherished traditions.

Lawrence entered the navy as a midshipman (1798) and fought against the Barbary pirates. He was first lieutenant to Stephen Decatur when the USS *Philadelphia*, which had been captured by the Tripolitans, was destroyed in Tripoli harbour by Decatur-led forces (1804). During the War of 1812 Lawrence commanded the USS *Hornet* in the capture of HMS *Peacock*. Shortly thereafter he was promoted to captain of the frigate *Chesapeake*. On June 1, 1813, the *Chesapeake* accepted HMS *Shannon*'s challenge to a sea fight off Boston. The *Chesapeake* was decisively defeated in less than an hour and Lawrence was mortally wounded.

THOMAS MACDONOUGH
(b. Dec. 31, 1783, the Trap, Del.— d. Nov. 10, 1825, at sea en route from the Mediterranean Sea to New York City)

U.S. naval officer Thomas Macdonough won one of the most important victories in the War of 1812 at the Battle of Plattsburg (or Lake Champlain) against the British.

Entering the navy as a midshipman in 1800, Macdonough saw service during the U.S. war with Tripoli (1801–05). When the War of 1812 broke out, his major assignment was to cruise the lakes between Canada and the United States. When enemy ground forces threatened Plattsburg, N.Y.—the U.S. Army headquarters on the northern frontier—Macdonough's foresight and painstaking preparation for battle paid off. On Sept. 11, 1814, his 14-ship fleet met the British in the harbour and after several hours of severe fighting forced the 16-vessel squadron to surrender, thus saving New York and Vermont from invasion.

The victory brought Macdonough the thanks of the U.S. Congress and promotion to captain. More important, it left the British no grounds for territorial claims in the Great Lakes area at the peace negotiations that followed. In failing health, he died en route home after serving on various European assignments.

Oliver Hazard Perry
(b. Aug. 20, 1785, South Kingston, R.I.—d. Aug. 23, 1819, at sea)

U.S. naval officer Oliver Hazard Perry became a national hero when he defeated a British squadron in the Battle of Lake Erie.

Appointed a midshipman at 14, Perry served in both the West Indies and the Mediterranean until February 1813, when he was sent to Erie, Pa., to complete the building of a U.S. squadron to challenge British control of the Great Lakes.

By early autumn he had assembled a fleet of 10 small vessels and was ready to engage the enemy. When the battle was joined on September 10, Perry's fleet was greatly superior in short-range firepower but only slightly superior at long range; a light wind prevented him from closing in quickly on the six British warships commanded by R.H. Barclay. When

Perry's flagship, the *Lawrence*, was disabled, he transferred to the *Niagara*, winning the battle within the next 15 minutes by sailing directly into the British line, firing broadside. In his official report of the British surrender he said, "We have met the enemy and they are ours."

Perry's successful action at Lake Erie helped ensure U.S. control of the Northwest; it also raised him to a position of national eminence and earned him promotion to the rank of captain. He commanded the *Java* in the Mediterranean (1816–17) and a small U.S. fleet sent to the South Atlantic (1819) to bring under control certain vessels that were preying on American shipping out of Buenos Aires and Venezuela. On the return trip he contracted yellow fever and died.

Zebulon Montgomery Pike
(b. Jan. 5, 1779, Lamberton, N.J.— d. April 27, 1813, York, Ont., Can.)

U.S. army officer and explorer Zebulon Montgomery Pike, for whom Pikes Peak in Colorado was named, was killed while serving his country during the War of 1812.

In 1805 Pike, then an army lieutenant, led a 20-man exploring party to the headwaters of the Mississippi River with instructions to discover the river's source, negotiate peace treaties with Indian tribes, and assert the legal claim of the United States to the area. Pike travelled 2,000 miles (3,200 km) by boat and on

Shown c. 1806, Zebulon Montgomery Pike died while fighting in the attack on York, Ontario (now Toronto). MPI/ Hulton Archive/Getty Images

encountered the Front Range of the Rocky Mountains. After trying unsuccessfully to scale the mountain peak later named for Pike, the party proceeded southward to northern New Mexico, where they were apprehended by Spanish officials on the charge of illegal entry into New Mexico. They were escorted across Texas to the Spanish–American border at Natchitoches, La., where on July 1, 1807, they were released.

Pike's report on Santa Fe, with information noting particularly the military weakness of the capital and the lucrativeness of the overland trade with Mexico, stimulated the expansionist movement into Texas. Pike served in the War of 1812, attaining the rank of brigadier general. He was killed in action during the attack on York.

DAVID PORTER
(b. Feb. 1, 1780, Boston, Mass.— d. March 3, 1843, Pera, Tur.)

U.S. naval officer David Porter commanded the frigate *Essex* on its two-year expedition against British shipping during the War of 1812.

Young Porter early accompanied his father—who had been a naval commander during the American Revolution—on sea voyages. He became a midshipman in 1798, was promoted to lieutenant in 1799, and took part in the undeclared war against France (1799) and the war with Tripoli (1801–05).

Promoted to captain in 1812, Porter won a formidable reputation as commander

foot from St. Louis, Mo., to Leech and Sandy lakes, in northern Minnesota. He erroneously identified Leech Lake as the river's source.

In July 1806 Pike was dispatched to the Southwest to explore the Arkansas and Red rivers and to obtain information about the adjacent Spanish territory. Pike established an outpost near the site of present-day Pueblo, Colo., and then led his party northwest, where they

of the *Essex* in the next two years. His was the first U.S. warship to become active in Pacific waters. He captured a large number of British whaling vessels and took possession of Nuku Hiva, the largest of the Marquesas Islands, in November 1813. Finally, in February 1814, he was blockaded by British frigates in the harbour of Valparaíso, Chile, and was defeated at the end of March.

After serving on the new Board of Naval Commissioners from 1815 to 1823, Porter commanded a squadron sent to the West Indies to suppress piracy. When one of his officers landed in Puerto Rico and was imprisoned by the Spanish authorities, Porter sent in an armed force and demanded an apology. For this unauthorized action, he was recalled (December 1824), court-martialed, and suspended from duty. Resigning his commission, he accepted appointment as commander in chief of the Mexican navy (1826–29), then fighting Spain.

Upon returning to the United States, he was sent to Algiers as U.S. consul general (1830), and then to Constantinople (1831), where, in 1841, he became minister. He was the father of U.S. naval officer David Dixon Porter.

WINFIELD SCOTT
(b. June 13, 1786, Petersburg, Va.— d. May 29, 1866, West Point, N.Y.)

American army officer Winfield Scott held the rank of general in three wars and was the unsuccessful Whig candidate for president in 1852. He was the foremost American military figure between the Revolution and the Civil War.

Scott was commissioned a captain of artillery in 1808 and fought on the Niagara frontier in the War of 1812. He was captured by the British in that campaign, but he was exchanged in 1813 and went on to fight in the battles of Chippewa (July 5, 1814) and Lundy's Lane (July 25), where his success made him a national hero. By war's end he had attained the rank of major general. Scott remained in military service, studying tactics in Europe and taking a deep interest in maintaining a well-trained and disciplined U.S. Army. In 1838 he supervised the removal of the Cherokee Indians from Georgia and other Southern states to reservations west of the Mississippi River. Scott became commanding general of the U.S. Army in 1841 and served in that capacity until 1861.

With the outbreak of the Mexican-American War (1846–48), Scott recommended Gen. Zachary Taylor for command of the U.S. forces. When Taylor appeared to be making little progress, however, Scott set out himself with a supplementary force on a seaborne invasion of Mexico that captured Veracruz (March 1847). Six months later, after a series of victories, including those at Cerro Gordo, Contreras, Churubusco, Molino del Rey, and Chapultepec, Scott entered Mexico City on September 14, thus ending the war. For this service he was honoured by appointment to the brevet rank of lieutenant general. Despite—or perhaps because of—the fact that he was clearly the most capable American military

Shown c. 1860, U.S. Army Gen. Winfield Scott was known as "Old Fuss and Feathers." Spencer Arnold/Hulton Archive/Getty Images

he was promoted to lieutenant general, becoming the first man since George Washington to hold that rank. Scott was still commander in chief of the U.S. Army when the Civil War broke out in April 1861, but his proposed strategy of splitting the Confederacy—the plan eventually adopted—was ridiculed. Age forced his retirement the following November.

SAMUEL SMITH
(b. July 27, 1752, Carlisle, Pa.—d. April 22, 1839, Baltimore, Md.)

U.S. soldier and politician Samuel Smith is best known as the commander of land and sea forces that defended Baltimore from the British during the War of 1812.

Smith grew up in Baltimore, to which his family had moved in 1760. The son of a wealthy merchant, he joined the family business after lengthy travels in Europe.

Smith fought in the American Revolution, participating in the Battle of Long Island and spending the winter with George Washington at Valley Forge. As commander of Fort Mifflin, he helped prevent Gen. William Howe's fleet from coming to the aid of Gen. John Burgoyne, contributing to the crucial American victory at Saratoga in 1777.

After the Revolution, Smith returned to Baltimore, where he became quite wealthy through land speculation as well as the family mercantile concerns. His main interest turned to politics. From 1793 to 1803 he won election four times to the U.S. House of Representatives, and from 1803 to 1815 he held a seat in the Senate.

leader of his time, Scott was bedeviled by political opposition throughout his career. And though he was highly popular with his men, he earned the nickname "Old Fuss and Feathers" because of his emphasis on military formalities and proprieties.

A prominent Whig, Scott won his party's presidential nomination in 1852 but lost the election to Democrat Franklin Pierce, mainly because the Whigs were divided over the issue of slavery. In 1855

During the British invasion of Maryland in 1814, Smith led about 13,000 troops in defending Baltimore. The Americans repulsed the invaders and inflicted heavy losses on them. The American-held citadel Fort McHenry withstood a two-day bombardment (inspiring Francis Scott Key to compose "The Star-Spangled Banner") before the British finally withdrew.

In 1816 Smith returned to the House of Representatives where he stayed until once again moving over to the Senate in 1822. He held his Senate seat until 1833, marking 40 continuous years in Congress. Then in 1835—at the age of 83—he took command of the state militia and put down riots in Baltimore. The grateful city elected Smith mayor, and he served in that capacity until 1838, one year before his death.

THE BRITISH SIDE

Among those who fought for the British cause in the War of 1812 were several generals whose defense of Canada against American incursions ultimately set the stage for it to emerge as a sovereign country. Also fighting on the British side was a famous Native American chief who hoped that the British would help his people keep their land.

SIR ISAAC BROCK
(b. Oct. 6, 1769, St. Peter Port, Guernsey, Channel Islands—d. Oct. 13, 1812, Queenston, Upper Can. [now Ontario])

British soldier and administrator Sir Isaac Brock was popularly known as the "Hero of Upper Canada" during the War of 1812.

Brock entered the British army as an ensign in 1785. He was made lieutenant colonel of the 49th Regiment in 1797, and in 1802 he was sent to Canada, where he was promoted to colonel in 1805 and major general in 1811. In 1810 he assumed command over all troops in Upper Canada (now Ontario), and the following year he took over the civil administration of the province as well. In 1812, with the outbreak of war between Great Britain and the United States, he energetically undertook the defense of Upper Canada against invasion and organized the militia. On Aug. 15, 1812, with British and Native American troops, against great odds, he took Detroit from U.S. forces; for this achievement he was awarded a knighthood of the Order of the Bath. On October 13 his troops defeated U.S. forces at the Battle of Queenston Heights on the Niagara frontier, but during the battle he was mortally wounded.

SIR GEORGE PREVOST, 1ST BARONET
(b. May 19, 1767, New Jersey—d. Jan. 5, 1816, London, Eng.)

Born in colonial New Jersey, George Prevost became a soldier in the service of Great Britain. He also served as governor in chief (1811–15) of Upper and Lower Canada (now Ontario and Quebec) and was known for his conciliatory policies toward French Canadians.

Prevost attained the rank of major in the British army by 1790. From 1794 to 1796 he saw active service in the West Indies; in 1798, as a brigadier general, he was made lieutenant governor of St. Lucia. He dealt successfully with the French there, adopting a policy of conciliation toward them, no doubt facilitated by his fluency in French. He was created a baronet in 1805 for his services in the West Indies.

In 1808 Prevost went to Nova Scotia as lieutenant governor. Four years later he was transferred to Quebec, where he was administrator of Lower Canada, then governor in chief of both Canadas. The previous governor, Sir James Craig, had alienated many of the French Canadians, but Prevost endeavoured to meet their demands. During the War of 1812, Prevost commanded the British forces in Canada; his military reputation was marred by two incidents: in 1813 he withdrew after a successful attack on Sackets Harbor, N.Y., and in 1814 he was defeated at Plattsburgh, N.Y., another baffling retreat. Prevost was recalled to London in 1815 to face a court-martial, but he died before it was held.

TECUMSEH
(b. 1768, Old Piqua, in modern Clark County, Ohio—d. Oct. 5, 1813, near Thames River, Upper Can.)

Shawnee Indian chief Tecumseh, long an opponent of the expanding new American republic, died in battle while fighting on the British side during the War of 1812.

As a boy during the American Revolution, Tecumseh participated in combined British and Indian attacks on American colonists. In 1794 he fought unsuccessfully against Gen. Anthony Wayne. With inexhaustible energy, Tecumseh began to form an Indian confederation to resist white pressure. He made long journeys in a vast territory, from the Ozarks to New York and from Iowa to Florida, gaining recruits (particularly among the tribes of the Creek Confederacy, to which his mother's tribe belonged). The tide of settlers had pushed game from the Indians' hunting grounds, and, as a result, the Indian economy had broken down.

In 1811, while Tecumseh was in the South, William Henry Harrison, governor of the Indiana Territory, marched up the Wabash River and camped near his settlement. Tecumseh's brother, known as the Prophet, unwisely attacked Harrison's camp and was so decisively defeated in the ensuing Battle of Tippecanoe that his followers dispersed, and he, having lost his prestige, fled to Canada and ceased to be a factor in Tecumseh's plans.

Seeing the approach of war (the War of 1812) between the Americans and British, Tecumseh assembled his followers and joined the British forces at Fort Malden on the Canadian side of the Detroit River. There he brought together perhaps the most formidable force ever commanded by a North American Indian, an accomplishment that was a decisive factor in the capture of Detroit and of 2,500 U.S. soldiers (1812).

Shawnee chief and British ally Tecumseh as painted by Mathais Noheimer, January 1790. MPI/Hulton Archive/ Getty Images

Fired with the promise of triumph after the fall of Detroit, Tecumseh departed on another long journey to arouse the tribes, which resulted in the uprising of the Alabama Creeks in response to his oratory, though the Chickasaws, Choctaws, and Cherokees rebuffed him. He returned north and joined the British general Henry A. Procter in his invasion of Ohio. Together they besieged Fort Meigs, held by William Henry Harrison, on the Maumee River above Toledo, where by a stratagem Tecumseh intercepted and destroyed a brigade of Kentuckians under Colonel William Dudley that had been coming to Harrison's relief. He and Procter failed to capture the fort, however, and were put on the defensive by Oliver Hazard Perry's decisive victory over the British fleet on Lake Erie (Sept. 10, 1813). Harrison thereupon invaded Canada. Tecumseh and his Indians reluctantly accompanied the retiring British, whom Harrison pursued to the Thames River, in present-day southern Ontario. There, on Oct. 5, 1813, the British and Indians were routed, and Harrison won control of the Northwest. Tecumseh, directing most of the fighting, was killed. His body was carried from the field and buried secretly in a grave that has never been discovered. Nor has it ever been determined who killed Tecumseh. Tecumseh's death marked the end of Indian resistance in the Ohio River valley and in most of the lower Midwest and South, and soon thereafter the depleted tribes were transported beyond the Mississippi River.

CHAPTER 11

NONMILITARY FIGURES OF THE WAR OF 1812

A s in the American Revolution, some of the most important efforts on behalf of the United States during the War of 1812 came not from military men or politicians but from civilians, including a philanthropist, who influenced the outcome, and a poet, who framed the way it is remembered.

THE AMERICAN SIDE

JOHN ARMSTRONG
(b. Nov. 25, 1758, Carlisle, Pa.—d. April 1, 1843, Red Hook, N.Y.)

American soldier, diplomat, and politician John Armstrong, who, as U.S. secretary of war during the War of 1812, was blamed for the British capture of Washington, D.C.

Armstrong fought in the Revolution and, as an officer in the Continental Army, was apparently the author of the Newburgh Addresses attacking Congress. After the war, he entered politics in New York, serving briefly as U.S. senator, and from 1804 to 1810 was U.S. minister to France. When the War of 1812 began, Armstrong served as a brigadier general and, from February 1813 until September 1814, as secretary of war under Pres. James Madison, with whom he shared blame for the failure to provide men and equipment to protect Washington, D.C., from British troops, who burned the

Capitol on Aug. 24, 1814. Unpopularity forced Armstrong to resign his cabinet position.

GEORGE CABOT
(b. Jan. 16, 1752, Salem, Mass.— d. April 18, 1823, Boston, Mass.)

Powerful Federalist Party leader George Cabot is remembered for his opposition to the War of 1812 and the role he played in the wartime Hartford Convention.

After studying at Harvard, Cabot went to sea. He became a shipowner and successful merchant, retiring from business in 1794. Cabot was a member of the Massachusetts Constitutional Convention (1779–80), of the state Senate (1783), and of the Massachusetts convention that ratified the federal Constitution (1788). He served in the U.S. Senate (1791–96), where he was a leading supporter of the financial policies of treasury secretary Alexander Hamilton, and in 1793 he was named a director of the Bank of the United States. He was president of the Hartford Convention, a secret meeting called on Dec. 15, 1814, to express the opposition of the New England Federalists to the War of 1812. Its report of Jan. 5, 1815, attacking President James Madison's administration and the war, aroused charges of lack of patriotism from which the party, already unpopular, never recovered.

HENRY CLAY
(b. April 12, 1777, Hanover County, Va.,—d. June 29, 1852, Washington, D.C.)

U.S. politician Henry Clay practiced law from 1797 in Virginia and then in Kentucky, where he served in the state legislature (1803–09). He was elected to the U.S. House of Representatives (1811–14, 1815–21, 1823–25); as House speaker (1811–14), he was one of the leaders who pushed the country into the War of 1812. He also served as a member of the commission at Ghent that drew up the terms of peace with Britain in 1814. He supported a national economic policy of protective tariffs, known as the American System, a national bank, and improvements to internal transportation. His support of the Missouri Compromise earned him the nicknames "The Great Pacificator" and "The Great Compromiser." After his bid for the presidency in 1824 fell short, Clay threw his support to John Quincy Adams, who made him his secretary of state (1825–29). He served in the U.S. Senate (1806–07, 1810–11, and 1831–42), where he supported the compromise tariff of 1833. He was the National Republican Party candidate for president in 1832 and the Whig Party candidate in 1844. In his last Senate term (1849–52) he argued strongly for passage of the Compromise of 1850.

ALBERT GALLATIN
(b. Jan. 29, 1761, Geneva, Switz.— d. Aug. 12, 1849, Astoria, N.Y.)

Albert Gallatin, the fourth U.S. secretary of the Treasury (1801–14), insisted upon a continuity of sound governmental fiscal

Shown in an 1840 engraving after the painting by Alonzo Chappel, Albert Gallatin was a peace negotiator for the War of 1812. Hulton Archive/ Getty Images

policies when the Republican (Jeffersonian) Party assumed national political power, and he was instrumental in negotiating an end to the War of 1812.

Gallatin plunged into business and public life after immigrating to the New World at age 19. Settling in Pennsylvania, he became a mainstay of the anti-Federalists (and, later, the Jeffersonian Republicans) in that area and in 1795

was elected to the House of Representatives. There he inaugurated the House Committee on Finance, which later grew into the powerful Ways and Means Committee. In 1797–98 he helped to reduce Federalist-sponsored expenditures aimed at promoting hostilities with France. He was bitterly denounced by Federalists in Congress, and, when the Alien and Sedition Acts were passed in 1798, Thomas Jefferson believed they were partly intended to drive Gallatin from office.

As secretary of the Treasury, Gallatin stressed simplicity in government and termination of the public debt. Despite heavy naval expenditures and the $15,000,000 Louisiana Purchase (1803), he managed to reduce the public debt by $23,000,000 within eight years.

The declaration of war with Great Britain in 1812 shattered all of Gallatin's most cherished schemes, for he felt war to be fatal to the nation's prosperity and progress. He therefore put the nation's finances in the best order he could and set himself to attain an early peace. Grasping at Russia's proffered mediation of the war, he sailed for Europe in May 1813. Refusing to deal through Russia, Great Britain expressed its willingness to proceed with direct negotiations, and commissioners from the two countries finally met at Ghent in August 1814. In the tedious discussions that followed, Gallatin played the leading role, preserving peace among his colleagues and establishing an enviable reputation as a diplomat. Peace was signed in the Treaty of Ghent (December 24).

While still in Europe, Gallatin was appointed minister to France (served 1816–23), after which he returned to the United States, only to be embroiled in a bitter intraparty political struggle. After serving briefly as minister to Great Britain (1826–27), he retired from public life and became president of the National (later the Gallatin) Bank in New York City (1831–39). A student of the Indian tribes in North America, he founded the American Ethnological Society of New York (1842) and has sometimes been called the "father of American ethnology."

STEPHEN GIRARD
(b. May 20, 1750, Bordeaux, France— d. Dec. 26, 1831, Philadelphia, Pa.)

American financier and philanthropist Stephen Girard played a crucial role in the War of 1812 through his purchase of government bonds that provided economic support for continuation of U.S. military campaigns.

Girard shipped out to sea at the age of 14 and by 1774 was captain of a ship involved in U.S. coastal trade with the West Indies. Stymied by British blockades of U.S. seaports during the Revolution, he settled in Philadelphia but resumed maritime trading after the war. He developed a worldwide trading fleet and scrupulously efficient business methods that laid the foundation of his fortune. In 1812 he bought out the first Bank of the United States, after its charter had expired. He renamed it the Bank of Stephen Girard, which became known as the "sheet anchor" of government credit during the War of 1812. Toward the end of the war, when U.S. credit was at its lowest ebb, his subscription for 95 percent of the government war loan issue enabled the United States to carry on the war. Subsequently he was one of Philadelphia's most noted civic leaders.

Girard bequeathed nearly his entire fortune to social welfare institutions, including an endowment for a Philadelphia college for male orphans, founded as the Stephen Girard College in 1833.

FRANCIS SCOTT KEY
(b. Aug. 1, 1779, Frederick County, Md.—d. Jan. 11, 1843, Baltimore, Md.)

Although a lawyer by training, Francis Scott Key is best known as the author of the poem that provided the lyrics to the U.S. national anthem, "The Star-Spangled Banner."

In September 1814, after the burning of the city of Washington by the British during the War of 1812, Key was sent to the British fleet in Chesapeake Bay to secure the release of his friend William Beanes, who had been captured after the defeat of the U.S. forces at Bladensburg, Md. He was detained aboard ship during the shelling of Fort McHenry, one of the forts that successfully defended Baltimore. During the night of the bombardment, September 13–14, Key's anxiety was at

Francis Scott Key, c. 1805. Hulton Archive/Getty Images

high pitch, and in the morning when he saw the American flag still flying over the fortress, he wrote "The Star-Spangled Banner." Released that day, he rewrote the poem in a Baltimore hotel. It was printed anonymously under the title "Defence of Fort M'Henry" and on September 20 was published by the *Baltimore Patriot*. Set to the tune of an English drinking song, "To Anacreon in Heaven," it soon became popular throughout the nation. It was later adopted by the army and navy as the national anthem, and in 1931 it was officially adopted by Congress.

JAMES MADISON
(b. March 16, 1751, Port Conway, Va.— d. June 28, 1836, Montpelier, Va.)

James Madison was serving as the fourth president of the United States (1809–17) when the War of 1812 broke out and oversaw its conduct.

EARLY LIFE

After graduating from the College of New Jersey (now Princeton University), he served in the Virginia state legislature (1776–80, 1784–86). At the Constitutional Convention (1787), his Virginia, or large-state, Plan furnished the Constitution's basic framework and guiding principles, earning him the title "father of the Constitution." To promote its ratification, he collaborated with Alexander Hamilton and John Jay on the Federalist Papers, a series of articles on the Constitution and republican government published in newspapers in 1787–88 (Madison wrote 29 of the 85 articles). In the U.S. House of Representatives (1789–97), he sponsored the Bill of Rights. He split with Hamilton over the existence of an implied congressional power to create a national bank; Madison denied such a power, though later, as president, he requested a national bank from Congress. In protest of the Alien and Sedition Acts, he drafted one of the Virginia and Kentucky Resolutions in 1798 (Thomas Jefferson drafted the other). From 1801 to 1809 he was Jefferson's secretary of state.

MADISON'S PRESIDENCY

Although he was accused of weakness in dealing with France and England, Madison won the presidency in 1808 by publishing his vigorous diplomatic dispatches. Faced with a senatorial cabal on taking office, he made a senator's lacklustre brother, Robert Smith, secretary of state and wrote all important diplomatic letters for two years before replacing him with James Monroe. Although he had fully supported Jefferson's wartime shipping embargo, Madison reversed his predecessor's policy two weeks after assuming the presidency by secretly notifying both Great Britain and France, then at war, that, in his opinion, if the country addressed should stop interfering with U.S. commerce and the other belligerent continued to do so, "Congress will, at the next ensuing session, authorize acts of hostility . . . against the other."

An agreement with England providing for repeal of its Orders in Council, which limited trade by neutral nations with France, collapsed because the British minister violated his instructions; he concealed the requirements that the United States continue its trade embargo against France, renounce wartime trade with Britain's enemies, and authorize England to capture any U.S. vessel attempting to trade with France. Madison expelled the minister's successor for charging, falsely, that the president had been aware of the violation.

Believing that England was bent on permanent suppression of American commerce, Madison proclaimed nonintercourse with England on Nov. 2, 1810, and notified France on the same day that this would "necessarily lead to war" unless England stopped its impressment

James Madison, fourth president of the United States and co-author of the Federalist papers, c. 1810. Hulton Archive/ Getty Images

of American seamen and seizure of American goods and vessels. One week earlier, unknown to Congress (in recess) or the public, he had taken armed possession of the Spanish province of West Florida, claimed as part of the Louisiana Purchase. He was reelected in 1812, despite strong opposition and the vigorous candidacy of DeWitt Clinton.

With his actions buried in secrecy, Federalists and politicians pictured Madison as a timorous pacifist dragged into the War of 1812 (1812–15) by congressional War Hawks, and they denounced the conflict as "Mr. Madison's War." In fact, the president had sought peace but accepted war as inevitable. As wartime commander in chief he was hampered by the refusal of Congress to heed pleas for naval and military development and made the initial error of entrusting army command to aging veterans of the Revolution. The small U.S. Navy sparkled, but on land defeat followed defeat.

By 1814, however, Madison had lowered the average age of generals from 60 to 36 years; victories resulted, ending a war the principal cause of which had been removed by revocation of the Orders in Council the day before the conflict began. Contemporary public opinion in the United States, Canada, England, and continental Europe proclaimed the result a U.S. triumph. Still the country would never forget the ignominy of the president and his wife having to flee in the face of advancing British troops bent on laying waste to Washington, D.C., including setting afire the executive mansion, the Capitol, and other public buildings.

The Federalist Party was killed by its opposition to the war, and the president was lifted to a pinnacle of popularity. Madison's greatest fault was delay in discharging incompetent subordinates, including Secretary of War John Armstrong, who had scoffed at the president's repeated warnings of a coming British attack on Washington and ignored presidential orders for its defense. During Madison's second term (1813–17) the second Bank of the United States was chartered and the first U.S. protective tariff was imposed.

On leaving the presidency, Madison was eulogized at a Washington mass meeting for having won national power and glory "without infringing a political, civil, or religious right." Even in the face of sabotage of war operations by New England Federalists, he had lived up to the maxim he laid down in 1793 when he had said:

If we advert to the nature of republican government we shall find that the censorial power is in the people over the government, and not in the government over the people.

He retired to his Virginia estate, Montpelier, with his wife, Dolley (1768–1849), whose political acumen he had long prized. He participated in Jefferson's creation of the University of Virginia, later serving as its rector (1826–36), and produced numerous articles and letters on political topics.

Thomas Pinckney
(b. Oct. 23, 1750, Charleston, S.C.—d. Nov. 2, 1828, Charleston)

American soldier, politician, and diplomat Thomas Pinckney served as a general during the War of 1812, but he made his biggest contribution to American history as the negotiator of Pinckney's Treaty (Oct. 27, 1795) with Spain.

After military service in the American Revolutionary War, Pinckney, a younger brother of the diplomat Charles Cotesworth Pinckney, turned to law and politics. He served as governor of South Carolina (1787–89) and as president of the state convention that ratified the U.S. Constitution. As U.S. minister to Great Britain (1792–96) and envoy extraordinary to Spain in 1795, he negotiated the Treaty of San Lorenzo, or Pinckney's Treaty.

Pinckney was the unsuccessful Federalist candidate for vice president in 1796. He was a member of the U.S. House of Representatives (1797–1801) and a major general in the War of 1812. Upon retiring from public life, he practiced law and was a frequent contributor to the Southern Agriculturist.

Pushmataha
(b. c. 1765, on Noxuba Creek [now in Mississippi—d. Dec. 24, 1824, Washington, D.C.)

Choctaw Indian chief Pushmataha contributed to the American success in the War of 1812 by fostering the alliance of the Choctaw with the United States in the Creek War (1813–14).

In 1805, shortly after being elected chief, he signed the Treaty of Mount Dexter, ceding much of his people's land in Alabama and Mississippi for white occupancy. His opposition was important to the failure of the Shawnee chief Tecumseh's effort to include the Southern Indians in his antiwhite confederation (1811). Pushmataha persuaded the Choctaw to ally themselves with the United States during the Creek War (1813–14) and fought with distinction in the Battle of Holy Ground (Econochaca), Dec. 23, 1813. He made further land cessions in 1816 and 1820.

THE BRITISH SIDE

Between 1812 and 1814, much attention in Britain was focused on fighting the Napoleonic wars. But several notable British politicians were equally engaged in the conduct of the War of 1812.

Robert Banks Jenkinson, 2nd earl of Liverpool
(b. June 7, 1770, London, Eng.—d. Dec. 4, 1828, Fife House, Whitehall, London)

The long tenure of Lord Liverpool as the British prime minister (June 8, 1812–Feb. 17, 1827) began about the same time as the War of 1812 and extended well beyond the war's completion. Yet despite his long premiership, Liverpool was overshadowed by the greater political imaginativeness of his colleagues, George Canning and Viscount Castlereagh (afterward 2nd Marquess of Londonderry), and by the military prowess of the duke of Wellington.

Entering the House of Commons in 1790, Jenkinson soon became a leading Tory, serving as a member of the Board of Control for India (1793–96), master of the Royal Mint (1799–1801), foreign secretary (1801–04), home secretary (1804–06, 1807–09), and secretary for war and the colonies (1809–12). As foreign secretary he negotiated the short-lived Treaty of Amiens (signed March 27, 1802) with Napoleonic France.

After the assassination of Prime Minister Spencer Perceval (May 11, 1812), Liverpool reluctantly took his place, hoping to find and train a more brilliant successor. The War of 1812 with the United States and the final campaigns of the Napoleonic Wars were fought during his premiership. At the Congress of Vienna (1814–15), he strenuously urged the international abolition of the slave trade; within a few years the other European powers accepted this view.

In 1819 he strengthened the British monetary system by restoring the gold standard. Throughout his tenure he insisted that ecclesiastical and other appointments be justified by merit rather than by influence. Less enlightened was his attitude toward civil disturbances following industrial and agricultural failures: he suspended the Habeas Corpus Act for Great Britain in 1817 and for

Ireland in 1822 and imposed other repressive measures in 1819. His position on proposals to repeal the Corn Laws (import duties on foreign foodstuffs) and to grant political rights to Roman Catholics was equivocal. After nearly 15 years in office, he was forced to retire because of a paralytic stroke.

SPENCER PERCEVAL
(b. Nov. 1, 1762, London, Eng.— d. May 11, 1812, London)

Spencer Perceval served as the prime minister of Britain during the run-up to the War of 1812. He was assassinated about one month before war was declared.

The second son of the 2nd earl of Egmont, Perceval was educated at Harrow and at Trinity College, Cambridge. He was called to the bar by Lincoln's Inn in 1786 and became a king's counsel in 1796. In that same year he entered Parliament, where his rise to power was facilitated through his contacts with William Pitt the Younger. On the formation of the government of Henry Addington (1801–04), which succeeded that of Pitt, he was appointed solicitor general. From 1802 and through Pitt's second administration (1804–06) he was attorney general.

When King George III dismissed William Grenville's ministry in March 1807, Perceval, an ardent opponent of Catholic emancipation, became chancellor of the Exchequer and chancellor of

IN FOCUS: THE TREATY OF GHENT

Signed on Dec. 24, 1814, in Ghent, Belg., the Treaty of Ghent between Great Britain and the United States ended the War of 1812 on the general basis of the status quo antebellum (maintaining the prewar conditions). Because the military positions for each side were so well balanced, neither country could obtain desired concessions. No mention was made in the peace settlement of neutral rights, particularly concerning the impressment of seamen—one of the prime reasons the United States had gone to war.

Expansionist interests in the American Northwest were better served, since all British-held territory in this area was surrendered to the United States. This severance of British–American Indian ties led in 1814 and 1815 to a number of treaties of allegiance and land transfer between the Indians and the United States and thus opened the way to American settlement of the Northwest. The treaty also provided that certain boundary disputes between Canada and the United States be referred to arbitration commissions, and both the U.S. and British governments agreed to use their best efforts to abolish the international slave trade.

Based on the situation before the war, the Treaty of Ghent did not resolve the issues that had caused the war, but at that point Britain was too weary to win it, and the U.S. government deemed not losing it a tolerable substitute for victory. Nevertheless, many Americans became convinced that they had won the contest.

Unaware of the treaty, British forces under Edward Pakenham assaulted New Orleans on Jan. 8, 1815, and were soundly defeated by Andrew Jackson's ragtag army, an event that contributed to the notion of a U.S. triumph. The unanimous ratification by the U.S. Senate of the Treaty of Ghent and the celebrations that followed cloaked the fact that the United States had achieved none of its objectives.

Contention in the United States had hobbled the war effort, and domestic disaffection had menaced the Union, but after the war a surge of patriotism inspired Americans to pursue national goals. Contrary to American expectations, Canada remained British and eventually developed its own national identity, partly from pride over repulsing U.S. invasions. Meanwhile, Britain's influence among the northwestern Indians was forever ended, and American expansion in that region proceeded unchecked. In the South, the Creek War opened a large part of that region for settlement and led to the events that persuaded Spain to cede Florida to the United States in 1821.

The most enduring international consequence of the war was in the arbitration clauses of Ghent, perhaps the treaty's most important feature. Its arrangements to settle outstanding disagreements established methods that could adapt to changing U.S. administrations, British ministries, and world events. There lay the seeds of an Anglo-American comity that would weather future disagreements to sustain the longest unfortified border in the world.

the duchy of Lancaster under the 3rd Duke of Portland, whom he succeeded as prime minister on Oct. 4, 1809. His administration was marked by strong opposition to the tolerant views that had ruined his predecessors, and he is one of the few English statesmen of the period notorious for his extreme religious intolerance. He was a man of a cold, ungenial nature. Perceval was shot and killed in the House of Commons by John Bellingham, a deranged man who had vainly applied to him for redress of a personal complaint against the government.

FINAL STAGES OF WAR AND AFTERMATH

Peace talks began at Ghent (in modern Belgium) in August 1814, but, with France defeated and Napoleon sent into exile on the island of Elba in April 1814, the British stalled while waiting for news of a decisive victory in America. Most Britons were angry that the United States had become an unwitting ally of Napoleon, but even that sentiment was half-hearted among a people who had been at war in Europe for more than 20 years.

Consequently, after learning of British defeats in Plattsburgh and Baltimore and upon the advice of the Duke of Wellington, commander of the British army at the Battle of Waterloo, the British government moved to make peace.

GLOSSARY

abortive Failing to succeed; imperfectly developed.

advert Turn attention (to).

barkentine Sailing ship with at least three masts, the foremast of which has a square sail.

bill of lading A document issued by a carrier to a shipper, acknowledging the receipt of specific goods and specifying their method of transport.

brevet An honorary promotion wherein a military officer's rank, but not pay, is raised.

broadside The simultaneous discharge of all the guns on a warship.

bulwark A wall of earth built for defense; rampart.

capitulation Surrender.

confluence A coming together of people or things.

embargo Any restriction imposed on commerce or imports.

feint A mock movement made in one direction to distract attention from the real point of attack.

frigate A three-masted, fully rigged vessel, with its armament carried on a single gun deck and with additional guns on the poop and forecastle.

House of Burgesses The lower house of Virginia's colonial legislature.

inalienable Untransferable.

loyalist A person who is loyal to the existing government.

matériel Ammunition, weapons, and other military equipment.

mercenaries Soldiers for hire.

paternalistic authority A governing body that supplies the needs and regulates the behaviour of those under its control.

peruke From the French *perruque*, a wig for men that was fashionable in the 17th and 18th centuries.

plenipotentiary A diplomatic agent who has the authority to conduct business on behalf of a government.

polemicist A person engaged in the practice of disputing religious, political, and philosophical ideas.

privateer A privately owned armed ship commissioned by a government to fight enemy ships. Also, the commander of such a vessel.

protracted Prolonged; drawn out.

quartering Providing room and board for soldiers in private homes.

redress The setting right of wrongs.

riposte A quick sharp return in speech or action.

sedition Inciting rebellion against the government.

sloop A quick, single-masted boat.

spoliation An act of plundering.

vis inertiae Lack of activity; slow to action.

writ A formal order that is under seal.

American Revolution

Bernard Bailyn, *The Ideological Origins of the American Revolution*, enlarged ed. (1992), examines the transmission of English Republican ideology and its American reception. John Richard Alden, *The American Revolution, 1775–1783* (1954, reissued 1987), is distinguished for its political and military analyses. Jack P. Greene (ed.), *The American Revolution: Its Character and Limits* (1987), contains a valuable collection of essays. Robert Middlekauff, *The Glorious Cause: The American Revolution, 1763–1789* (1982, reprinted 1985), examines the Revolution from a somewhat older point of view than is now fashionable. Piers Mackesy, *The War for America, 1775–1783* (1964, reissued 1993), explains the British side of the war. J.G.A. Pocock (ed.), *Three British Revolutions: 1641, 1688, 1776* (1980), sets the American Revolution in the historical context of British experience. Military histories include John Shy, *Toward Lexington: The Role of the British Army in the Coming of the American Revolution* (1965), on the British army in America; Don Higginbotham, *The War of American Independence: Military Attitudes, Policies, and Practice, 1763–1789* (1971, reprinted 1983), which shows the interrelationship of military and political developments; Charles Royster, *A Revolutionary People at War: The Continental Army and American Character, 1775–1783* (1979, reissued 1986); and William M. Fowler, Jr., *Rebels Under Sail* (1976), on the American navy.

War of 1812

David S. Heidler and Jeanne T. Heidler, *The War of 1812* (2002), contains essays that examine the causes of the war, the diplomatic ramifications, and the military conduct of the conflict. David S. Heidler and Jeanne T. Heidler (eds.), *Encyclopedia of the War of 1812* (1997, reissued 2004), is the only all-inclusive reference work on the war that examines its causes as well as its social, military, political, and diplomatic facets.

Donald R. Hickey, *The War of 1812: A Forgotten Conflict* (1989, reissued 1995), is a good one-volume narrative of the war that emphasizes the politics of the clash. J. C. A. Stagg, *Mr. Madison's War: Politics, Diplomacy, and Warfare in the Early American Republic, 1783–1830* (1983), is an exemplary examination of the civil-military relations in the United States during the war.

Richard V. Barbuto, *Niagara 1814: America Invades Canada* (2000), offers an excellent analysis of this pivotal theatre of the war. J. Mackay Hitsman, *The Incredible War of 1812: A Military History*, rev. ed. updated by Donald E. Graves (1999), examines the war on the border from the Canadian viewpoint. Pierre Berton, *Flames Across the Border:*

The Canadian-American Tragedy, 1813–1814 (1981, reissued 2001), views the beginning of Canadian national identity as originating in the war on the border. Robert Gardner (ed.), *The Naval War of 1812* (1998), provides some of the latest scholarship on the naval war. C. Edward Skeen, *Citizen Soldiers in the War of 1812* (1999), examines the role of militia in the war. Sandy Antal, *A Wampum Denied: Procter's War of 1812* (1997), is an interesting revisionist examination of Britain's war in the Northwest that sees British efforts there as largely successful.